contents

Cover image courtesy BBC Picture Library

crime time 2.3  stuff

distribution

turnaround

printing

caledonian international book publishing, glasgow

editorial

editor:

barry forshaw

advertising, founding editor:

paul duncan

reviews/fiction/design:

peter dillon-parkin, with an assist from gavin holland. ta!

advertising

please fax or phone paul duncan (01203 315864) for rates, or write to the editorial address.

subscriptions

crime time subscriptions, 18 coleswood rd, harpenden, herts al5 1eq

legal stuff

crime time is © 1998 ct publishing isbn 1-9020020-6-7

tirade

A HIGHLY EXPENSIVE survey carried out for this magazine (utilising hundreds of computers and round-the-clock volunteers) has determined that most of our readers feel they have a book in them. But is it a book that anyone other than your mothers would want to read? Agents, if they deign to look at tyro writers' work, will point out that publishers are *"looking for someone in the Grisham/King/Clancy vein…but different"*. Or, alternatively, *"there are too many Grisham/King/Clancy clones around at present"*. Getting something published is a Herculean task (even in this magazine), and then the publishers' reps will intone to glazed-eyed booksellers *"this is definitely the new Grisham/King/Clancy"*. After that first book, the polarities of choice are movie options or bargain-bin oblivion.

But what budding writer is ever put off by the vagaries of publishing? And nor should they be—many a favourite writer of the CT team could paper the proverbial bedroom with rejection slips. But we want to make things a tad easier for our readers, philanthropists that we are. And among the articles on Sax Rohmer's time as a Boy Scout or Agatha Christie's stint as an LAPD painclotheswoman, you'll find the odd item on how to polish your writing craft—and how to get published. No guarantees, of course, but advice from editors, agents and the like. Who knows, you may be reading your own career overview in these very pages before too long.

The first word on our new format is hearteningly positive—which is not to say that more changes may not be on the way (we like assaulting the status quo). And, hopefully, there's enough in this issue to tempt anyone who's shelled out our modest cover price.

Finally, our Gentleman Columnist (and, when not at a hunt meeting, novelist), Mark Timlin, writes from his armchair at the Reform Club to point out that that (pace his reference in this issue to Fred Willard's *Down on Ponce* being favourite for the John Creasey Award), he wrote the reference to crawling across glass before he knew the result. Mr. Timlin will be shedding only the blood of his characters, not his own.

Barry Forshaw

THE FIRST THING you'll have noticed about this issue is the photo cover featuring the splendid Warren Clarke and Colin Buchanan as Dalziel and Pascoe. Ta to the BBC Photo Library for letting us use it gratis for our Reg Hill feature. The second thing is the price. Both are aimed to let us sell substantially more copies of your favourite crime fiction magazine.

The re-jigging to 192 pages has meant me fiddling with the format yet again, assisted by the lovely Gavin Holland, who designed the 'telescopic sight' icons that we've used everywhere. Gavin is a vastly talented dance musician and web designer, and if you need either side of his personality (or both – he provides music for web sites) you can contact him through CT or by entering move.to/deepblue in your web browser or email him at gavin.holland@btinternet.com.

I know that many of you entertain the fallacy that this organ is produced in the luxury offices of a mighty publishing combine. Well we do now *have* offices, but the move to them (over Christmas, natch) and to the new size and price has meant chaos has ensued. If there is anything that you've written/expected to see/wanted for Christmas missing, sorry. It should be here in the next two issues, in which all our existing inventory of interviews, fiction and reviews will finally find a berth.

Peter Dillon-Parkin

adrian muller

CWA AWARD SHORTLISTS AND WINNERS

Announced in November were the nominations for the Macallan sponsored Crime Writers' Association's Dagger Awards:

GOLD AND SILVER DAGGERS FOR BEST NOVEL:

Geoffrey Archer for *Fire Hawk* (Century)

Nicholas Blincoe for *Manchester Slingback* (Picador)

Michael Dibdin for *A Long Finish* (Faber & Faber)

Reginald Hill for *On Beulah Height* (HarperCollins)

James Lee Burke for *Sunset Limited* (Orion)

George P. Pelecanos for *King Suckerman* (Serpent's Tail)

THE SHORT STORY DAGGER:

Chaz Brenchley for *Master Eld, His Wayzgoose* (from *Shakespearean Detectives*, ed. Mike Ashley, published by Robinson

Ian Rankin for 'Unknown Pleasures' (from *Mean Times*, edited by Jerry Sykes, published by The Do-Not Press)

Ian Rankin for 'The Hanged Man' (broadcast on BBC Radio)

Jerry Sykes for 'Roots' (from *Mean Times*, edited by Jerry Sykes, published by The Do-Not Press

THE GOLD DAGGER FOR NON-FICTION:

Sean O'Callaghan for *The Informer* (Bantam)

Gitta Sereny for *Cries Unheard* (Macmillan)

Donald Thomas for *The Victorian Underworld* (John Murray)

During the *Dead on Deansgate* convention in October, it was announced that Denise Mina was the 1998 winner of the CWA John Creasey Award for best crime novel by a first time author. Mina's debut, *Garnethill*, is a psychological thriller published by Bantam. (Shortlisted were: *The Locust Farm* by Jeremy Dronfield, and *Down on Ponce* by Fred Willard)

Also revealed at the Manchester convention was the winner of the Crime Writers' Association's new competition for unpublished crime writers. Julianne Denby's successful entry, the opening chapter to her (as yet unpublished) novel *Stone Baby*, was published in the book supplement of *The Sunday Times*.

(For another chance to read the first chapter of *Stone Baby*, together with details of the 1999 CWA New Writing Competition, buy the next issue of *Crime Time*)

PAULA GOSLING

After a three-year sabbatical, award winning crime writer Paula Gosling is back with a new novel from LittleBrown. *Death and Shadows* will be published in February and, judging by the promo blurb, it would seem that the new mystery revisits the location of the author's 1992 mystery *The Body in Blackwater Bay*.

POISONED PEN PRESS

This US publishing company, a spin-off from Arizona crime fiction bookstore The Poisoned Pen, is going from strength to strength. Edgar nominated for their first book, they have gone on to publish first instalments from out-of-print mystery series by both American and

Anne Perry

British authors. Their latest 'missing first', P.C. Doherty's *Death of a King*, using the latest technology called 'flash publishing'. This printing process, together with the company's agreement with US distributor Ingrams, makes it financially viable for a book to be reprinted at a minimum order of twenty-five copies, thereby allowing it to remain available indefinitely.

For details of Poisoned Pen Press books check with booksellers listed below 'New Crime Novels', or contact

**The Poisoned Pen Press,
6962 E 1st Ave Suite 103,
Scottsdale AZ 85251.
Fax: (602) 949-1707, email:
sales@poisonedpenpress.com**

ANNE PERRY

Best known for her historical crime novels, Anne Perry is widening her writing skills and has sold the rights to Headline for a fantasy trilogy featuring a heroine called Tathea. Headline, who already publish Perry's historical series featuring William Monk, will soon be publishing future Pitt titles as well (HarperCollins publish

their last Pitt novel, *Ashworth Hall*, in December). Of the fantasy trilogy Perry says, *"The best fantasies are explorations of, perhaps not so much good and evil, but of right and wrong."* The first instalment is due next year.

PAST POISONINGS

Due to brisk sales, *Past Poisonings*, the historical crime fiction anthology dedicated to Ellis Peters, may well become an annual publication. Certainly plans are well under way for a 1999 volume, and if this too is equally successful further short stories will be commissioned.

MINETTE WALTERS

Not only does the best-selling author have a new psychological suspense novel out, *The Breaker*, but two of her books are currently in (post) production at the BBC. James Wilby and Dervla Kirwan will star in *The Dark Room*, scheduled for an Easter broadcast. Before then fans can watch a dramatisation of *The Echo* at Christmas. The cast includes Joely Richardson and Anton Lesser, but playing the lead is Clive Owen who may well find himself in a series inspired by the novel. Walters has already written a story-line for a TV follow-up.

Currently the author is completing a 20.000 word novelette which will be the free gift for anyone buying books to the value of £10.00 in Holland's Crime and Thriller Month in June 1999.

MAXIM JAKUBOWKSI

Besides editing a new instalment of *Fresh Blood* (including entries by Lee Child, Peter Guttridge, and the award winning Denise Mina—see above), Murder One owner Jakubowski will be organising the Crime Weekend for the London Festival of Literature to be held in late March or early April. One of the special guests will be Walter Mosely.

LIZ EVANS

JFK is Missing is Liz Evans' sequel to last year's highly entertaining *Who Killed Marilyn Monroe*. Neither novel will answer any questions that the Warren Commission might have had, but fans of Grace Smith will be glad to see the PI back.

US CRIME FICTION AWARDS

THE ANTHONY AWARDS

Best Novel: S. J. Rozan for *No Colder Place*

Best First Novel: Lee Child for *The Killing Floor*

Best Paperback Original: Rick Riordan for *Big Red Tequila*

Best Short Story: Jan Grape for 'Front Row Seat'; and Edward D. Hoch for 'One Bag of Coconuts'

Best Cover Art: Michael Kellner for *Night Dogs* by Kent Anderson (Dennis McMillan edition)

THE MACAVITY AWARDS:

Best Novel: Deborah Crombie for *Dreaming of the Bones*

Best First Novel: Penny Warner for *Dead Body Language*

Best Short Story: Peter Robinson for 'Two Ladies of Rose Cottage'

Best Non-fiction: *Deadly Women* (Editors: Jan Grape and Dean James)

THE SHAMUS AWARDS

Best Novel: Terrance Faherty for *Come Back Dead*

Best First Novel: Rick Rirodan for *Big Red Tequila*

Best Paperback Original: Laura Lipman for *Charm City*

Best Short Story: Carolyn Wheat for 'Love Me for my Yellow Hair Alone'

THE TIMES CRIME FICTION SUPPLEMENT

Damn! The cunning plan to include Mark Timlin in *The Times'* 100 Masters of Crime (and thereby avoiding his the scorn) failed! Oh well, a column by Timlin wouldn't be a column by Timlin if he didn't try to stir up some controversy, and he did make some valid points in *A Personal View* in *Crime Time* 2.2. There were some odd 'masters' and notable exclusions. Unfortunately *The Times* failed to mention how the 100 listed authors had been chosen, so here follows a brief clarification.

The supplement's shining example was an annual Dutch guide that lists every crime and thriller author in print in that language. Time and space did not allow this in *The Times'* version. Having less than a week to put the British crime fiction supplement together—not weeks—the organisers decided that they would try and promote those who would most benefit from the guide: living authors currently in print in Britain. *The Times*, however, insisted that its readers would expect to find the likes of Agatha Christie, and Dashiell Hammett listed as well, so some of the founding mothers and fathers of the various crime fiction genres were also included. The end result was a highly a successful—but, by its nature, an obviously flawed—supplement that pretty much covered the whole spectrum of crime fiction available in Britain.

Discussions with *The Times* are currently underway for a 1999 crime fiction supplement, and it is hoped that increased publishing will allow more space and therefore a more inclusive line-up of authors.

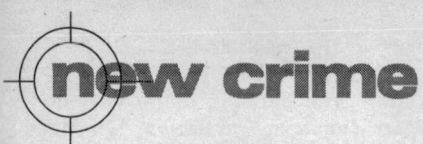

new crime

NOVEMBER

Geoffrey Archer, *Fist of Fire*. Century, £15.99.

David Baldacci, *The Winner*, Simon & Shuster, £9.99.

T.R. Bowen, *The Death of Amy Parish* (debut crime novel, new series), Michael Joseph, £5.99.

Simon Brett, *Mrs Pargeter's Point of Honour* (Mrs Pargeter), Macmillan, £16.99.

Jane Brindle, *The Hiding Game*, Headline, £16.99.

Agatha Christie (& Charles Osborne), *Black Coffee* (Hercule Poirot), HarperCollins, £15.99.

Elizabeth Corley, *Requiem Mass* (DCI Andrew Fenwick, new series), Headline, £16.99

Liz Evans, *JFK is Missing* (Grace Smith), Orion, £5.99.

John Francome, *Safe Bet*, Headline, £16.99.

Kinky Friedman, *Blast From the Past* (Kinky Friedman), Faber & Faber, £9.99.

Ann Granger, *Running Scared* (Fran Varady), Headline, £16.99.

Peter Guttridge, *Two to Tango*, Headline, £16.99.

Sparkle Hayter, *The Last Manly Man* (Robin Hudson), No Exit Press, £10.00.

Juliet Hebden, *Pel is Provoked*, Constable, £16.99.

Tom Holland, *The Sleeper in the Sands*, LittleBrown, £15.99.

Michael Jecks, *The Leper's Return* (Sir Baldwin Furnshill), Headline, £16.99.

Anthony Masters, *The Good and Faithful Servant* (Daniel Boyd, new series), Constable, £16.99.

Jennie Melville, *Stone Dead* (CS Charmian Daniels), Macmillan, £16.99.

Richard Montanari, *The Violent Hour*, Michael Joseph, £5.99.

Bill Napier, *Nemesis*, Headline, £12.99.

Frank Palmer, *Final Score* (Phil 'Sweeney' Todd), Constable, £16.99.

George Pelecanos, *Nick's Trip* (Nick Stefanos), Serpent's Tail, £7.99.

Sharon Penman, *Cruel as the Grave* (Justin de Quincey), Michael Joseph, £15.99.

Richard Pitman, *No Place to Hide*, Hodder & Stoughton, £16.99.

Candace Robb, *A Gift of Sanctuary* (Owen Archer), Heineman, £10.00.

Barrie Roberts, *Sherlock Holmes and the Royal Flush* (Sherlock Holmes), Constable, £16.99.

Laura Joh Rowland, *The Concubine's Tattoo*, Headline, £16.99.

Paul Thomas, *Guerrilla Season* (Tito Ihaka), Vista, £5.99.

Marilyn Todd, *Wolf Whistle* (Claudia Seferius), Macmillan, £16.99.

Martyn Waites, *Little Triggers*, Piatkus, £17.99.

Various (Otto Penzler, editor), *Criminal Records* (short stories), Orion, £9.99/£16.99.

DECEMBER

Paul Bennett, *False Profits* (Nick Shannon), LittleBrown, £5.99.

Mary Clayton, *Death is the Inheritance* (John Reynolds), Headline, £16.99.

Iris Collier, *Innocent Blood* (CI Douglas MacBride), Piatkus, £16.99.

Kit Craig, *Some Safe Place*, Headline, £16.99.

Rankin Davis, *The Oath*, Hodder & Stoughton, £16.99.

Emer Gillespie, *Virtual Stranger* (Karen McDade, new series), Headline, £16.99.

Cynthia Harrod-Eagles, *Shallow Grave* (DI Bill Slider), LittleBrown, £16.99.

Jane Jakeman, *Fool's Gold* (Lord Ambrose Malfine), Headline, £16.99.

Fergus Linehan, *The Safe House*, Macmillan, £16.99.

Phillip M. Margolin, *The Undertaker's Widow*, Little, Brown, £9.99.

Edward Marston, *The Wildcats of Exeter* (Domesday Chronicles), Headline, £16.99.

Nick Oldham, *One Dead Witness*, Headline, £16.99.

Yang-May Ooi, *The Flame Tree* (debut crime novel), Hodder & Stoughton, £16.99.

Anne Perry, *Ashworth Hall* (Thomas and Charlotte Pitt), HarperCollins, £15.99.

Mark Ramsden, *The Dark Magus and the Sacred Whore*, Serpent's Tail, £7.99.

Mark T. Sullivan, *Ghost Dance*, Hodder & Stoughton, £16.99.

Craig Thomas, *Slipping into the Shadow*, Little, Brown, £15.99.

EARLY 1999

Lisa Appignanesi, *The Dead of Winter*, Bantam, £15.99.

Jimmy Boyle, *Hero of the Underworld*, Serpent's Tail, £9.99.

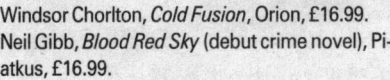

Windsor Chorlton, *Cold Fusion*, Orion, £16.99.
Neil Gibb, *Blood Red Sky* (debut crime novel), Piatkus, £16.99.
Laurie King, *The Birth of a New Moon* (non-series), HarperCollins, £15.99.
Diane Langford, *Left for Dead*, Serpent's Tail, £7.99.
Martin Limon, *Slicky Boys* (Sueno & Bascom), Serpent's Tail, £8.99.
Maureen O'Brien, *Deception*, Constable, £16.99.
Carol O'Connell, *Judas Child* (non-series), Hutchinson, £10.00.
Jerry Raine, Frankie Bosser Comes Home, Gollancz, £9.99.
Ian Rankin, *Dead Souls* (Inspector Rebus), Orion, £16.99.
Eric Reich, *The Lost Son*, Serpent's Tail, £8.99.
Gerald Seymour, *The Road Past Nowhere*, Bantam, £16.99.
Jenny Siler, *Easy Money* (debut crime novel), Orion, £9.99.

For further information on the above titles, or to order books, contact:

Crime in Store, 14 Bedford Street, Covent Garden, London WC2E 9HE.
Tel: +44-171-379-3795, fax: +44-171-379-8988.
Email: CrimeBks@aol.com
Website: http://www.ndirect.co.uk/~ecorrigan/cis/crimeinstore.htm

Murder One, 71-73 Charing Cross Road, London WC2H 0AA.
Tel: 0171-734-3483, fax: +44-171-734-3429.
Email: 106562.2021@compuserve.com
Website: http://www.murderone.co.uk

The Mysterious Bookshop, 82 Marylebone High Street, London W1M 3DE.
Tel: 0171-486-8975, fax: +44-171-486-8953.
Email: MysteriousLON@compuserve.com
Website:
http://www.MysteriousBookshop.com

Post Mortem Books, 58 Stanford Avenue, Hassocks, Sussex BN6 8JH.
Tel: 01273-843066, fax: 00-44-1273-845090.
Email: ralph@pmbooks.demon.co.uk
Website:
http://www.postmortembooks.co.uk

If you wish your shop or website to be included in sources *write or email the editorial address with your details*

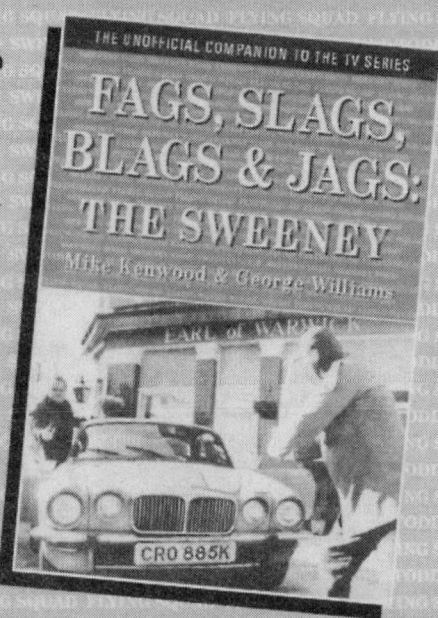

i am a sparkle hayter limited edition (1 of 1)
maxim jakubowski

ONCE A YEAR, the creme de la creme (and other hangers-on) of the crime and mystery field gather for Bouchercon, the world mystery convention. This year's proceedings, the 29th instalment of the convention, took place in Philadelphia from October 1st to 4th, and attracted the usual stellar cast, including a particularly strong contingent of British authors.

Many of these travelled up on a mystery train of sorts from New York's Penn station, still fresh from the New York is Book Country fair on the previous Sunday where crime and mystery also made an impressive showing. NYIBC is a unique event where the upper part of 5th Avenue is closed off to traffic and becomes a day-long book fair with hundred of stands from publishers, booksellers, dealers and various literary organisations lining the famous canyon of 5th Avenue. Nearly 100,000 people attended in the strong September sun and the queues for signings of crime writers were by far the most impressive, as writers met their public at stalls set up by the New York mystery bookstores and the Mystery Writers of America. In attendance were Mary Higgins Clark, Ed McBain, Donald E. Westlake, George Pelecanos, Lawrence Block (sporting a devilish goatee which had disappeared by the time he reached Philadelphia) and over a hundred others. If only London could host a similar public event! Sadly, the organisers of next year's London Festival of Literature 'The Word' (for which I

am consulting on the crime events) have declined a Charing Cross Road event, because of the unpredictable nature of the British weather.

So, there we were, bleary-eyed on the Thursday morning annexing the Amtrak train to Philadelphia, survivors of the 5th Avenue bash. Lauren Henderson (with dark glasses hiding the damage of earlier wild birthday celebrations), white-collar noir maven Jason Starr and myself, augmented by more recent arrival Jim Driver of the Do-Not Press, Martin Edwards and a gaggle of local criminals: mystery academic BJ Rahn, Parnell Hall, Martin and Annette Meyers and legendary crime editor (and Bouchercon guest) Ruth Cavin, who still edits crime with vigour and acute perception well into her 70s. I'm sorry to report the journey was without incident; you just can't live a life of crime all hours of the day!

In addition to Ruth Cavin, Bouchercon's other principal guests were Carl Hiaasen looking as ever, in the immortal words of the one and only Mike Ripley, like 'a junior CIA trainee', International Guest of Honour Janwillem van de Wetering, serene as a zen monk (which he once was), scriptwriter and producer Tom Fontana, the creator TV series *Homicide*, and our very own Jonathan Gash as an ebullient Toastmaster.

Organised by recidivist fan Deen Kogan and her committee, this year's Bouchercon was one of the best organised in years and attendance broke the 2,000 mark, with an overpowering choice of panels spread over four days in six separate streams, involving all the 300 writers present. In addition, the double-size book room was a veritable Ali Baba's cave for die-hard collectors and readers alike, even if some of the prices for old or rare books were out of the reach of common mortals (Ian Rankin's first book at nearly $1,000, a rare David Goodis at $4,000, and hyper firsts by Patricia Cornwell, Lindsey Davis and Minette Walters approaching $800!).

And that well-known crime reader President Bill Clinton was also in town! Albeit for a fund-raiser rather than the convention, although he reputedly made a detour by the Franklin Plaza Hotel where we were all gathered. Knowing how the Clinton imprimatur has boosted the careers of Walter Mosley, Stephen Hunter and others, needless to say there were hordes of mystery writers all too ready to brave the security heavies to generously give him their latest, in the hope of a future quote or a photograph of him clutching their book descending the steps of Airforce One. I actually had to be restrained by my own American publishers, who somehow thought that my last two crime novels sported inappropriate titles for the likes of Bill Clinton in the wake of the Monica Lewinsky affair. So, what is wrong about such evocative titles as 'It's You That I Want To Kiss' and 'Because She Thought She Loved Me'? Anyway, as we say in the biz, they're available in all good bookshops and probably not in WH Smith, Bill, so you know where to find them...

No one can do justice to a Bouchercon as so much is going on all the time, in addition to the obligatory socialising in the lobby, at the awkwardly-shaped bar, in the book room. My own panel on Noir with Jason Starr, KJA Wishnia, Dennis Lehane, SJ Rozan and Philip Reed, played to a standing room only audience and offered new definitions of noir above and beyond the rainbow (nice to know that I am now known for sleaze noir, which beats coun-

try, white collar, urban, neo and other types of noir—if you're a pornographer, flaunt it, I say!). Amongst the myriad other panels and events were the compulsory legal, historical, Golden Age, procedural, real-life crime, collecting and other panels but also more uncommon subjects like Fire Marshalls and Arson Dogs, Killing Cats and Other Taboos, Dental Forensics, Vidocq, Japanese mystery fiction. Something for everyone and more.

So who did you miss? In addition to the aforementioned hardy train travellers, the British contingent included: Peter Chambers, music agent and author Paul Charles (just a stop-over for him on an American tour which included Jackson Browne's 50th birthday party in LA), Lee Child, Penelope Evans, Frances Fyfield, CWA Chairman Janet Laurence (who organised a British breakfast for us colonial scribes to display our wares to American publishers and specialist bookstore owners), Michael Z Lewin (OK, so he's American but he's lived in Somerset forever..), Val McDermid, Susan Moody, Ian Rankin, Peter Robinson, Michelle Spring and Christopher West.

And then there were the American writers. 200 or so you might not have heard of plus Neil Albert, Linda Barnes, Eleanor Taylor Bland, Anthony Bruno, Dorothy Cannell, Stephen Cannell (of Rockford Files and A-Team fame), P.M. Carlson, Harlan Coben, Margaret Coel, Max Alan Collins, Michael Collins, Michael Connelly, Robert Crais, Deborah Crombie, Dorothy Salisbury Davis, Janet Dawson, Carole Nelson Douglas, Tony Dunbar, Loren D. Estleman, Linda Faistein, Philip Jose Farmer, GM Ford, John Gilstrap, Leslie Glass, Ellen Godfrey, Ron Goulart, Robert Greer, Jane Haddam, Matthew Hall, Charlaine Harris, Lee Harris, Ellen Hart, Pete Hautman, Sparkle Hayter, Jeremiah Healy, William Heffernan, Sue Henry, Tami Hoag, Edward D. Hoch, Susan Isaacs, Jon A. Jackson, J. Robert Janes, Stuart M. Kaminsky, Lee Killough, Martha C. Lawrence, Paul Levine, Laura Lippman, Gayle Lynds, Margaret Maron, Sujata Massey, Stephanie Barron, Archer Mayor, Claire McNab, Miriam Grace Monfredo, Sharan Newman, Joyce Carol Oates, Abigail Padgett, Ridley Pearson, George Pelecanos, Gary Phillips, Robert Randisi, Rick Riordan, Candace Robb, Gillian Roberts, Les Roberts, Lynda S. Robinson, Laura Joh Rowland, Tom Savage, Lisa Scottoline, Robert Skinner, Elizabeth Daniels Squire, Dana Stabenow, William G. Tapply, Charles Todd, Walter Wager, Marilyn Wallace, Valerie Wilson Wesley, John Westermann, Eric Wright, RD Zimmerman and Sharon Zukowski. And that was only the tip of the iceberg... That's what Bouchercon is all about, authors galore (and publishers and agents and fascinated fans in tow).

The Anthony Awards named in memory of famed writer and critic Anthony Boucher were announced and given out at a brunch on Sunday 4th. See *Bullets* in this issue for the results. As successful as it was, the Philadelphia Bouchercon also, for many of us, failed to catch fire as some previous ones did, but that is very much in the eye of the beholder. Somehow, the sheer size and labyrinthine meanders of the hotel took their toll for many. But a convention is only as good as you make it, so as a parting shot, some striking memories of the event: Ian Rankin, arriving at the convention after a 36 hour journey from Edinburgh to London to New York to Philadelphia with attendant delays and airline/airport hassles, clad in a kilt and making it to the stage barely 10 minutes before his appearance on the panel discussing series writing. Having survived that, he then took a place in the bar for the following seven hours without food and, somewhat under the influence, having to find his own hotel at 3 in the morning in the darkness of downtown Philadelphia, not the safest of places, and escaping bodily harm from drunks and derelicts offended by his 'dress' by an inch or two. The hardy creator of Inspector Rebus has now sworn not to wear a kilt in public again. At any rate in America!

Dennis McMillan, independent publisher extraordinaire from Tucson, Arizona and his splendid taste in clothing. Every day a different flashy silk suit, homburg or fancy hat, Hawaiian shirt and 30s two-tone shoes. A picture of elegance which no other publisher or convention guest could even approach.

Miss Lauren Henderson, a refugee from the Tuscan hinterland, who skirts seemed to get tighter and shorter by the day as her cleavage increased. A hit with the boys. Now we know where her heroine Sam Jones gets her bad habits from.

The deep basso-profundo voice of rap expert and LA hardboiler Gary Phillips resonating triumphantly from one end of the convention to the other. This man needs no protection.

And finally, my own modest attempt at doing a Hunter S. Thompson and turning a convention report into a tale of gonzo: at the charity auction, I mistakenly took pity on the kind offer from scintillating Canadian writing lasses Sparkle Hayter and Alison Gordon to offer a tattoo, that I bid a meagre five dollars over the floor bid and surprisingly won. The ceremony was held in public, caught on digital camera and probably is by now all over the web. And no, I didn't bid enough to be able to chose the body part of my choice, so my arm it was, and a heart signed Sparkle. I hasten to add that the unique decoration was in henna and temporary and, by the time you read this, will have faded into memory. And, yes, Sparkle, the audience probably did see your ass as you bent over me in your act of artistry in a micro-skirt that kept moving up. Authors will do anything to publicise their new books, won't they? So, if you wish to meet your favourite authors getting up to nonsense and mischief, book now for next year's Bouchercon. It takes place in Milwaukee in October 1999. See you there; I'll be the one hiding from Sparkle Hayter lest she wishes to decorate me again...

roman blood
steven saylor in britain

HE'S IN BRITAIN to promote his new book, *A Murder on the Appian Way*. His publishers, Robinson Books, have taken him to the Roman town of Chichester to give a talk in a museum. Speaking to Steven Saylor on the Sunday after this event, I find myself reminding him that the modest numbers attending give no indication of how seriously Saylor is taken in this country. In fact, few would dispute that Saylor is now the leading light of the brand of historical fiction best described as whodunits in ancient Rome. Actually, Saylor is sanguine about his visit (he's appreciative of the fact that he got to see Chichester, and seems to know that from *Roman Blood* onwards, his following has been snowballing).

That first book demonstrated a remarkable legerdemain: his Roman sleuth, Gordianus the Finder, was a strikingly rounded creation catapulted into a labyrinthine plot involving even the saturnine dictator Sulla. But most enjoyable of all was the astonishingly rich historical detail, freighted into the narrative with total assurance and never once seeming forced. I break the ice by persuading him that on his next visit, he should try to get to Thomas Hardy's Dorchester (every street of which, as Hardy said, "shows forth old Rome"). And Saylor soon proves a

barry forshaw

delight to talk to, comparing the statuary chosen for his UK covers with the collage and art elements of the original American designs. Did he realise just how overcrowded the field he was entering would become? He tells me that after submitting *Roman Blood* to his publishers, he encountered Colleen McCullough's *First Man in Rome* and then the much-acclaimed Roman novels of Lindsey Davies. But he seems unfazed by the strength of his rivals – his own historic credentials are impeccable, and he wears his narrative skills with a quiet self-confidence.

Was it the politics and power plays of the day that drew him to the era? To some degree, he replies, but as the period of the Republic he deals with is so well known, it's often a question of tackling those fascinating areas which are both like and unlike our own. If litigation, for instance, doesn't prove a successful way of dealing with an opponent, then assassination is another option (one wonders if these books are wish fulfilment reading for any of our politicians).

While all the books (including *Catilina's Riddle* and the remarkable *Arms of Nemesis*) present a cornucopia of delights, one remembers the structural strength of the first, *Roman Blood*. The dictator Sulla is a powerful unseen presence throughout the book, but is (surprisingly) brought on *deus ex machina* with the same kind of assurance Saylor demonstrates in including Cicero as one of his characters – in fact, the latter hires the cynical Gordianus to help on a murder case he's dealing with. And Crassus, memorably incarnated by

Olivier in Kubrick's *Spartacus*, also figures. Did this movie, recently reissued with the censorship cuts reinstated, influence Saylor? He concedes that it did – although Howard Fast's original concept, with the left-wing emphasis given to Spartacus, is not the route pursued by Saylor himself. Another influence, surprisingly, is Tolkien: his marvellously created world being a source of inspiration (as is, less surprisingly, John Le Carré – one can sense echoes of Smiley in Gordianus' dogged pursuit of the facts). And Saylor even acknowledges the curious echoes of science fiction in his work – again via a carefully created world (although Saylor can spin elaborate filigrees on established facts of history).

And Saylor clearly enjoys the gently educative aspect of his books: we all feel a lttle better-read in history after a trip through Gordianus' intrigue-filled Eternal City (how, for instance, Romans never dump faeces over their back walls – this is how provincials unwittingly betray their unsophisticated origins) But, first and foremost, Saylor is a thriller writer of conviction and authority.

What is he working on now? For another publisher (and to appear in the spring of the year 2000) *Honour the Dead* is set in America in 1885, has a Jack the Ripper connection, and features the writer O'Henry: the man who made the twist ending his very own. It's not hard to predict that the ranks of Saylor followers will have grown considerably by the Millennium, and that more than a few of them will be ready to follow him in any new directions he takes.

crime on campus
st. hilda's crime and mystery weekend

ST. HILDA'S is Oxford's only remaining all-female student college. However, for the past five years, during the summer holidays, the doors have been opened to both genders for the annual Crime and Mystery Weekend. Past weekends have concentrated on such varied topics as Oxford Women Crime Writers, the Golden Age of crime fiction, Historical Crime Fiction, and Crime Fiction in Academia. This year's theme was the Police Detective in Crime Fiction.

In a departure from the hectic schedules of the previous two years, organisers Kate Charles, author of clerical mysteries, and Eileen Roberts, St. Hilda's Development Officer, ensured that the 1998 meeting was more relaxed. A late start on Friday the 21st of August allowed most speakers and participants to arrive without too much of a rush. Those who arrived early used the time to explore the town centre and its historic colleges.

The first event, a pre-dinner wine reception, began at 6.30pm and was held in the beautiful college grounds overlooking the river Cherwell. The crowd included people from all over the world, many of them familiar faces from past weekends, and some of them former graduates from the college. It was also nice to see that authors who would not be speaking attended the weekend. (They included Ann Granger, Lesley Grant-Adamson, Janet Laurence, Susan Moody, and Betty Rowlands)

After a delicious three course dinner, the first speaker was a former 'St. Hilda's girl': Dr. Elizabeth Neville, Chief Constable of Wiltshire Police Force. Without dampening the buoyant atmosphere, Dr. Neville gave a very informative description of the scale and detail that goes into a murder investigation. She also pointed out that, prior to any trial, a follow-up investigation had to be mounted to prove that no-one but the accused could be responsible for the crime. Following dinner many people gathered in the Senior Commons Room to socialise before retiring for the night.

adrian muller

Following a choice of an English or Continental breakfast, the crowd gathered in the Vernon Harcourt Room for the first of the talks. Before the proceedings started Kate Charles introduced the person who would be chairing events: author Robert Barnard. His fellow crime writer Edward Marston had been the Chairman for at least two of the previous St. Hilda's conventions, and Barnard had a tough act to follow. However, he did so masterfully and in his own unique, and very entertaining style. After explaining the agenda for the weekend, Barnard introduced the first speaker David Williams.

A former Advertising Executive, Williams wowed everyone by arriving in a very stylish Rolls Royce, and fittingly spoke about 'Gentlemen versus Players'. Williams is the creator of two series sleuths: amateur detective Mark Treasure, an International Banker; and Welsh policeman Chief Inspector Merlin Parry. The author started his writing career with the Treasure series, and due to their varied locale the policemen changed from book to book, often finding themselves the butt for the humour. Then, to widen his audience, Williams went on to write about policeman Merlin Parry. Having written from both perspectives Williams had come to the conclusion that fictional policemen are mostly limited by professional restraint, whereas the amateur sleuth is more often bound by moral obligation.

The title of Dorothy Simpson's talk was 'The Yawn Factor: Problems of Writing a Series'. Simpson, after two stand-alone suspense novels, decided she would try her hand at a murder mystery. Since she did not want to find herself in the trap of having to write about someone she would grow tired of, she very carefully went about creating a series character. Part of the solution to this problem was to create a wide cast of characters to support her hero, Detective Inspector Luke Thanet. Consequently Thanet found himself with a side-kick and a happy family life. The only aspect that still causes problems are the confrontations with murder victims. How many different ways can an author write about what effect violent death has on an investigating officer?, Simpson wondered.

'When is an Police Officer not a Police Officer?' asked writer H.R.F. Keating. The answer, he concluded, was: when created by H.R.F. Keating. The author is best known for his series featuring Indian Inspector Ghote, but recently Keating has started a second series featuring a string of police detectives facing various moral dilemmas. In the first of these books, *The Rich Detective*, the central character had left the police force after winning the jackpot in a lottery. However, even in civilian life the former Police Officer still finds himself caught up in trying to solve the last case he was involved with.

In the first (and subsequent) coffee and tea breaks the audience and speakers flocked to buy books at the Crime in Store bookstall, or briefly went outside to stretch their legs and catch a fresh breath of air.

Anne Perry, soon to widen her writing scope by having the her first fantasy novel published, was more than capable to talk about 'Looking for the Real Victorian Policeman'. Not only has she written two Victorian crime series set fifty years apart, she recently found herself back in the middle of the last century when 'a Hitchcock' as an extra on the set of *The Cater Street Hangman*. Should the feature length television adaptation of the first Pitt mystery prove successful, it may well become a series. At St. Hilda's Perry spoke about the trying times many policemen faced after the force was first set up.

Leaping forward to the very recent history, the title of Andrew Taylor's talk was 'A Necessary Nuisance ?: The Police Officer in Crime Novels Set in the Past'. His Lydmouth series, which start in the early 1950s, are set in a small fictional town on the Welsh border near the Forest of Dean. He felt that one of the protagonists in this crime series had to be a policemen as a private investigator would not be believable in that locale at that moment in time. Taylor also spoke about the policemen of Margery Allingham (Albert Campion), Michael Innes (John Appleby), and Ngiao Marsh (Roderick Alleyn). He suggested that part of these authors' success was due to flattering their readers into believing that they were on the same level as their gentleman sleuths.

After an extended lunch break everyone reassembled for the afternoon sessions which was led by Gwendoline Butler who spoke about 'The Historical Background to Charmian Daniels'. Some fans of the Charmian Daniels series may not be aware that it is Butler who writes them

under the pseudonym Jennie Melville. (Under her own name the author is best known for the novels featuring Inspector John Coffin). Butler said she was convinced that women have played a role in detecting crime throughout time—very likely if one knows that in some societies it was women who implemented law. Wanting to give women credit as detectors of crime she created Charmian Daniels, not an amateur, but a dedicated and professional policewoman.

Priscilla Masters asked the question: 'Joanna—A Suitable Woman for the Job?'. At the outset of her series featuring Detective Inspector Joanna Piercey, Masters intended to focus on Joanna's gender without making a big issue of it. Based on feedback from a contact in the police force, the author was able to establish that Joanna is a credible protagonist, and that her male side-kick, who is prone to bigotry, scarily is actually liked by some policemen.

After another brief break Anthea Fraser spoke about 'Planning a Murder'. For her a welcome change from the Golden Age was that crime novels were now more character- rather than plot driven. So, like Dorothy Simpson, Fraser set about establishing a history outside the police force for protagonists Detective Chief Inspector Webb and Detective Sergeant Jackson. Besides having had the benefit of quizzing a policeman about procedure, Fraser also sifts through her nightly dreams as they have been the source of at least one novel and several short stories.

June Thomson, the author of several Sherlock Holmes pastiches and a splendid biography called *Holmes & Watson*, also has written a series featuring Inspector Finch (renamed Inspector Rudd for US editions). Before starting on the police procedurals she weighed the pros and cons of writing about a policeman versus a private investigator, and the bigger credibility attached to a police series won out. Influenced by Simenon's Maigret, Thomson decided that her protagonist also had to be a man due to the limited involvement of woman in the police force in the early 1970s.

In the evening, after another choice dinner, Guest Speaker and crime writer Catherine Aird charmed her audience with a set of entertaining anecdotes. As the local doctor her father would be called upon by the police to identify any strange bones that may have been found in the area. Naturally her mother was far from happy when, on one occasion, she found them strewn over the kitchen table. Before the evening drew to a close, people either continued to chat in the SCR, or retired early in preparation for the final day of the weekend.

The usual breakfast was followed by some free time in which people either found themselves reading the Sunday newspapers in the SCR, checking out the Oxford sights, or attending the Sunday service at St. Cross Church, the church were Lord Peter Wimsey and Harriet Vane were married.

At 11.30am all reconvened in the Vernon Harcourt Room for the first of the last day's final sessions. In her talk, titled 'How Lady Molly Finally Reached Scotland Yard', Joan Lock gave a spellbounding account of the long struggle women had in gaining access to, and equal status in the British police force. Not surprisingly the early struggle matched and had close links with the Suffrage. However, it wasn't until the Equal Opportunities Act of 1976 that policewomen 'officially' obtained the same rights as their male counterparts. These and other accounts can be found in Lock's non-fiction accounts of police history. The Lady Molly referred to is Baroness Orczy's *Lady Molly of Scotland Yard*, a creation by the woman who wrote the Scarlet Pimpernel series.

Following Lock, who herself was a policewoman, a soon-to-be husband-and-wife team of police officers spoke. Phil Gormley, a senior officer, and his partner Claire, a Family Liaisons Officer between the police and the families of those involved in crimes, spoke about 'Murder: Fact and Fiction'. Gormley, a Detective Chief Inspector, was able to add further details to those described on Friday evening by the Chief Constable of Wiltshire. From the description of his partner-to-be, the counselling bereaved families, it became quite obvious that her role as Family Liaisons Officer is one of the most traumatic jobs imaginable.

With the knowledge that many of those serving in the police force do have the compassion and integrity the job calls for, everyone moved to the dining hall for a traditional Sunday roast lunch.

Heartily contented though, due to travelling arrangements of some, fewer in numbers everyone gathered to hear Stuart Pawson talk about his 'Limestone Cowboy'. Pawson recalled questioning Reginald Hill's parentage on the discovery that Hill had beaten him to the idea of creating a police series set in a Yorkshire coal-mining society. However with Dalziel and Pascoe already in existence, Pawson wisely decided to relocate his Charlie Priest novels to Halifax. The soil type in the Halifax area is a clue to the title of Pawson's very funny account of the creation of his sleuth.

Unfortunately for M.C. Beaton, her experience of seeing her Scottish policeman Hamish Macbeth adapted for television in no way matched her talk called 'Romancing the Police'. It turned out that the idea for Hamish came to the author on 5th Avenue in New York, and the highland area where he patrols in fact only has had two murders in the last hundred years. Bye the time the policeman and supporting cast made it to the small screen, they were almost unrecognisable to Beaton. So much so that she began having second thoughts about allowing her other series character, Agatha Raisin, to make the transition to television as well. Unfortunately actress Penelope Keith seems to be indecisive about taking on the role, so for the time being we are unlikely to know if she will do the part justice.

More people left in the weekend's final tea-break, and they missed an excellent summary of gentleman sleuths in the talk by Dean James. In 'Murder Most Genteel: Margery Allingham, Ngaio Marsh, Josephine Tey

and the World of the Golden Age Police Detective' he pointed out similarities, differences, and described character traits of the protagonists by the Golden Age authors. James, co-author of the superb reference book *By a Woman's Hand*, not only was informative, but he also shared in the key element he said his subjects provided: entertainment.

The weekend's last speaker was Nancy Ellen Talburt, an academic and, like Dean James, from the United States. In many ways she followed James' route when speaking about 'Dalgliesh and Morse: A Policeman's Lot—in Love—is Not a Happy One'. Both policemen of her title put their jobs before personal relationships, making the prospect of happy, romantic companionship unlikely. However, according to Talburt, Colin Dexter may still have one more Morse to write so, for him at least, there is still hope.

Since Robert Barnard has hardly got a mention in this report, it may seem that he was an ineffectual Chairman. Nothing could be less so. I have already mentioned that he carried out his task in a masterful, unique, and very entertaining fashion. He unobtrusively kept everyone to their allotted time, fielded the crowd for questions, and created interesting debates between the authors and their audience after all the talks. In short, we can only hope that he will be asked back for next year's St. Hilda's conference.

Another St. Hilda's? Yes! After thanking all the participants Eileen Roberts announced that it will be held same time, same place, next year: 20—

23 August. Even the theme and some of the speakers were revealed. Talking about 'Partners in Crime' will be: Kate Charles, Natasha Cooper, Ann Granger, Janet Neel, Anne Perry, Betty Rowlands, Andrew Taylor, with more names to follow. Those who attended can only applaud Kate Charles and Eileen Roberts for pulling off another great Mystery Weekend, and look forward to next year.

For details of the 6th St. Hilda's Crime and Mystery Weekend (20—23 August 1999), please contact Eileen Roberts, Development Office, St. Hilda's College, Oxford OX4 1DY, United Kingdom.

a quick word with...
...robert harris

SOMETIMES A THRILLER comes along which changes the face of the whole genre. Such a book a) enjoys phenomenal sales, b) generates many imitations, c) has an indifferent movie made of it, and d) is a book the author finds very hard to follow up. Such a book was *Gorky Park*, and for a time it looked like Robert Harris' remarkable *Fatherland* was another example. The success that this picture of a murder investigation by a sympathetic cop in a Nazi Germany that just happened to have won the Second World War, was both superbly written and characterised, with a white-hot thriller pace and a sense of locale that brilliantly demonstrated the author's research. Harris' new book *Archangel* has triumphantly shown that this ex-political columnist is not a one-trick pony. In a Moscow hotel room a British academic (who life is not treating well) is drinking Scotch with the former

barry
forshaw

bodyguard of Stalin's brutal chief of police Beria. And soon we're in pursuit of the dictator's lost notebook, stolen by Beria and the bodyguard when they encounter the dying dictator after his assault on a young girl. Harris manages to top all the action set pieces of his earlier books (including the second, the powerful *Enigma*) while providing the kind of rich and detailed settings that his mentors Graham Greene and Eric Ambler traded in. Le Carré's influence is in there too – and who can call that a bad thing? The academic anti-hero, Kelso, is marvellously sympathetic and low-key, and his sinister nemesis, murdering his way towards the Holy Grail of the lost notebook gives a pulse-racing edge to the narrative.

Harris joined the BBC in 1978 from Cambridge and worked on various prestigious news shows before becoming Political Editor of The Observer, and (in 1989) a weekly columnist for the Sunday Times. His famous study of the Hitler diaries fraud, Selling Hitler, made a perfect prelude to this latest book, and his knowledge of the arcane byways of politics give a tangy sense of truth to his writing. There's a superb scene in *Archangel* in which a party functionary, trying to deport Kelso, lets rip with a diatribe against the West's refusal to let modern-day Russia forget Stalin and his legacy.

Harris has always been an expert on Nazi Germany (it's one of the reasons why *Fatherland* convinces from page one), but the recent resurgence of Fascism in Europe – and the continuing anti-Semitism and totalitarian leanings of the old Russian empire – has convinced him that Russia is the place the West should watch. He sees the neo-fascists of Germany as small beer, compared to a country constantly on the brink, as Russia is.

In the new book the hero is the antithesis of James Bond. Like Ambler and Greene's shabby heroes, he is no superhero, and his faltering efforts to get at the truth are shot through with a genuine sense of danger. Harris is uninterested in the kind of hero who has a gadget for every occasion, and the plots of most thrillers bore him rigid. For those who agree with him, *Archangel* will come as the proverbial breath of fresh air. And those who have read only *Fatherland* because of the astonishing amount of attention it attracted (Tony Blair was an early champion), there's a reason to go back and pick up the overlooked *Enigma* which Mick Jagger is currently producing as a film from a Tom Stoppard screenplay. Mel Gibson has just bought the film rights to *Archangel*, and all of this pretty conclusively proves that Harris has laid to rest the one-book-wonder syndrome.

the false pretences of
margaret yorke
barry forshaw

MARGARET YORKE is well aware of the fact that no crime writer writes in blithe isolation from the facts of bookselling. Over the years in which she has built up a considerable following for her elegant, restrained (yet disturbing) thrillers, she has become acquainted with such things as the significance of her surname's position in the alphabet (which dictates the fact that her books will usually be on the lower shelves of bookstores). And she knows her strengths: she is not an urban writer, and if the big-town-based passages of her books have the tang of authenticity, that is as much due to her voracious consumption of information from street-wise relatives.

But Yorke is no Christie – her characters are given a roundedness that the most famous of women crime writers could only have dreamt of. Her new book from Little, Brown, *False Pretences*, has an interesting title in light of her avowed reluctance to deal in Cornwell-style blood-letting: Yorke, beneath the ordered surfaces, is one tough writer.

Yorke tells me that her interest in psychology is the determining factor in her writing, and despite her pleasant and easy-going manner, it quickly becomes apparent that she takes her craft very seriously. Although she is prepared to do the obligatory appearances that are part of a writer's life, she is bemused by writers who seem to spend more time at events than writing. And writing for her is both a discipline and a pleasure – the greatest satisfaction comes from the fleshing out of an initial concept. She doesn't, however, feel that a writer should work in total isolation, and values the feedback from readers – even if that feedback is negative. And her tenure as chairperson of the Crime

Writers Association was something she undertook fully conscious of the responsibility it entailed. It is hard to imagine that she would be too fazed by the hostility to the CWA shown by certain writers for this very magazine (step forward, Mr Timlin) – although she clearly does not live in a home counties ivory tower. Speaking to her, one is aware of a sharp perception of how her words are being received – and a readiness to acknowledge that a writer must tackle issues that aren't always comfortable.

I ask if her considerable track record makes producing a book like *False Pretences* more challenging, given the expectation of her regular readers. She replies that she writes what she can write, and doesn't think about meeting any self-imposed targets. And all the appearances are that her readers are more than happy for her to continue to do that.

trouble is my business
william b field

A VERY TALL MAN boards the train at Welling-borough. He has stacked-up dreadlocks in the style of Jazzie B., and a single gold earring. He is at least six foot four. A horizontal scar crosses the bridge of his nose—itself the source of a story or two. He doesn't have to ask other commuters to move; they part instantly, like God letting Moses into the buffet car. As it's rush hour, the best clue to their behaviour adorns the back of his black bomber jacket: 'Pyramid Security'. As Raymond Chandler might say, trouble is his business.

Everyone has a story to tell about close encounters with a nightclub bouncer like the one on the Midland Mainline. Those steroid-fuelled gorillas with close-cropped scalps and sovereign rings, pedantic over whether or not it's a polo shirt you're wearing. When not hospitalising your mates they're flirting with female customers, regardless of the wishes of nearby boyfriends. Conversation revolves around fights, sex and bodybuilding, the holy trinity of the security trade. When not in the gym, they spend their days in the jobs where brawn always triumphs over brain. In crime fiction they endanger our detective heroes with beatings or worse; where would *Get Carter* be without a hard doorman or two? It takes Moose Malloy, not Marlowe, to sort out the one in *Farewell My Lovely*. By now this repertoire should sound familiar and—like most stereotypes—there's perhaps a grain of truth in there somewhere. However, clubbers who let such images inform a night out are ignoring the way that the noble art of bouncing is changing.

Tales of sex and searches don't come cheap, so it's worth saying how I got here. What seems like a long time ago I was watching my paid employment slacken off. Being of solid frame and calm temperament—some

might say with the obligatory colourful past— I replied to a discreet 'security operatives' vacancy in the local paper. Before long I was working weekends—on top door, on corners, and floating, to use the lingo—in a cavernous Yorkshire nightclub. Needless to say, the sort of situations intrinsic to the job—sometimes brutal, sometimes surreal—flowed thicker and faster than the pints consumed all around us. Trouble became my business too.

'Trouble' can be as simple as tantrums thrown by 'over-eighteens' who get turned away after stuttering through fictitious dates of birth. It gets tenser when negotiating with the men who'd 'forgotten' they had knives— and in one case a pair of *nanchaku*s—down their socks. Just to keep us on our toes, Saturday nights sometimes climax in a full-scale bar brawl with stools and foreheads coming in from all directions. We're good at confiscating harmless Swiss army knife keyrings, but not so hot on smuggled CS gas canisters, as we've sometimes found out at closing time. 'Domestics' lead to endless daft confrontations: just when you think you've persuaded a couple to calm down, you unite them against you. In turn, the price of getting a good armlock on the husband is a chair on the head from his better half.

Older lads would tell you stories to make your (cropped) hair stand on end, such as 1980s football crews with crossbows and hatchets paying a visit. "We'd smoke 'em, then they'd come looking for us the next week. It got to the stage where we was expecting bazookas," confided Jerry, resplendent in short dreadlocks and with biceps the size of human heads. On a nervous night you'd console yourself with the knowledge that it was worse in neighbouring Leeds. Top Cats—clientele 70% male—is the place with doormen who've fought everyone. Mutter the club's name within one's earshot during his off-duty pint, and watch him reach silently for a set of brass knuckles. Even if this is an urban myth, it no doubt feeds on the sour grapes thrown up by years of ejecting awkward customers.

Going equipped though is usually as unnecessary as it's officially forbidden. In practice, a mixture of cool-headedness and psychology is enough to do the trick. Cold stares are a fair match for the Dutch courage of most customers, who also fear that years of bodybuilding or bricklaying lurk beneath our bomber jackets.

Some of us also take gentlemen's protective sportswear seriously. It's no good being a mighty oak if a single kick to the acorns can take you down: gonads are great for evening the odds. But like boxers and their gumshields, carry anything more than this and you're breaking the rules. Shady practices including the use of weapons have encouraged investigative journalists and legislators alike to scrutinise the security trade. Concerns about drug-dealing—fuelled by a recent documentary whose wired-for-sound reporter

became a Nottingham doorman—did little to improve our image. If the programme is to be believed, then things had got out of control there, the opportunities proving just too lucrative. Deciding on admissions to city centre night-spots means excluding rival drug dealers, thereby ensuring that punters would score from security staff prepared to supply that demand. Whereas once you had to be streetwise to approach bouncers for drugs, television encouraged any fool to try it on. Even the more straight-laced punters started ticking us off about the dangers of E, regardless of the facts.

The more I worked in nightclubs, the more I reconsidered my former belief that 'the bouncers always start it'. Everyone else seems to still share this view: in my time there the venue received just one customer's letter of thanks after we pulled her clear of some routine mayhem. A normal postbag was nothing but complaints. Two rather litigious examples illustrate this point. First came a letter from someone's mother, complaining that her son had been set upon by eight bouncers on the dancefloor, causing him to develop bulimia, which endangered his mortgage repayments. A horrific story, no doubt—but for the fact we'd had only four staff downstairs that night. (The swift appearance of health and money troubles within three days of the alleged incident was also slightly suspect, and the threatened legal action didn't materialise.) Equally daft was the woman who broke a tooth on the lollipop she was eating, who then blamed us for not warning her of the dangers. It ended in some energetic tag wrestling and me opening a fire exit with her boyfriend's chest, all to a Donna Summer soundtrack.

Perhaps strangely, it is precisely complaints of this nature to which the industry is most receptive these days. One indication of this is the growing demand for women security staff, influenced by a new etiquette in society. 'Risk awareness' drives everything. On one hand more searches occur because venues are more nervous about drugs and weapons. On the other, they fear complaints of doormen behaving improperly when searching female customers. Simultaneous pressures to avoid danger *and* litigation lead to door policies that try to please everyone all of the time. This creates new opportunities the women joining the trade, most of whom are also as tough and reliable (and often as idiosyncratic) as their male counterparts. It is a shame that the women are not recruited on the strength of these qualities alone, rather than as an accommodation to contemporary paranoia about bad behaviour.

As you might expect, such vacancies attract a fair number of ex-army types and martial arts enthusiasts. But overall the women who work doors are harder to pigeonhole than the men. For instance, Trish is an animated, heavily-built mother whose three young sons take up her days. Bouncing has given her an independent income and something new to do at night. Popular with the patrons of rock night, she makes it her self-appointed job to liven up their lives. The contrast with Fi couldn't be more striking. Tiny and immaculately tanned, she spends her days in the fashion trade and nights working doors. Both see the job as a bit of a laugh, but turn into hardcases the moment they sense trouble. Trish lets the men know that when they've taken the banter too far, becoming inflexible over who can't come in 'and telling them to arseholes', as she puts it. Provided the walkie-talkies are working, Fi has an ear for situations and is often first on the scene. Once she hears the cue to move—such as her infamous boyfriend and his brother telling a punter 'right, we've asked you nicely'—you fear for the sound barrier.

I sometimes wonder how long bouncing can continue to work in the old way. There is a big push on to professionalise the whole operation. The Northern Council for Further Education now runs a diploma course in 'door supervision'. The question of etiquette—political correctness, if you like—has had widespread repercussions for the industry as a whole. Renaming bouncers and doormen as 'security operatives' is just one example; drilling them with the jargon of equal opportunities is another. In the last year I have attended three training sessions designed to bring me up to speed with this caring nineties environment. Experience may tell you that there are only two ways of involuntarily leaving a club—through an open door or a closed one—but now it has to be done in a sensitive way.

This has been made clear to us on numerous occasions. Thus 'drugs awareness training' means understanding rave culture before ejecting someone who is tripping off their face. We're also assessed on whether we know how to get through a number of 'scenarios'. 'Two lesbians are kissing in the bar when a customer complains. How do you react?' (Much sniggering follows.) 'What do you do when an Islamic fundamentalist approaches you and complains he is trying to eat but there are women around him?' Provide the right answers and you're on course for a rewarding job with late hours. The people setting these little teasers don't seem to realise that real-life situations take more than a textbook approach to solve them. Just in case applicants had set their hearts on other perks, we were also told to 'be nice, be polite—but no snogging or exchanging phone numbers—it doesn't look professional'.

Redefining the trade in these terms has led to the adoption of licensing schemes by many local authorities. Licensing applications, which involve police checks for criminal records, include a form with all the jargon about being caring, sharing and sensitive. I contacted several local authorities for comments on this peculiar new trend, but they wanted all enquiries in writing first, to pass on to their lawyers before answering my questions. They're even cautious about commenting on their precautions. Fights, sex and searches are giving way to an anodyne age of 'safety first'. 'Trouble is my business' is no longer the right expression, but 'risk avoidance is my profession' just hasn't got the same ring to it.

ALLISON & BUSBY
FOR CRIME NOVELS PAR EXCELLENCE

Sold for UK Television
Roy Lewis
The Cross Bearer

'...adroit use of archeological know-how, with north-east locations as fresh
as the wind from the moors' *Literary Review*

'Especially recommended for the history buffs' *Financial Times*

The fabled treasure of the Knights Templar is a matter of myth and legend.
A man claims to know where it is hidden: intrigued Landon agrees to help find it.
The search turns violent and Landon finds himself plunged into a dangerous
vortex of murder, Masonic intimidation and corruption. Soon he is fighting
for his life in the darkness of the Templar tomb of the Cross Bearer.

14 December 1998   208pp   074900388X   £5.99pb

Other crime available from Allison & Busby

Brian Battison
The Witch's Familiar
0749003103   £5.99
Michael Bond
Monsieur Pamplemousse Afloat
0749003472   £5.99pb
Monsieur Pamplemousse Omnibus, Vol 1
0749003529   £9.99pb
Ann Cleeves
A Day in the Death of Dorothea Cassidy
0749003073   £5.99pb
Killjoy
0749003502   £5.99pb
John Gano
Inspector Proby's Christmas
0749002972   £5.99pb
Bartholomew Gill
The Death of a Joyce Scholar
0749003723   £5.99pb
Ted Lewis
Get Carter
0749001216   £5.99pb

Priscilla Masters
Catch the Fallen Sparrow
0749003022   £5.99pb
Winding up the Serpent
0749003715   £5.99pb
Jenny Melville
The Woman Who was Not There
0749003162   £5.99pb
Frank Palmer
Dark Forest
074903251   £5.99pb
Red Gutter
0749003367   £5.99pb
Sax Rohmer
Fu Manchu Omnibus, Vol 1
0749002719   £9.99pb
Fu Manchu Omnibus, Vol 2
0749002220   £9.99pb
Fu Manchu Omnibus, Vol 3
0749002271   £9.99pb
Frank Smith
Fatal Flaw
0749003200   £5.99pb

http://www.allisonandbusby.ltd.uk

interview

john milne:
alive and kicking
mark campbell

JOHN MILNE was born in Bermondsey in 1952, and trained as a painter before he decided to pursue a literary career. He's the author of four crime novels featuring one-legged private detective Jimmy Jenner, *Dead Birds*, *Shadow Play*, *Daddy's Girl* and — new in October 1998 from No Exit Press — *Alive & Kicking*. He has also written for *Bergerac*, *Eastenders*, *Lovejoy*, *The Bill*, *Boon*, *Taggart*, *Wycliffe* and *Silent Witness*. Not bad going.

Milne is a large man, and thoughtful with it. Sitting in the massive new Weatherspoons pub an High Holborn, his voice barely rises above the cacophony of noise that surrounds our snug. But what he's got to say is carefully considered, concisely articulated, and throws fascinating insight into the murky world of both publishing and television production. Over the last decade and a half, he's had his fingers in pretty much every crime series of note on the box, Oh, yes, and *Pie In The Sky* too. He could, it he wanted, be an egotistical pain in the neck. (I would be.) But — and here's the good news — he's Mr Modesty himself

What did you want to be at school? Did you particular want to be a writer?

No, I never intended to be a writer at all — I became one by chance. I went to art school when I was in my mid-twenties, and after I left I couldn't afford anywhere to paint. So I worked at the Post Office, and I wrote my first novel during my breaks and in the evenings, I sold it to the first person who read it, Christopher Sinclair Stevenson. It went like magic. I thought that was normal, but it took me years to work out that everyone else had a terrible time getting published. I thought it was always going to be like that, but it wasn't. Only then did the game begin.

Did it get harder after that?

Much harder.

Why?

I think people found it very difficult to know which pigeon hole to put my novels into. My relationship with mass-market publishers grew more and more difficult. I didn't like them.

Did they try and force you to edit your manuscript to suit their tastes?

They did quite a bit of that, yeah. I

had a terrible time with one woman who had been editing Douglas Adams in a very cocky way, and seemed to think that she could continue in the same way with me. At that stage I was with Heinemann, and in the end it got to the point where I couldn't talk to her, I couldn't have anything to do with her. I can't be treated like that by anyone,

What category do you feel your novels do fall into? Literary noir?

They have become that now, yeah, although I don't know that I intended them to be. Writing a crime novel is a bit like being a narrative painter or something. What you're doing is allowing the form to carry a great deal of the burden. Everybody knows what the form is — or thinks they know — and within that you can, to use 'form' in another sense, formally write in a way that expresses you best. Does that make sense?

Yes. You must enjoy working in the crime genre. All your novels are crime based, aren't they?

No, they're not, not really. The earlier novels are much more literary. I won prizes, council fellowships and all that kind of thing, but there was a natural level that they weren't going to go above, I think.

How did you start working for television?

A bloke who used to produce *Bergerac* had read some of my stuff, and he rang me up and said "*Do you want to have a go at writing for it?*" So I did.

And what was that like?

Terrific. I loved it. I loved the industrial quality of television scriptwriting; I liked the idea of doing something which is crafted well, which addresses a large audience. I wrote it for three series, in fact I wrote the last *Bergerac* of all.

I watched some of the later episodes, and I felt things had gone a little OTT. Helicopters, explosions, terrorists — all an one little island?

Well, there were no terrorists or helicopters in mine, but I do agree that having it all happen on Jersey is a fantasy!

Did you find the discipline hard?

No, I found it quite easy really. I'm surprised that I did, because I didn't have any drama in my background. I'm probably aided by the fact that in my books I write a series of pictures with the voice of this man [John Jenner] overlaying them. That's especially true of the latest one, Alive And Kicking.

What did you do after *Bergerac*?

I started to write for *The Bill* at the same time as *Bergerac*. Later on I worked on *Eastenders*. Then, without really meaning to do it, I became a kind of specialist who wrote episodes for crime series. I worked on little gems that everyone's forgotten, like Sam Saturday, about a Jewish policeman. I did a couple of *Lovejoy*s, and I rather liked that. I did a load of episodes of *Pie In The Sky* — I think I probably wrote about ten of those — and the guy who invented it is a great mate of mine.

Eastenders doesn't quite fit with the others you've done…

No, well I'd worked on *The Bill*, and the producer went off and worked for *Eastenders* and asked me if I would go and work for it, which I did. So I did that for a year, But I think they all hated me, and only put up with me while this guy was producing it. As soon as he left, I was out.

Why did they hate you?

Well, I can think of lots of reasons. I think they found me a very difficult person — I do have a very clear idea of what I want to write and how I want to write it, and I can be very impatient. There's a kind of production line of Oxford graduates going to the BBC and emerging two years' later as fully-fledged scriptwriters. The first script-editor I worked with on *Bergerac* used to teach these people at the BBC and said to me, "*You'd be as well served if you went down any dole queue and picked out people at random.*"

Have things changed much since you began scriptwriting?

Often it's luck — if you meet people you're likely to get on with, you can do things with them. There's no real order. Although lots of young, very inexperienced producers and script-editors are absolutely useless, some of them aren't — some of them are bloody brilliant. You have to keep things open, so you don't make a mistake or not recognise who those people are.

What about the Jenner books? How did they come about?

I can remember being on a No 22 bus going past the old Bishopsgate Station, and thinking 'I would like to write this character.' I could almost see him waiting for a bus.

Why has he only got one leg?

So he can't run after people and bash them up. Everything he does he's got to use his head. Sometimes he's violent, but not usually, and it's always for a very good reason.

Some of the decisions were dead easy — I gave him my background, my age, so I didn't have to struggle to remember what things held remember, There are lots of bits of true stories that I pinched. He comes from Bermondsey and he has my voice, but he's not me. I gave him roughly my birthdate so I know he'll remember the 1966 World Cup very well. It just seemed to me that he needed to be planted in the world in order to be a real person with a real London voice. Quite often, you're reading a story and you think, 'Where's this person from?' Sometimes characters have attributes that are bolted unto them, and I hope that's not the case with Jenner.

Do the plots arrive organically or do you sit down and formulate them

from page one?

A bit of each. Writing for television is really very mechanical – you have to have a beginning, middle and end. But novel writing can get away from that. I write the end quite early on and put it in the drawer, so that the tyranny of getting there has gone away. It's just a silly psychological game I play with myself. Actually, I never use that ending — I always write another one!

Did It bother you that Martin Amis stole your title, *London Fields*?

I wrote to him, and said, *"I'm told you're writing a book which you're calling* London Fields — *is there any truth in it?"* So he wrote back and said, *"Oh dear, I knew this would happen, my wife said it would."* But clearly I'm not Julian Barnes or Clive James, so he decided to blunder on and use it. There was no apology or even the slightest hint of regret. So I wrote to him again and said, *"By the way, I'm writing a book called* Money — *do you think it'll get me any?"* End of correspondence.

You haven't got much time for him, then?

He's a very fluent, very able writer, but for my money he's a bit cruel. I mean, you can say that in general about post-modernist literature, but with Amis, there's a lack of humanity, a lack of sympathy, which I find pretty disgusting,

Why the ten year gap since the previous Jenner novel?

Partly because when I fell out with Heinemann, I fell about with then very spectacularly. After disagreeing with Douglas Adams' editor, about a year passed and then a woman rang me up and said, *"Hello, I'm so-and-so, I'm your new editor. Could I see your novel?"*

So I took my novel down there, to Michelin House, and when I got to the front door, this girl on reception said, *"All deliveries have to go round the back."* So I said, *"They may well do, but I'm a writer not a delivery driver."* So she said very nicely, *"Please could you take it round the back, otherwise it makes it very difficult for me."* So I shut the door, and went round the back, and there was this Irish guy at the back door. Re pointed over to the other side of this room and said, *"You have to put your stuff over there and wait for someone to sign it in."* So I said, *"I'm not doing that. You're on the back door, I've brought round my book to the back door, here you are."* I put it on the counter, and he ran around the table, grabbed the manuscript, dashed it onto the floor and said, *"Listen, you cunt, either you take it with you, or you put it over there."* Now I guess this man wanted to fight me, although I hadn't insulted him, but I certainly didn't want a fight. So I picked it up, with as much poise as I could muster, tucked it inside my bag and cycled home again. (Laughs)

I then rang this woman and she said, *"Oh, I'm terrible sorry,"* but she never did much about it. And I realised that actually these people were giving the game away — there was something very anti-author about them, It's very interesting, because you don't find this attitude with booksellers — I have to say this, because my wife's a bookseller.

Booksellers, by and large, are interested in fucking books. But people in publishing, quite a lot of them, are just interested in next year's car. What famous people they've met, what account they've got, every bloody thing except this difficult man with this bundle of paper under his arm. And so I kind of fell out of the whole thing completely. I didn't need it, because although I was tinkering away at writing fiction, I was also doing this television stuff, and that engaged me more fully.

Why the switch to No Exit Press?

My wife worked in Waterstones in Earls Court, and the manager there, David Creek, was a friend of Ion Mills [publisher of No Exit]. I'd known Ion since I did freelance work in Time Out. And this guy said he knew Ion was interested in my work, and my wife started this campaign of nipping at my ankles, till eventually Ion and I got together. I think Ion is a pretty heavenly publisher. He's interested in the text, he listens to what you've got to say, he's interested in what my opinions are about the typeface, the cover — he's like a bloke who's publishing what he'd like to read. That worked for me, so I was able to do something again. I'd kept saying to my friends over the years that I hadn't finished this latest novel, and they kept saying to me, *"You have, haven't you — you've been lying."* And I realised that I had, and all I had to do was simply cut it back to a reasonable size, which is what I've done.

And No Exit are republishing your backlist?

Yes, I hold all the rights, but the early ones are so different, they're much more literary, much more playing games with words, I think we need to be focused. We're saying, *"Here are the Jenner novels,"* and Ion has decided in his wisdom to take a punt on doing them again. That's no problem, No Exit is a publisher of specialist crime, so that's great. If we do other things later on, then we'll do them.

What's your favourite TV programme?

Match Of The Day, with QPR!

What's your favourite book? Do you have one?

Not really. I love Patrick O'Brien's novels,

Any crime writing heroes?

Yeah, Chandler. Elmore Leonard. It's not to do with their names or reputations; it's to do with a certain way in which they deal with language, which I find very engaging. Too often crime writing is an excuse for rather impoverished writers to get published. I used to review crime novels for *Time Out*, I read hundreds of them, and the percentage of them that were good was tiny.

What are you doing now?

I'm writing another of the Jenner books and I'm also writing some films for C4. They're called Future Shock; they're documentaries set in the near future, about technology. They have no crime story input at all.

interview

reginald hill
adrian muller

"You can't tell people how to write books,"
states Reginald Hill. "The only advice I give
aspiring writers is that, when you have
finished your first novel, immediately start
writing your second because now you will
have a faint idea of how it is done." Smiling,
he adds, "And don't sit around waiting for
publishers to come pushing wheelbarrows
full of money—they won't."

Acting on this directive himself, the

novelist completed his first manuscript,
Fell of Dark, *and shortly afterwards*
started work on his first published novel,
A Clubabble Woman. *Since the latter*
appeared in 1970, Hill has had a further
twenty-nine books published under his own
name, and another twelve under three
pseudonyms. Best known for his novels
featuring Yorkshire policemen Andy
Dalziel and Peter Pascoe, the author has
also written three highly enjoyable books
about Joe Sixsmith, a private investigator
operating in Luton. Besides wining two
Crime Writers' Association Daggers for his
writing, Reginald Hill was also awarded
the CWA Diamond Dagger for his
outstanding contribution to the genre.
Following the publication of On Beulah
Height *earlier this year, the imminent*
republication of Fell of Dark *in December,*
and the prospect of a new instalment in
the Sixsmith series in 1999, Adrian Muller
spoke to the author about his writing career.

When asked to give some brief
details about his background Reginald
Hill reels off the essentials without a
moment's pause. "I was born in 1936
in West Hartlepool, County Durham,

and I was brought up in Cumberland in Carlisle from the age of two or three. Education: Carlisle Grammar School, followed by two years national service. Lance Corporal, unpaid—unappreciated—in the Border Regiment. Then three years at Oxford—St.Catherine's—followed by a year in Edinburgh as a British Council Overseas Students Officer. After that I went into teaching as a secondary school teacher down in Essex. Later, I became a lecturer in a college of education in Yorkshire where I remained until I gave up the day job in 1980 and went into full-time writing." Aware that it is his writing that most people are interested in, Hill slows down to reflect a little further. "The first book came out in 1970 and during the 70s, I gradually felt myself changing from being a college lecturer who wrote fiction on the side to being a novelist who did some college lecturing. So, at the end of the decade, I came clean and took the big leap into the unknown," he says, smiling.

One of the things that makes Reginald Hill's writing such a pleasure to read is his ability to conjure up realistic portrayals of not only characters from different social backgrounds, but also those from different generations. Does the author feel that his career in education helped him in his writing? "I couldn't say consciously that it helped, but looking back it probably did," Hill says after a moment's reflection. "A lot of people wondered whether being separated from the world of work might affect my writing, 'Where are you going to get your characters from?', but I never found any trouble in still being able to reach into my knowledge or my imagination."

The answer to whether his choice to become a teacher had been a conscious one comes after an interesting diversion. "Back in the good old days if you had a degree, especially if it was from one of the old universities, there was none of this business of graduate unemployment," he explains. "People used to come out to Oxford to interview *us*. They would take a suite of rooms at one of the local hostelries and the young undergrads would go around and pick and choose. We had a very different world outlook than the poor kids nowadays. You got to an age where you thought 'Oh, I need a job', and you looked around and the world was full of a variety of them. I thought I would give teaching a try to see if I liked it and found out that I did. It was as simple as that."

Hill has fond recollections of both his students and his colleagues, and adds that he has always enjoyed people's company. "Perhaps something of this comes out in my writing," he says, "or perhaps it comes from the same spring of wanting to communicate. I have never really been one for analysing myself and trying to work out where it all comes from."

Having started reading and making up stories at a very early age, the first adult fiction Reginald Hill encountered was crime fiction. "I came from a very ordinary working class background. There weren't a lot of books in our house, but my mother was a great enthusiast of the golden age of crime writing," he remembers. "When I was going down to the children's library, my mother would ask me to pop into the 'big' library and ask if they had anything new by Agatha Christie or the likes. After a while I started wandering into the big library and began investigating the shelves myself. So my toes were dipped into crime fiction at a very early age."

Hill does not feel that any particular crime author has been of influence on his work. "It was the idea of the novel as a vehicle for telling a story about crime and detection that was very early imprinted on my mind," he explains. Smiling he recalls, "In my middle teens I decided I was going to sit down and write a great crime story but it never came to anything."

A few years later Reginald Hill became what he calls a literary snob. "I suddenly realised I was enjoying the great novelists, Dickens, Hardy, and Austen, and crime fiction became rather beneath my notice for a while. My ambitions changed. I now wanted to write not thrillers or detective stories but the great English novel. I have still have a bottom drawer full of first chapters somewhere."

The latter remark is typically self-depreciating for the author. Over the years the entertaining whodunits he first wrote have become increasingly ambitious in content and style. Without much effort a case could be made that Hill has become an author of literary novels, but when pressed on this point, he will only say, "As mature years came upon me, I looked back and I could see that the snobbish distinction I made in

my late teens and perhaps early twenties between serious fiction and popular fiction was indeed foolish. Yet, I think it is a distinction that some of the more unimaginative critics still try to make. I would like to feel that I am writing in the main stream tradition of the English novel. My great novel loves are very much in the 19th century—Dickens, Austen, Thackeray, Trollope—and I would be unhappy to feel that some influence of theirs didn't show somewhere in my work." Taking stock of his present-day situation he adds, "These days I write the books I want to write without any glance either towards popularity or indeed reputation. It's a nice situation to be in."

By the time Reginald Hill reached the age of thirty, only some of his poetry had been published. It wasn't until the author and his wife moved from Essex to Yorkshire that Hill found time to sit down and write *Fell of Dark*. "My wife stayed down in Essex to sell our house while I was camping in a Yorkshire house without any social life," he says. "I was just starting a new job so I didn't know anybody, and suddenly there was time to not only write, but to actually finish something I was writing. That was *Fell of Dark*. Curiously it opens within two-and-a-half miles from where I am presently sitting in my study. The wheel has come full circle."

Fell of Dark, part detective story and part psychological thriller, is about a man arriving in Cumbria, and subsequently being suspected of murdering two girls. "I wrote it and sent it off," Hill says, "and via a convergence of circumstances, which often happens in publishing, it ended up being the second of my books to be published." This December, almost a quarter of a decade after *Fell of Dark* first appeared, HarperCollins will be republishing the novel in both hard- and paperback editions.

Over the years Hill has written numerous stand-alone novels, under his own name as well as under his three pseudonyms: Dick Morland, Patrick Ruell (before they married, Hill's wife was named Patricia Ruell), and Charles Underhill. "There is a lot of variety there," the author says of his early output. "When I started writing it was really as if I was relieved to discover that I knew I could do it, and so I was very productive in those early years. At the beginning of the 70's I had three books published in a single year! I couldn't manage that now, but I really just wanted to try all forms of writing."

The pseudonyms came about after Hill's publisher turned down a non-detective manuscript. "This was the first of the Patrick Ruell books," the author recalls. "HarperCollins suggested that someone else might be interested in publishing it, and when I found another publisher they said, 'Well, we think it would be a good idea for you to use a pseudonym in order not to confuse your readership.' As my readership then consisted of my close friends, relatives and a few hundred others I didn't think there was going to be much chance of confusing them, but being young and always afraid at

REGINALD HILL

THE WOOD BEYOND

FEATURING DALZIEL AND PASCOE

NOW A MAJOR TV SERIES

that stage that the publishers would take away their money and give it to someone else, I went along with it, and this was repeated on two further occasions."

Describing the nature of the books he wrote under the pen-names Hill says, "The Ruell books were, I suppose, thrillers in the sense that they weren't about the investigation of a crime. They had a strong adventure element in them. Those I wrote as Charles Underhill were tongue-in-cheek historical novels, and the Dick Morlands were science fiction."

Besides crime fiction, some of the other non-series books the author has written under his own name are war novels. "*No Man's Land* is set during the First World War and it probably was my first expression of interest in the fate of the unfortunates who got shot for desertion and other alleged crimes. They were really books with an individual idea, situation or character which I felt interested in exploring at that time."

The novels Hill is best known for are those featuring Superintendent Andy Dalziel (pronounced Dee-ell) and Sergeant (later Inspector) Peter Pascoe. As strange as it may seem sixteen instalments down the line, *A Clubbable Woman* was never intended to develop into a series. "It was the second book I wrote. Then I did another couple of books, probably the first of what turned out to be the Ruell books. At some point I thought 'That chap Dalziel, there's a bit more life in him.'"

So was Dalziel intended to be the central character? "Well no, quite the reverse in fact," Hill says. "When I started it was Pascoe who was the main character in my mind. Pascoe was the character with whom I at that time, as the writer, identified with: youngish, graduate, the same kind of interests as myself. Andy Dalziel was much more intended to be the foil to Pascoe, the rather old fashioned, seat-of-the-pants, rather brutish, non-cerebral kind of cop, but it didn't quite work out like that. Dalziel in concept was perhaps intended as a caricature, but I found that as I worked with him he ceased to be so. He became larger than life but not in any way false to life. They became equal in their billing and then, increasingly over the years, I had to make a conscious effort to stop Andy

Dalziel from taking over completely, to retain the balance and to ensure that Peter Pascoe got his fair share of the action."

In recent instalments Peter Pascoe has been showing signs of disenchantment with his role in the police force. It even seems that he might consider resigning. That, however, the author is adamant, will not happen. "The whole point about Pascoe is that he is very much at the centre of the books' ongoing dynamic," Hill says. "I think of Pascoe as being a kind of everyman, with the good and the bad angel sitting on either side of his shoulders—just as with the heroes in the old morality plays. Of course the good angel and the bad angel are interchangeable in this case, they being his wife, Ellie Pascoe, on the one side, and Andy Dalziel on the other."

Describing the flip sides of Pascoe's conscience the creator says, "When she was first introduced Ellie was very suspicious of the police force and the attitudes of people like Dalziel. Dalziel of course was also a very great influence on Pascoe. From time to time Pascoe now realises that he has said or done something which is 'Dalzielesque', that he is beginning to think like the fat bastard. But Dalziel and Ellie have also developed. They aren't static, and they have undergone changes in attitude as well."

As a further indication that Peter won't be making any drastic career changes, Reginald Hill points out that Pascoe is still very much active in law enforcement in *One Small Step*, his tongue-in-cheek novella set in the next century. When the first murder occurs Peter Pascoe, now the British Justice Commissioner in the EuroFed Department, brings a gouty Andy Dalziel out of retirement, and together they solve the case.

Increasingly two of the secondary characters in the Dalziel and Pascoe novels have come to the foreground. As more of Sergeant Edgar 'Wieldy' Wield and WPC Shirley Novello's background is revealed, their fans can expect larger roles for both of them in the future. Of Wield and Novello the author says, "Their first appearance in the books weren't earth shattering. They didn't step forward as major characters, but as I wrote more about them I found myself discovering more of their background. One of the delights of writing a series is that it gives you time to take what are small characters, to look more closely at them, and to develop them further. With Wield for instance, in his first appearance he is just a remarkably ugly police sergeant. Nobody really understood quite what he was about. He was very efficient, but what went on behind his ravaged exterior no one could work out. At that point I didn't say 'This chap is gay and I'm hiding it for a later book'. The next time he appeared I thought 'What are you using this exterior, this forbidding ugliness, in fact to hide?' I realised that he was gay, and I was able to take this further. It was a fascinating idea back in the late 70's. I don't know what the situation of a gay cop is nowadays—an openly gay cop—but I'm certain back then it was not a very comfortable one, and this is why he kept his gayness well hidden. Over the years I have been able to let the other characters get to know him better in the same ways as I have. I don't think I could have done that in a single book. At least not in a single Dalziel and Pascoe book, it would have had to have been about Wield and nobody else. The same applies to Novello. She initially made a brief appearance in *The Wood Beyond*, but there was a larger role for her in *On Beulah Height* which I could develop, and she will develop further. She's another individual at large in the police force trying to come to terms with herself and the job. Exactly how characters are going to develop I don't know in advance, and if I did I would get bored."

The latter statement raises the question which of the two main plotting categories Reginald Hill falls into: does he decide in advance how a book will develop and end, or does he find himself as surprised as his readers by the turn of events? "I suppose both and neither," he says almost apologetically. "There have been occasions when I have been very aware of exactly how a book was going to end, and the problem then has been to get to that end. At other times you start off with an idea without knowing how it will develop."

Taking *On Beulah Height* as an example he says, "I had this idea about a sunken village in a reservoir and it coming back up and bringing the past with it. Then the other ideas started falling around it: Mahler's *Kindertotenlieder*—his 'Songs for Dead

Children', and using those songs as epigraphs to underpin this story about losing children. Gradually I started planing the book before I actually wrote bits of it. Then I started seeing that the *Lieder* could be much more organic, that rather than these epigraphs having an ornamental effect, that they could be incorporated in the book in a much more integral role."

To allow him to include the song-cycle in the text, Reginald Hill translated the German lyrics into the Yorkshire idiom of one of the central characters in the book. Then he further included the factual history of the cycle in the introduction to a fictional compact disc. Hill also especially wrote a children's story for *On Beulah Height*. "I added a further element of losing a child," says Hill. "Not through abuse or abduction, but through illness. *Nina and the Nix* is the externalisation of what I think is every parents' greatest fear. The Nix is a water goblin who comes out to steal children." Initially the author wrote the story for his own point of reference, but on completion Hill realised that it might benefit readers if they had access to the tale as well.

The inclusion of lyrics, a children's story, and interview transcripts in *On Beulah Height*, together with diary entries in *The Wood Beyond*, the previous Dalziel and Pascoe novel, go some way to explain why Reginald Hill does not feel trapped writing about series characters. Without compromising the logical development of the two policemen and their friends and family, the author transposes them into the

stories he wants to tell. He admits as much himself. "For the past few years any idea I get, any area that I really want to explore, I now tend to think about in terms of plots for Dalziel and Pascoe novels. I have found the series to be incredibly elastic," he says, not without some relief. "It's been a gradual realisation. As the books have gone on I have extended them in all kinds of ways; in terms of theme and in the way the story has been told. It means that when I've got a theme I want to explore, that I can really go at it in a much more wholehearted manor because I am not having to devise and introduce totally new characters. I've got this steady core of people who are developing and growing, but I am totally familiar with them. The danger of any series is that familiarity can lead to staleness. We can all think of series in which the author is merely rewriting the same story and changing a bit of the plot, adding a few names here and there. Often I have enjoyed reading the same story written by some people again and again and again, but I haven't wanted to do that myself. What I have been trying to do with Dalziel and Pascoe is to find new stories to tell, new ideas to play with, giving me the chance to use ongoing characters without being boring."

After the appalling portrayal of Dalziel and Pascoe in the television adaptation of *A Pinch of Snuff*, many of Reginald Hill's colleagues feel that he has been extremely fortunate in the more recent adaptations by the BBC. Rumour has it that Hill purposely organised an alcoholic CWA meeting on the evening of the first episode of *A Pinch of Snuff*. He managed to get his fellow CWA members so drunk that the few who did see the broadcast were unable to remember much the following morning. Asked if this account is true, Hill manages a beatific expression of innocence.

"Many people feel that I have been lucky with the new adaptations and I feel it as well," he admits. "Mind you, the expert opinion was that the Yorkshire TV production would render Dalziel and Pascoe unsellable to other companies for at least five years. Since Portobello Productions and the BBC came along within that time one wonders what those expert opinions were based on."

In hindsight it was obvious that, with Hale and Pace playing the policemen, Yorkshire TV was hoping to tap into the format of comic actors starring in successful television adaptations. The important distinction the production company failed to make was that Hale and Pace were comedians and not actors known for comic roles (which was the case with David 'Inspector Frost' Jason for instance).

With the much-respected Warren Clarke as Andy Dalziel and the relatively unknown Colin Buchanan as Peter Pascoe, the makers of the new feature length dramas didn't take any risks and went for experienced performers with a wide range of acting ability.

"A question I get often these days is whether I now think of Warren Clarke and Colin Buchanan as Dalziel and Pascoe," Hill says. "The answer to that

Courtesy BBC Picture Library

is 'No, absolutely not.'" Whilst the author is delighted with the casting he points out that Warren Clarke is about seven stone underweight for the role of Dalziel. "But," he adds, "I can't imagine anyone being the 'real' Dalziel, or indeed the 'real' Pascoe. It doesn't matter. What mattered to me was the intent of the BBC, guided by the people at Portobello, to try to get into the scripts the important elements from the books."

Even when watching the BBC/Portobello productions of his books, it took some time before Reginald Hill could make the necessary mind swing to appreciate the adaptations. "At first I couldn't see them as television. I was watching them as versions of my books and judging them against that. It has taken a bit of time for the understanding to sink in, but now I can sit back and enjoy the adaptations for what they are. I would still be distraught if they did anything which betrayed the characters or my plots but they haven't. So far they are keeping in touch with me and staying true to the books."

In the novels and feature length television episodes it is only at first glance that Andy Dalziel appears to be the foil for more sophisticated counterparts. Through experience Peter Pascoe and observant fans have come to know better. Whereas Pascoe has been relatively straightforward to understand, Dalziel is far more of a puzzle. When asked about this Reginald Hill smiles and says, "To put it at its most vulgar: if Dalziel farts at a funeral, it is not because he is a coarse, or a flatulent and insensitive man. It is because that fart at that particular moment has got some purpose. The point about Dalziel is that he never does anything without a meaning. He is a man very much in control. If you look at the way Dalziel dresses, when he first appears he is wearing an old suit which age has given a sheen, a patina of shininess, which when he scratches himself—as he does frequently, leaves the mark of his nails on the cloth. Yet when he wants to he can appear extraordinarily smart. As I reveal in one book, he has his best suits especially made from the best Bradford cloth by a very good tailor who he has got banged up for some crime in an open prison somewhere. Dalziel is no slouch or anyone's fool, but he rarely sees the need to impress people. He influences people and he makes them move in the directions he wants them to."

A further hint at Dalziel's intelligence and learning is his immediate grasp of moments where someone is trying to get the better of him; he also frequently understands references people wouldn't necessarily expect him to get the meaning of. What can Hill say about Andy Dalziel's background? "He probably left school at fifteen, or thereabouts, before going into the police force. His father was a Scot who came down to Yorkshire and got married to Yorkshire lass, so they would have given him a great respect for education."

That being the case, why does Dalziel give Pascoe such a hard time about being a graduate? Is it something that Dalziel envies? "It's an interesting idea," Hill says, seemingly uncertain himself. "Certainly he mocks, he has got that element of northern down-to-earthiness in him. He mocks the need of people to stay on at school into their twenties when they could be out doing things, but I certainly don't think he is unappreciative of what it is possible to learn in higher education. He just doesn't feel the need to fall over himself to show any admiration, or indeed envy, of it. Dalziel is together enough not to feel envy. He is happy with who he is, which is why he does not have any ambitions to go beyond being head of Yorkshire CID. He looks at the Assistant Chief Constable, the Deputy Chief Constable, and the Chief Constable with a rather patronising air.

They *think* they are in charge but he *knows* he really is. I think it was in *Child's Play* that the Assistant Chief Constable has ambitions to become Chief Constable when the latter is about to retire. That is the last thing Dalziel wanted, so he set about making damn sure that he didn't get the job. He wouldn't want to have someone he regards as a prat in charge of him."

Besides winning the CWA Cartier Diamond Dagger for his overall contribution to crime fiction, Reginald Hill is also the recipient of two Golden Daggers: for his novel *Bones and Silence*, and for his short story *On the Psychiatrist's Couch*. Hill loves writing short stories but, comparing them to novels, he says, "I find that proportionately the short story takes far, far more time to write. I forget who said 'I am writing you a long letter because I do not have time to write you a short one', but I feel the same about short stories. I don't have enough time to get them into the shape in which I feel happy for people to read them. One of those unfortunate things is that aspiring writers often start by writing short stories because they are short, but in fact they are the most difficult to do well."

These days readers are most likely to find short stories in a book collection by a single author, or otherwise in anthologies. Hill's 'On the Psychiatrist's Couch' appeared in *Whydunnit, The 1997 CWA Anthology*, published by Severn House. Of anthologies he says, "If you have got twelve short stories in a book you will invariably find that three of them are very good; then

there's another three which are pretty good but which could have done with a bit more work; a further three which are a bit ragged really, and the author perhaps ought to have spent another couple of weeks at them; and then three which should never have been published and would never have been published had it not been for the eminent names which are attached to them. I really can't understand how people can let some short stories go out under their names. Usually I wait until I'm invited to submit one. Someone will say 'I'm desperate for a short story, can you help'. Only if there's enough time, if they don't need it for another two or three months, and if I feel that I can fit it in, will I'll see what ideas I have scribbled down," the author concludes.

Joe Sixsmith went through various incarnations—including a short story called *Bring Back The Cat!*—before he finally made his appearance in *Blood Sympathy*, a full-length novel. According to Reginald Hill, Joe's first appearance was a total non-appearance. "Way back in the early 70's, after my one and only television play—*An Affair of Honour*—had been broadcast, the BBC commissioned me to write another one. So I wrote something with this character called Joe Sixsmith in it. I duly got paid but, for reasons best known to the British Broadcasting Company, he never made it onto the screen. Perhaps they didn't feel that in 1973 the great British public was ready for a black detective from the working classes who had been made redundant. Many years later, someone asked me for a short story and—nothing is ever lost with me, it stays in my mind or goes into my desk drawer—Joe Sixsmith popped into my mind. I said yes and dug out this old tv script. Of course the script was very different from the story, but I liked the character, the situation, and the title, so I wrote *Bring Back the Cat!*, which went down very well. Eventually it appeared in the *Oxford Book of English Detective Stories*, which was very flattering."

Joe Sixsmith is about as far away as you can get from a character like Andy Dalziel. In the books it seems that nearly everyone uses the odd bit of bad language bar Joe; he won't say anything worse than "shoot". So how does a black, middle-aged, unemployed lathe worker become a private investigator in Luton? "I have always felt that that the private eye was very much something American, particular to American society. A hard-nosed gumshoe always strikes me as being a bit false in a British environment, so I didn't want Joe to be anything like that. What I hope I have done is to invent a very engaging guy. He's just a nice chap who wants to live and let live. Yet, there is a little bit more to him than just that. Deep down inside him he's got a very strong sense of justice, of right and wrong. It is his reaction to being the subject of the manifest unjustness of suddenly being dumped out of your job, your livelihood, and all your expectations for the future by a recession. Yet he is not resentful and doesn't brood on it."

Did Hill always envisage Joe as being black? "I think it was a further way of stressing differences. In the short story he walks into this very middle class Home Counties set-up in search of a lost cat. Instead he discovers all kinds of nastinesses and ends up, of course, rescuing the cat and solving the case. The woman who hires him does so without realising what she is getting—she just picked a private detective from the Yellow Pages. When she answers the door and there is this small, balding black man in a jacket which is getting a bit faded at the edges, who announces that he is the detective, she is rather taken aback," he says with a smile.

Before the interview draws to a close, Reginald Hill gives a glimpse of what readers can expect in the near future. First up is another book featuring Joe. "The new Sixsmith called *Singing the Sadness* will appear in 1999. In it Joe and the chapel choir enter a competition in darkest Wales and Joe gets involved in all kinds of mayhem among the Welsh." Not forgetting the fans of his police duo Hill concludes, "At the moment I am working on a new Dalziel and Pascoe, or would be if I wasn't doing this interview. I won't tell you too much about that, but certainly they go onward and I hope upward, and they will continue to do so for a long time to come."

bibliography

DALZIEL & PASCOE
A Clubbable Woman (HarperCollins, 1970)
Ruling Passion (HarperCollins, 1973)
An Advancement of Learning (Harper-Collins, 1973)
An April Shroud (HarperCollins, 1975)
A Pinch of Snuff (HarperCollins, 1978)
A Killing Kindness (HarperCollins, 1980)
Deadheads (HarperCollins, 1983)
Exit Lines (HarperCollins, 1984)
Child's Play (HarperCollins, 1987)
Under World (HarperCollins, 1988)
Bones and Silence (HarperCollins, 1990)
Recalled to Life (HarperCollins, 1992)
The Wood Beyond (HarperCollins, 1996)
On Beulah Height (HarperCollins, 1998)

JOE SIXSMITH
Blood Sympathy (HarperCollins, 1993)
Born Guilty (HarperCollins, 1995)
Killing the Lawyers (HarperCollins, 1997)

NON-SERIES BOOKS AS REGINALD HILL
Fell of Dark (HarperCollins, 1971)
A Fairly Dangerous Thing (HarperCollins, 1972)
A Very Good Hater (HarperCollins, 1974)
Another Death in Venice (HarperCollins, 1976)
The Spy's Wife (HarperCollins, 1980)
Who Guards a Prince? (HarperCollins, 1982)
Traitor's Blood (HarperCollins, 1983)
The Collaborators (HarperCollins, 1987)
Pictures of Perfection (HarperCollins, 1994)
The Four Clubs (Severn House, 1997)

AS PATRICK RUELL
The Castle of the Demon (John Long, 1971)
Red Christmas (John Long, 1972)
Death Takes the Low Road (Hutchinson, 1974)
Urn Burial (Hutchinson, 1975)
The Long Kill (Methuen, 1986)
Death of a Doormouse (Methuen, 1987)
Dream of Darkness (Methuen, 1989)
The Only Game (HarperCollins, 1991)

AS DICK MORLAND
Heart Clock (Faber, 1973)
Albion (Faber, 1973)

AS CHARLES UNDERHILL
Captain Fantom (Hutchinson, 1978)
The Forging of Fantom (Hutchinson, 1979)

SHORT STORY COLLECTIONS
Pascoe's Ghost (HarperCollins, 1979)
There Are No Ghosts in the Soviet Union (HarperCollins, 1987)
Brother's Keeper (Eurographica, 1992)
Asking For The Moon (HarperCollins, 1996)

the entropy kid:
steve aylett
barry forshaw

Steve Aylett, in just three novels, has cornered the market in hip, mordant and highly individual crime fiction – if it's crime fiction he writes. As Phoenix House publishes his latest, Slaughtermatic, *we try to find out what's behind the dark glasses.*

Is your new book a lampoon of the crime genre?

Yeah, *Slaughtermatic* is a sort of crime satire. When people ask about it who haven't read my other stuff, I save time by calling it a kind of *Catch 22* but about crime and law, rather than war. I mean that it's a similar satire of aspects of authority, of manipulations too extreme to process or even talk about in everyday chat. And there's some nice gunplay in there too, and jokes about dogs and so on.

The guns are quite unusual.

Well I burnt out straight gun fetishism in the course of doing *The Crime Studio*—that sort of shoot-out just feels like noise now, it doesn't mean anything. So I started to give the guns meanings by inventing software-enhanced guns, fire-by-wires, like the Zero Approach gun which scans the targets aura to see whether they're asking for it, as it were—it seeks their consent. Then there are guns that fire calories, drugs, ideas, charm, guns that ignore the target, guns that can be set for a certain demographic range, guns that can be set for Mexicans, randomizers, glass guns, tantrum guns, all this. So when a shoot-out happens, it means something, it can be like a philosophical exchange. The Crime Bill means people have to design and produce untraceable one-off firearms and that leads to a little bit of inventiveness at least, which is at a premium these days. So you have Hitachis, Mitsubishis, and Macs of course. There are also Microsoft guns, though they take a long time to fire.

Do you read a lot of crime?

A fair bit, but not only crime. A lot of crime readers can be a bit isolationist about the genre, though I think they're not at all precious within it— they'll judge stuff on its merit and not on the author's name, which is good. I've only been duffed up a couple of times for suggesting that Crais improved on Parker's Spenser and Hawk books with his Cole and Pike stuff. I think it's a travesty that Parker was given *Poodle Springs* to finish. Chandler would have pulled stuff out of the hat as that book went on. They should have given it to Walter Mosley at least—though I suppose he wasn't such a big deal then. But the thing is I think most crime, reported and fictionalised, is flat and uninventive. The thing of some guy with a stocking over his head walking into a bank with a gun—the most interesting thing is the stocking. I think that's why a lot of people get into that game, they're into that. it's the only situation in which it's socially acceptable to wear a stocking over your head—as many of your male readers will know from bitter

experience. And even when they wear the mask of some celebrity it's always the same people, you know, Ronald Reagan or Daffy Duck or something. But they don't put the voice on— everyone knows it's not really Daffy. And they should choose a more idiosyncratic celebrity—Alan Bennett, for instance, you know, and do the voice and everything. So anyway in *Slaughtermatic* these crime impresarios try to art their capers by embedding ideas in them, so it's sort of sarcastic crime. They call it headcrime. A simple example of this, and one which has actually been done, is to break in somewhere and perform an elaborate costume drama for the surveillance cameras, so this silent spectacle is discovered in the morning. But never looking into camera or acknowledging it. A whole frilly-cuffed *School For Fops* being performed on that nightmare-quality silent video. And that one's quite harmless too. Fiercer crimes may involve taking an authority's argument to its logical conclusion. Taking to heart American military procedure and killing hundreds of people in a pre-emptive strike.

Would you say the satirical aspect is about the individual against society?

It's society against the individual. It seems childish but I think it's important to remember who started it. If society declared a ceasefire with the individual, the individual would say great and abide by it with relief, but if the individual declares a ceasefire with society—and many do every day— society will just keep on battering away at them. I think it's good sense to know who is the aggressor, even if you have no defence at all.

Many people are lucky enough to be able to remember a teacher or mentor who was influential on them. Do you have such a figure?

No, I grew up in Bromley.

Is Beerlight based on Bromley?

No, Beerlight's based on a city on the East coast of America. Nothing happens in Bromley. I remember when the Brixton riots happened, I was eleven or twelve or something, and the shops in Bromley High Street were getting boarded up, as if the riots were going to catch on in Bromley, which was a funny idea. There weren't any drugs either except real make-do stuff like solvents, and people would inject lager intravenously. It was all that south-London DIY that kids got into around then. It was actually a nice, if uneventful, place to grow up.

Do you bear your potential readers in mind when writing, or do you write principally for yourself?

I write the kinds of books that I'd like to discover in a bookshop, you know, a real find—and a lot of people out there also thirst for that kind of book, so it works out okay. When I buy a book I invest not just money but hopes and expectations, you know— and when it doesn't live up to it, it's a personal insult. It's personal. And of course they almost never live up to it. I go for stuff that delivers hundreds of ideas on every page, as intense as a fever dream. Most books are dead on arrival, there's nothing there. So that leaves a gap in the market which is the size of the planet.

Do films and music inspire you?

Well, there's a bit of Orson Welles' *Touch of Evil* character in Henry Blince. Chief Blince is one of my favourite characters to write—he's in *The Crime Studio*, *Slaughtermatic*, and a few of the stories in the *Toxicology* collection that's coming out from Four Walls Eight Windows in America. And the third proper Beerlight book, as well, for 2000—he's in all of them. And there's a lot of music in the books—all the streets in Beerlight are named after something.

Should a writer be solitary or gregarious?

Well, both. I can't go out clubbing a lot or to the pub or whatever and expect to get anything done, it takes me ages to recover. I turned up in that *Disco Biscuits* anthology of rave writing but I'm sort of the odd one out in that I wrote about stuff other than just Oh gawd I was off me face and blah blah … and I also wrote grammatically. I've got great affection for that scene, it saved my generation's lives, but I was never robust enough to indulge like other people did. It's totally dead now, we're heading back into another sterile, early eighties kind of desert. But anyway, the basic answer is I'm mainly a sad hermit and that's how I get stuff done. Mostly I like it that way. there's no concept of privacy or personal space in England. Everything is everyone else's business. In America, people might intrude on you but at least they know they're doing it. I think the personal space thing is why we're a knife culture and they're a gun culture—in the States they keep their distance even when they're killing you.

Is there anything which you find

Distressingly brilliant'
THE GUARDIAN

SLAUGHTERMATIC

STEVE AYLETT

inherently funny?

Trousers, needless to say. Also steam, dogs, lard, hens, and anything spiral shaped which appears in an unexpected location. Nerves are also an important image for me, because they're creepy, funny and painful, and they're on the borderline between the body and the spirit, which also has those three qualities. *Bigot Hall* had a lot of nerve action, if I recall correctly.

Speaking of nerve, Lee Harvey Oswald is mentioned in both *The Crime Studio* and *Slaughtermatic*—do you have an interest in conspiracy theory?

Not in the usual sense, no. For me the interesting thing about the JFK murder is that something weird has happened around it—it's become completely mutable and postmodern—turned to shit, in other words. It's a swamp—anything at all can be argued about it. Evidence can be found to prove any theory at all regarding that. I could prove conclusively that I did it, and I wasn't even born yet. The same thing's shaping up around Mena Airport and Ives/Henry with the dozen or so gag murders, though it's still early enough to revolve only around Clinton and a few others—in another couple of years it'll include Rolf Harris and my mother. Although, admittedly, my mother was involved. But you can see the facts beginning to blur. James Milan was decapitated and the coroner ruled his death as due to natural causes. I hope that's the way I go—in my sleep, natural causes, head flying off, blood everywhere. Ever visit an old people's home? Bang, bang, bang, left, right and centre, like champagne corks. Absolute mayhem. But still for postmodernist bullshit, the law is streets ahead. Anyone who's sat in on an adversarial court case, seen the mechanisms of the law, the subjectivity, the basic disengagement from fact, truth thrown to the wind, it really is like being in the mouth of madness. The person who's in the right might win the case, but not because he's in the right—just for other, quite surreally disassociated reasons. Reality gets the kiss-off at the start. The lawyer Harpoon Specter is great to write, he's a monster who operates in that totally unanchored, mutable alternate dimension. He said right at the start of *The Crime Studio* The law is where reality goes to die—he knows this. In *Slaughtermatic* he talks about fractal litigation, where the flapping of a butterfly's wings on one side of the world results in a massive compensation claim on the other. All these characters are very articulate, they'll talk about the manipulations they're working. Even thugs as they die are fully aware and articulate so you get this constant eyes-open effect, nobody ever just goes off into the dark. you're wide awake through the whole nightmare. The book's structured like Dante's *Inferno*, but it starts off in hell and things get progressively worse. Anyone who's been alive for a while will know what I mean.

You talk about the brotherhood in *Slaughtermatic*, a merger between the police and the army. Do you believe this will happen?

I think the lines will blur in most places, toward a kind of national guard—I saw one of these blurred-line police at Gatwick Airport a couple of years ago, at WH Smiths, holding an H & K submachine gun. Guns scare me, I don't care who's holding it. So I look at this as I walk past, and this guy accosts me, asking for my passport and so on. It turned out it was just because I'd looked at him. I told him if he wanted to stand around with a submachine gun, he should get used to people looking at him. These people have forgotten what normal responses are, in a way. Mind you, if he didn't have the gun he'd probably stand around with his cock hanging out, so thank heaven for small mercies. Of course like most people who slag off the police, I'll run crying to them as soon as anything happens,

because there's no alternative body to run to. If there was a body which was honest and efficient, I'd go to that one instead.

Is there a city that gets your creative juices flowing more than any other?

I like cities that have got places to sit down. Chairs and so on. But without having to spend huge amounts of money to do so. New York's terrible for that. London has places to sit down, on the edge of buildings, but they've usually got protruding spikes. Many buildings in the Strand are like this. I suppose the alternative would be severe slopes, but then people would probably lie back on them, using those inflatable neck-pillows you take on a plane journey. I don't know, the world's gone mad.

What can you tell me about your next book?

In England there'll be *The Inflatable Volunteer*, where the main character's talking about his encounters with various forms of authority, and their effect on his nerves. In the States there'll be *Toxicology*, a collection of very concentrated satire stories, including Beerlight stuff. it's all the same to me, I'm just trying to make enough money to buy new ears.

Ears?

Well you can see how ragged these ones are.

We're discussing artificial ears?

The ones I have in mind are about the size of boxing gloves, and made of bronze.

Steve, thanks for talking to CT.

Are we finished?

interview

what's a girl gotta do?
sparkle hayter
adrian muller

YES, SPARKLE HAYTER is her real name. Sparkle Vera Lynnette Hayter to be exact, and her name is not the only thing that is unusual about the Canadian author. This is someone who grew up in a place where voting in radical conservatives was a step forward; someone who saw friends and colleagues die while she was covering the war in Afghanistan for CNN; this is also someone who has written and performed stand-up comedy. In her most recent venture Sparkle has combined her previous experiences as a journalist and comedienne by writing a series of humorous crime novels featuring Robin Hudson, a female television reporter who is demoted for burping—on air—during a presidential press conference at the White House. With her debut, What's a Girl Gotta Do, *the author won the Crime Writers of Canada's Arthur Ellis Award for Best First Mystery Novel, and since then the she has written three further instalments.* The Last Manly Man, *the most recent title, was published in Britain by No Exit Press in December.*

When meeting the attractive author, it is impossible not to ask the most obvious question first: how did Sparkle

Hayter come by her first name? "You know, my parents have never given me a straight answer on that," she says with a smile, "but I think there might have been heavy drinking involved." It doesn't take a genius to realise that Sparkle has been asked about this many times, but if she is bored by the question she doesn't give any signs of being so. She happily continues, "I thought it came from Dick Tracy—there was a Dick Tracy character called Sparkle Plenty, the daughter of B.O. Plenty and Gravel Gertie—but my father said he wasn't familiar with them. He said my name came to him in a vision, so again, all signs point to heavy drinking." What probably was supposed to be a wistful smile looks more like a grin when she adds that she can't even blame her name on her parents being hippies because she was born in 1958. "I have to carry my birth certificate around to prove my name. Would you like to see it?" she asks. She rumbles through her bag and brings out a dog-eared copy of the document. "People often ask me about my name because they think I'm making it up. So, rather than get into a big argument,

sparkle hayter

the last manly man

Tips Bridget Jones off the scales and steals her fags!

religious fundamentalism. Alberta was run by radio evangelists for about fifty years until 1970. Then we took a huge leap forward into the 20th century and elected radical conservatives." Radical conservatives are a huge leap forward? Sparkle grins widely, "It's a huge leap forward from radio preachers! It was a very lucrative business for the conservatives who even tried to print their own money. Anyway, there were so few liberals in Alberta that we could fit all of them in our living room, and we often did."

Due to her name and background Sparkle did not have an easy time as a child. "I was encouraged to speak my mind at home but it was not a very girl-friendly culture I grew up in, " she recalls. "In the playground I was the outcast, a 'cootie' girl, so instead I read a lot and I had a rich fantasy life. Plagiarising the plots from the *Bonanza* television series, I used to pretend I was a crime-fighting cowgirl, the leader of this army of virtuous men. My parents got sick of hearing my stories and taught me to write, that way I could write them down instead. That was the root of it all."

Unfortunately for Sparkle Hayter's protagonist Robin Hudson, she seems to share a parallel world with her creator. Not only were they both cootie girls, they also became acquainted with New York in a remarkably similar and eventful manner. Sparkle's experiences were fictionalised in her third book, *Revenge of the Cootie Girls*. "My girlfriend and I were squired around by these guys who took us to lots of fashion shows. We'd walk in with them and people would just give us free

I just show them the birth certificate, it's much easier."

According to her parents, Sparkle Hayter was always destined for a career in journalism. Born in Pouce Coupe, British Columbia—"the zero point in the Alaska Highway"—her father worked for *The Alaska Highway News*. On the night she was born he broke a big news story. "So my parents always say that I was born under a news star," Sparkle says. "Because of that scoop we moved to Edmonton, Alberta, where he got a job at *The Edmonton Journal*."

All things considered, it is not surprising that the author describes her parents as eccentric, but they were more than just that. "They were liberals," she says, "they were the only eccentric liberals in a hotbed of stuff. We thought it was because we were so sweet and Canadian," the writer says giggling. Only later did Sparkle realise that the men had a shady background.

Having enjoyed her visit to the Big Apple, Sparkle moved to the city in the early eighties. "I worked for CNN and decided I was going to write like Ernest Hemingway, I was going to be a serious journalist and write serious fiction." At CNN Sparkle was everything from assignment editor, to researcher, and producer. Still looking slightly disappointed she says, "I had a really pronounced Canadian accent, so I'd do all the reporting except they'd use somebody else's voice."

So, unlike Robin, she wasn't demoted for belching during a presidential press conference? With a rueful grin the ex-reporter says, "Well that did happen to me, but not exactly in those circumstances. Actually I burped during a news conference in Ottawa. That was something I extrapolated especially for Robin. I thought, 'Oh my god, what if I had been the Whitehouse correspondent. I'd stand up to ask my first question and... Burrrrp!'" The idea still makes her laugh.

When her American work visa expired in 1986, Sparkle Hayter used the opportunity to go backpacking around India and Pakistan. Events on this trip would prove to be highly influential on her later career as a writer of crime fiction. "Backpackers swap books with each other on the road," she explains, "and I traded some Graham Greenes for a bunch of humorous murder mysteries by Simon

Brett. I'd never read anything like them before and I just loved them. When I ran out of the Bretts I started writing my own story where I killed off people I had worked with at CNN. Later I rewrote it as *What's a Girl Gotta Do*. That's what got me into crime writing."

On her return from Southern Asia, however, Sparkle's journalistic ambitions still ruled supreme and she went back to the troubled region to cover the Afghanistan war. "I was still very serious about doing this bad Hemingway thing," she says smiling, "but I had not been able to go into Afghanistan whilst I was backpacking. I wanted to see what was going on over there, and I managed to visit a lot of the refugee camps in Pakistan. In 1988 I went back and lived in Peshawar, Pakistan, for a year before going into Afghanistan with the Mujahidin. It was a pretty hairy and crazy time."

Having been saved by both "godless communists and holy warriors of Islam", Sparkle found her time there to be a life changing experience. "It gives you a very broad view of humanity. It was one of those situations that teaches you that people are all the same once you take away politics and religion. It also made me realise that I didn't like seeing my friends getting killed. One of my housemates, Joe Gall, was killed and, later, also a brilliant and moderate Islamic scholar I knew... It is always the moderates who get killed by the fundamentalists. A lot of the Mudjahadin who I went into Afghanistan with didn't live through the war. You would see somebody you knew—some sweet person—you would see their face on the Wall of the Martyrs. This is a wall that is covered with pictures of the people who died fighting."

It was a reaction against this horror that further inspired the fledgling novelist to try her hand at crime fiction. "I decided murder mysteries were where I could make sure that the people who deserved to get killed, got killed. Often when people die it's hard to figure out who is responsible, but with murder there is a perpetrator, it's very clear cut and that appealed to me."

Besides having been a journalist Sparkle Hayter also was a stand-up comedienne for a while. Yet, these days she prefers to concentrate on her writing. "The comedy club scene in New York is littered with yobs now," she says, repeating the word 'yobs' again. "It's my new favourite word that I picked up in Britain." Then she continues, "There's so much comedy on television that people will just stay at home to watch it. What they do now is get these big parties of people into the clubs and my humour doesn't always play well with those crowds. I much prefer writing."

Not that Sparkle gets much time to do so. She frequently ends up touring four months of the year to promote a new book, and even on a promotional tour she spends a lot of time writing. "I prefer to write at night because I write better after midnight. Even if I get up early in the day my writing doesn't really gel until after 10.00 p.m., I don't know why. I'm just a night creature which is very hard because I keep wanting to go out to parties and drink cocktails." Sparkle comes close to

pouting but goes on to talk about how she constructs her novels instead. "I start with a plot and then I write and re-write and re-write and end up throwing most of it out because my books are not plot driven mysteries. They are much more character and idea driven. That's why I'm constantly re-working things until the editor literally wrenches it out of my hands telling me I can't make any more changes."

So, if her novels are not about plotting, what does the author think is the main attraction in her books? "I think people read me for the comedy, but the mystery is there as well. Sometimes it's just so far below the surface that it comes up like the Loch Ness monster," she says smiling. "Every book has it's own rhythm and once I find that rhythm then the book just happens."

In *What's a Girl Gotta Do*, the first in the Hudson series, Robin is still very much trying to live down the White House fiasco. Demoted to the Special Reports Unit at the All News Network she finds herself on an undercover assignment at a sperm bank with her loathsome boss Jerry Spurdle. Meanwhile, she also has to find time to clear her name when she becomes the prime suspect in a murder case of a blackmailer. Having used her wits, poisoned ivy, an Epilady, and a perfume atomiser filled with cayenne pepper as weapons, Robin survives to return in *Nice Girls Finish Last*, only to find herself assigned to another sordid special unit report on the New York S&M sex-club scene. This and the murder of her gynaecologist Robin can live with, but having to put up with a visit from her Aunt Maureen is asking to much, only then Aunt Maureen goes missing... Adding a new weapon to the arsenal—a hot-glue gun with two settings: steam and spray—Robin goes to the rescue. The insane, paranoid, and at times surreal comedy of the first two instalments is still very much present in *Revenge of the Cootie Girls*, but part of the mystery—Robin's reporter protégé, a wide-eyed, small-town girl, goes missing—makes way for the bonding process of a girls-night-out.

Like many of her colleagues Sparkle Hayter says that she does a lot more research than she ends up using in her books. Considering the subject matters in the books, this is a very scary thought. Robin's weapon arsenal for instance. "I have used the cayenne pepper in a spray cologne before they had commercial pepper sprays," Sparkle admits laughing. "I didn't use an Epilady as a weapon, but I once used it on my legs and I thought it would make a really good weapon." A wicked smile appears on her face when she says, "I love the idea that things which are supposed to make you more attractive end up being used to repel an attacker." As for the dangerous foliage she adds, "I looked into planting Poison Ivy and I went around all these gardening places. They looked at me as if I was nuts," she recalls giggling. "It turns out that it's actually against the law in a lot of states to knowingly grow noxious plants, and it would be hard to say it just grew naturally off your balcony in Manhattan."

With some of the research the author has help, or at least the companionship from a friend who is a

writer for the *New York Post*. "Andrea is game for anything," Sparkle says. "She'll get an article out of it and I'll use it in my books. So, for *Nice Girls Finish Last* we went to some S & M clubs and we met some dominatrixes and their slaves. Men came up to me and wanted to lick my boots." When asked if that was the strangest moment, she replies, "It's hard to pick out one strange thing but the woman who led her slave around like he was a dog in a kennel show was pretty weird." Sparkle goes on to reveal that Mistress Lena from the book is based on a real person. "I went to her apartment and she seemed very normal. She had fridge magnets on the refrigerator, her slave was dressed normally, but he waited on her hand and foot and didn't speak unless spoken to. It was just a very interesting control dynamic that played into what I was interested in: relationships between the genders, how they are changing, and how the control issue come into play."

The subject of relationships returns in *The Last Manly Man*, Sparkle's most recent Robin Hudson title. "It's kinda like a paranoid feminist fantasy," the author reveals, "but at the same time it's a love letter to men." Does this mean that her heroine will finally meet Mr. Right? "Well, she's trying not to be so afraid, so leery of men," Sparkle says. "She wants to get it together because she doesn't want to end up old and alone, paying a male nurse to change her diapers. She realises that if she is going to have a serious relationship she has to figure things out now, and she's trying to arrange it through her work so she can kill two birds with one stone."

In *The Last Manly Man* Robin is making a series of reports on 'the man of the future' and finds herself trying to figure out the opposite sex. What is it that she likes about them? She also comes to realise that sexism is a two way street, and that women perpetrate it on men as well as on each other. If this sounds as though the author is getting all serious on her fans, then they will be relieved to hear that there is little need for concern. Along the way the intrepid reporter stumbles across a mysterious chemical called Adam 1, encounters libidinous chimps and convention of drugged feminists, as well as discovering a secret world of men that Robin never knew existed. In short enough ingredients to ensure the liberal dose of offbeat humour that

readers have come to expect from the author.

After establishing a character, many writers start alternating their books with a second series or one-off novels. Can Sparkle Hayter see herself branching out? "Yes, I can," she says. "I'd really like to write something dark but probably nobody would publish it."

The author hopes that, one day, a deal with a television or film production company may give her the financial independence to pursue her other creative ideas. Not that she would sign over the rights to her heroine easily. "I'm really down on Hollywood because of the crap they're putting out," Sparkle says disgustedly. "You could feed a small nation on what they spend on some of these terrible movies. I just think that's a crime."

The film and television rights have attracted interest from numerous quarters. At one stage they were optioned by Janine Turner, the actress who played pilot Maggie O'Neal in *Northern Exposure*. "I mentioned Janine [in the acknowledgements to *Nice Girls Finish Last*]. She's a lovely person, and there was a lot of interest, but nothing happened," Sparkle explains. "Since then I've been really fussy." Worried that her creation might be sanitised, the ideal scenario for the author would be for an independent film company to adapt one of Robin's exploits. "That way I'd have a lot more input," is Sparkle's reasoning.

So who would she like to see playing Robin Hudson? Diplomatically she replies, "You know, as long as it was a multi-dimensional portrayal, I'd be happy for any good comic actress to take the part and make it her own." However, she adds, "I love Janeane Garofalo and Joan Cusack. Joan Cusack would be absolutely brilliant, but neither of them look like Rita Hayworth." Rita Hayworth? "My idea of Robin is that she thinks she looks like Rita Hayworth but that maybe she doesn't." So who would be Robin's preference? "Julia Roberts," Sparkle replies without a moments hesitation. "Robin is a little vain, so she would definitely go for a more glamorous choice. And Roberts does have that gawky, glam, red-headed thing going for her."

At the time of this interview, Sparkle Hayter was planning her next mystery which she intends to set at her current New York address, the Chelsea Hotel. This famous hotel has been host to such world-renowned guests as photographer Henri Cartier-Bresson, the eccentric 'Naked Civil Servant' Quentin Crisp, writers Dylan Thomas and Thomas Wolfe, and rock legend Sid Vicious. It's not difficult to imagine Sparkle fitting comfortably in this eclectic ambience.

Prior to her taking up residency at the Chelsea, the comic crime novelist had been passing her time in temporary accommodations. "My marriage had fallen apart, and my friends wouldn't let me sleep on their couches anymore because I'm too much of a slob," Sparkle says smiling in hindsight. "So I moved into this rundown little residential hotel, and on my floor there were three disgruntled postal workers and some guy who just stood around pumping iron all day." Unfortunately these weren't the only strange creatures the author had

to deal with. "We had really weird cockroaches there. The exterminator would come in and I don't know what kind of chemicals he used, but whatever it was, they mutated and they had too many legs, not enough legs, strange bumps... It was just a nightmare." Then one day, after a disastrous interview to share an apartment, Sparkle found herself walking past the Chelsea Hotel and, having wandered in on the off-chance, discovered the occupancy was half residential and half tourist, and that a room was available. "It was a total fluke," she says. "So I moved in with like 37 shopping bags filled papers and clothes. I thought it would be for just a few months, but it wasn't that much more expensive than an apartment, and I just fell in love with the place, so I ended up staying there. It's just an amazing, strange, other-worldly kind of place to live."

No shortage of character to write about then? "Endless possibilities," the author agrees with relish. "And I'm going to include some stories from the hotel's history. I talked to the management about it and they have been great. I've mentioned them in the acknowledgements of my previous books because they have really helped me out when I've been tapped out for money and stuff." Concluding Sparkle says, "The working title is *Murder at the Chelsea Hotel*, and I thought it would be really rather fun to try and write it as a classic mystery, but we'll see."

hot chicks, cool dudes and bad muthas:
ct's definitive guide to blaxploitation
charles waring

Blaxploitation: The Trailer

The recent success of Quentin Tarantino's *Jackie Brown* movie has created renewed interest in that

somewhat dubious form of Seventies entertainment known as the blaxploitation phenomenon. *Jackie Brown*, although ostensibly based on the novel *Rum Punch* by American crime writer Elmore Leonard, purports to be a homage to the blaxploitation film genre. The fact that Tarantino changed both the name and racial status of the book's heroine (originally Jackie Burke, a Caucasian airline cabin attendant), would seem to support this argument, particularly when the Hollywood wunderkind cast former blaxploitation goddess, Pam Grier, in the title role. The fact that the glamorous, pistol packin', kung fu-kicking Foxy Brown of the seventies has been transformed into a nineties' down-at-heel air stewardess, *Jackie Brown*, is a tad ironical, but more significantly, it illustrates how elements of a peripheral, almost cult form of entertainment have been absorbed into the movie mainstream.

Contrary to the assertions of some

observers, blaxploitation never really died. It may have shot its proverbial bolt prematurely after a glut of low-budget, sub-standard, derivative movies in the seventies, but its influence and impact has been far-reaching.

We funky dudes at CT aim to give you, the reader, the dirty low-down on the blaxploitation phenomenon, detailing its history, the significant movies and their stars, and of course, the glorious music that so often redeemed an execrable cinematic experience.

Blaxploitation—Opening Reel

The word blaxploitation is now regarded as a convenient term for labelling movies (and associated cultural paraphernalia) that were made in white Hollywood for consumption by America's black population. It's a word that has great resonance both culturally and historically, with different implications for black and for white.

Blaxploitation culture has a special place in the wider public consciousness, particularly in the UK, where it possesses a certain cachet for some sections of society. The cult popularity of blaxploitation movies has prompted the opening of nostalgic dance clubs (like *Shaft* in London), fashionable sartorial retro-chic in the clothing industry and the re-release on CD of much of the exciting music that graced the original soundtracks of blaxploitation movies.

A single utterance of the word 'blaxploitation' is, for many people, likely to conjure a wealth of vivid, admittedly stereotypical, imagery: bush-sized, kinky Afro-hair;

John Shaft's apartment - no, really! Dig it, Jive Turkeys!

voluminous flares; sky-scraping platform heels; expletive-ridden, ghetto jive-talk and irresistibly funky music led by rasping wah-wah guitars. Right on, baby!

However, it wasn't so long ago that blaxploitation was frowned upon by more radical and intellectual elements in both the black and liberal white population. The epithet was, after all, originally coined as a pejorative term, summing up Hollywood's cynical cash-in and subsequent exploitation of black people. Not just the directors and actors, but ultimately the audience, whose money they wanted. The phenomenal success of Melvin Van Peebles's *Sweet Sweetback's Baadasssss Song* alerted Hollywood to the potentially large, previously untapped black market.

The genre was vilified by many observers during a critical backlash

The Original Motion Picture Soundtrack Written & Performed by CURTIS MAYFIELD

Super Fly

period in the seventies and eighties. A shameful stigma was attached to blaxploitation's participants who were charged by some with 'selling out' to 'The Man' up in white Hollywood. In some ways, it was an understandable knee-jerk reaction. After all, many of the films were cartoon-like and one-dimensional, devoted to cheap, visceral thrills like sex and violence. Racial stereotypes abounded, often focusing on the white mythology of black sexuality.

But with the emergence in the late eighties and early nineties of exciting young black directorial talent like Spike Lee and John Singleton—many of whom had been weaned on a diet of blaxploitation entertainment—perceptions began to change, forcing ridicule and a sense of dishonour to give way to respect and ultimately reverence.

The 90's re-evaluation of the blaxploitation genre focused on the fact that seminal movies like *Shaft* and *Foxy Brown* provided an unprecedented creative platform for black movie-makers. It was a necessary evil, if you like, giving black directors, writers, actors and even technicians a valuable opportunity to work and express themselves within a new framework and even taste something of Hollywood's fame and glamour.

But as we shall discover, blaxploitation isn't just about movies. It's a multi-faceted, multi-media entertainment phenomenon, as much about music, literature and fashion as it is about motion pictures.

The History

So, how did it all begin? Well, to adequately understand the emergence of the blaxploitation phenomenon it is important to retrace the history of black cinema, examining the role of black people in the movies prior to the blaxploitation explosion of the 1970s.

In many ways, the historical legacy of the depiction of Afro-Americans by Hollywood would later dictate the blaxploitation agenda.

In the silent movies made in the early part of this century, black people were often required to play the role of slaves. Paradoxically, the only black roles of any consequence were almost always played by whites, 'blacking-up' in a bizarre tradition which Al Jolson popularised and was perpetuated right up to the 1970s in this country with the BBC's grotesque and surreal *Black and White Minstrel Show*.

But in 1914, the first all-black film in the shape of *Darktown Jubilee* was made. Ironically, and by a strange twist of fate, this was also the year that witnessed DW Griffith's controversial *The Birth Of A Nation* silent epic, featuring the faintly ridiculous but still insidious figures of hooded Ku Klux Klansmen propagating inflammatory anti-black sentiments. Griffith also made the first film (*One*

Exciting Night, 1928) that included the grotesque comic figure of the panic-stricken, eyeball-rolling black manservant, later to become a staple fixture of mainstream white American movies.

When the advent of sound revolutionised the movie industry in the early 1930s, films like *Hearts In Dixie* and King Vidor's *Hallelujah* became the first all-black talkies. One of the early black stars of the silver screen was the singer Paul Robeson, who appeared in a version of Eugene O'Neill's *The Emperor Jones*. In the 1940s, *Stormy Weather* and *Cabin In The Sky* represented creditable Hollywood attempts at all-black musicals but generally, the roles black actors had to play were demeaning, grotesquely exaggerated caricatures. Women were either portrayed as rotund, maternal figures ('Black Mamas') in domestic roles or as sexually promiscuous, wanton hussies. Black males were frequently depicted as emasculated, gangly, high-voiced clowns. Afro-Americans were almost always presented in a position of subservience in relation to whites. If they weren't delineated as servants then they were the next best thing: entertainers. These stereotypical figures were essentially viewed as intellectual and moral imbeciles; passive and non-threatening, providing humour at the expense of their own race. The famous role of Prissy played by black actress, Butterfly McQueen, in the epic southern saga *Gone With The Wind* is a prime example of blatant racial stereotyping.

However, after the Second World War, a new generation of black actors emerged. Urbane, articulate and sophisticated young men like Sidney

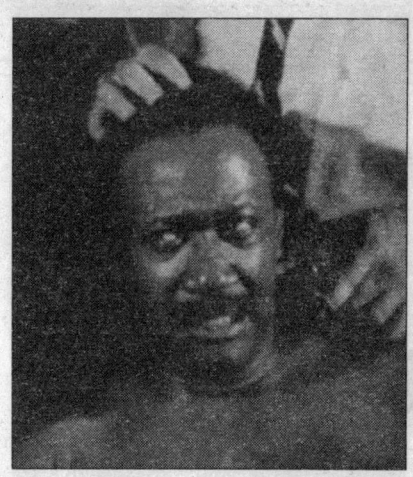

Sweet Sweetback's Baadasssss Song

Poitier and James Edwards made mould-breaking films like *Intruder In The Dust* and *Pinky* which examined the race issue that so preoccupied the American people.

By 1965's cold war thriller *The Bedford Incident*, Poitier's race was, for once, not an issue in the movie, and by the time of *In The Heat Of The Night*,(1966) its sequel *They Call Me Mr.Tibbs*(1970) and *Guess Who's Coming To Dinner*,(1968) Hollywood was beginning to reflect the changing social and political climate in America. As the Civil Rights movement gained momentum initiating black empowerment, so Tinseltown broadened the expressive parameters for black actors by beginning to repudiate the damaging racial stereotypes that had dominated for so long.

The positive black role model that Sidney Poitier presented in the two hugely successful Virgil Tibbs' films laid the foundations for what was to follow in the 1970s.

Other films that anticipated the genre

They got it goin' on. Yes they do!

were Jules Dassin's 1968 film *Uptight* (which was basically an all black re-working of a pre-war movie made by legendary director John Ford called *The Informer*) and perhaps more significantly, the 1970 film *Cotton Comes To Harlem*.

As some CT readers will know, the inspiration for this prototype blaxploitation flick came from crime writer, Chester Himes' book of the same name, featuring his popular Harlem-based detective duo, Gravedigger Jones and Coffin Ed Johnson (played by actors Godfrey Cambridge and Raymond St. Jacques respectively). This fast-paced, action-packed film presented a more realistic portrayal of contemporary black American ghetto-life, with its array of petty crooks, preachers, hookers, pimps and pushers.

But the film that really opened the floodgates for a new wave of black movie entertainment was the brainchild of a radical (some would say maverick) intellectual called Melvin Van Peebles.

Van Peebles was a highly gifted Chicago-born black American who had left America in disillusionment to make a name for himself in France (initially as a writer of five novels published in French). It was while residing in Paris that the multi-talented Van Peebles wrote and directed *La Permission* (aka *The Story Of A Three Day Pass*), a film that brought him both critical acclaim and international recognition. The film's success also provided Van Peebles with an opportunity to return to his homeland (he travelled as part of a French delegation) in order to attend the San Francisco Film festival where he was fêted by critics who, to quote the film maker's own words, "*didn't know I was an American, let alone black.*"

Van Peebles's growing international reputation finally opened Hollywood's gates in 1970, where he directed and wrote the satirical comedy *Watermelon Man*, a surreal, Kafka-esque fable of metamorphosis, in which a white man wakes up one morning to discover (to his horror) that he is black.

Frustrated by the restrictions of Hollywood's artistic straitjacket and at a crossroads of personal creative crisis, Van Peebles took a drive out to the Mojave desert. In his recently published film diaries, Van Peebles confessed that inspiration came to him in a moment of clarity induced by fevered masturbation amongst the sand and sagebrush!

The epiphany that Van Peebles experienced out in the desert prompted him to quit Hollywood and go it alone. He had a vision of what he called 'Guerilla Cinema', a subversive visual medium within which he would seek to undermine Hollywood's view of the world. The result was *Sweet Sweetback's Baadasssss Song*, an extraordinary movie written, directed, edited and produced by the fiercely autonomous Van Peebles.

The film made an unprecedented impact as an independent movie project, not only breaking box-office records but achieving endorsement by the revolutionary Black Panther political group.

But while *Sweetback* instigated a cinematic revolution in black cinema, the radical political shake-up that Van Peebles envisaged did not transpire. Any threat that Van Peebles may have posed to Hollywood was soon nullified.

Conscious of the large, potentially lucrative black audience that the success of *Sweetback* had exposed, Hollywood studios moved in on the action with their corporate muscle and suddenly began bankrolling a plethora of black movie projects. But to the disgust of ideological radicals like Van Peebles, the avant-garde expressionism and polemical manifesto of *Sweetback* had given way to the re-hashing of routine, hard-boiled thrillers, high on action but short on political substance. Art had been raped by commerce. Furthermore, it was the whites who were dictating the black movie agenda, reducing Van Peebles's incendiary revolutionary aspect to an inconsequential if not irrelevant side-issue. In fact, more whites than blacks were generally involved on the production, direction and writing side of things. It was indeed tantamount to exploitation, and hence the origination of the term blaxploitation.

Blaxploitation—The Main Picture

The films that followed in the pioneering wake of *Sweetback* established the vivid iconography that has become synonymous with the blaxploitation phenomenon: Afro-sporting, muscular,

Trouble Man

badmutha action heroes; jive-ass pimps gaudily dressed in fluorescent flares and foppish, wide-brimmed hats; superfly, foxy chicks turning Bruce Lee tricks in hot pants; and a motley assortment of sartorially challenged dudes, jive-turkeys, crackers and honkies accompanied by the sound of a funky backbeat supplied by soul superstars like Isaac Hayes, Curtis Mayfield and James Brown.

Shaft (1971), directed by Gordon Parks, established the blueprint for almost every other blaxploitation flick that followed in the 1970s. The eponymous hero (played by the then unknown male model and actor, Richard Roundtree) was a black private detective cast in the hard-boiled Raymond Chandler/Philip Marlowe mould. He was a prototype black action-hero: good-looking, athletic, smart and streetwise. He didn't take shit

Coffy

films that emulated *Shaft* (like *Superfly*, *Coffy*, *Black Caesar*, *The Mack*) fresh and exciting, particularly to black audiences who finally saw a more honest portrayal of black urban life up there on the silver screen. Black people were no longer peripheral figures in the movie business or just there to make up the numbers by providing token representation. Blaxploitation movies proved that black actors possessed a strong box-office appeal.

A slew of films (about 200 in all), good, bad and downright ugly, rode on the back of *Shaft*'s success in the seventies. It wasn't all macho, misogynistic posturing either. The voluptuous Amazonian figure of Pam Grier led the female charge as a gun totin' superbitch with hard-hitting movies like *Coffy* (1973) and *Foxy Brown* (1974). Regarded as a licence to print money, this badass, soul-sista formula was milked for all it was worth, producing many clones, but one particularly memorable character in the shape of *Cleopatra Jones*, a chic, Afro-topped, kung-fu kicker busting balls and drug cartels for the CIA (played by the six foot two statuesque figure of black supermodel Tamara Dobson).

At its zenith in the early seventies, the blaxploitation phenomenon also hijacked other movie genres, invading that sacred haven of rednecks, the western (*Thomasine And Bushrod* (1974)), horror movies (the spoof *Blacula* (1972) and *Abby*, a virtual rip-off of *The Exorcist*) and even martial arts films (*Blackbelt Jones*, 1974). Even James Bond could not escape the permeating influence of blaxploitation, as 1975's *Live and Let Die* (where Roger Moore dabbles with a voodoo high-priestess and *Superfly* drug dealers)

from no one, baby, whether it be ball-breaking cracker cops or jive-assed black gangsters!

Shaft also, somewhat humorously (and with tongue firmly in cheek) took advantage of white insecurities about black male sexual performance, depicting its hero as a 'sex machine to all the chicks' and hinting (in the second sequel, *Shaft Goes To Africa*) at the Private Eye's majestic physical endowment.

As the blaxploitation genre developed, so these racial stereotypes became even more exaggerated: so much so that the characters degenerated into comic book ciphers. Indeed, action took precedence over storyline, plot and character development. But the raw, visceral excitement of these films pushed aside any spurious notions more serious film-makers might have entertained of imparting any profound moral messages or political manifestos to their black cinema audience. It was entertainment, pure and simple.

Hampered by small budgets and unknown actors, blaxploitation movies compensated by providing big thrills and lashings of gratuitous violence. Sure, they were formulaic and cliché,-ridden, even naive, but these factors also made them refreshing in a perverse way. There was a vigour and creative zest that made the testifies.

But as blaxploitation culture infiltrated the mainstream, so it became more diluted to appeal to popular taste, leading inevitably to a new black stereotype: the *give me skin, blood* ghetto dude.

Every seventies TV cop show had its own jive-talkin' token blaxploitation character. The most famous of these was the sartorially-challenged, riotously camp Huggy Bear who routinely offered wardrobe tips to the Jaeger-sponsored detective duo of *Starsky And Hutch*.

In movies, a similar assimilation of ghetto-types became commonplace, as in Joel Schumacher's light comedy, *Car Wash* (1976), which represented the pinnacle of blaxploitation's watering-down.

But while elements from blaxploitation were being absorbed into mainstream culture, the quest for greater thrills and spills led hard-core directors down more preposterous creative avenues. Blinded by dollar signs, film-makers took the trash aesthetic to the very edge of taste, churning out lurid charnelhouses of movies: x-rated, profane, amoral, excessively violent and just plain cheap and nasty.

Black Caesar and *Slaughter's Big Rip Off* led the way in offal-drenched screen carnage while *Savage* deepened the comic-book effect with its surreal storyline about a black mercenary who teams up with a couple of scantily-attired foxy chicks to join a group of rebels in their quest to overthrow a South American dictator. Advertisements for the film bore this memorable legend: "*Men call him savage… women call him all the time!*"

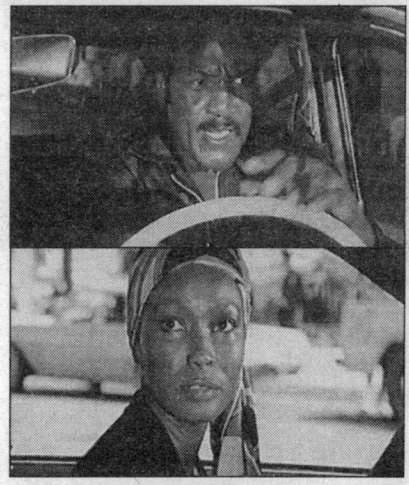

Jim Brown and Marlene Clark in Slaughter

One of the most popular blaxploitation films in the US has proved to be the risible but nevertheless entertaining *Dolemite*, starring Rudy Ray Moore as a night club entertainer framed by the infamous racketeer, 'Mr Big'. *Dolemite* gets his revenge big time in this lurid, gung-ho, kung-fu fable.

But perhaps the ultimate lapse in good taste and critical judgement manifested itself in the 1975 movie directed by Lee Frost entitled *Black Gestapo*, a bizarre tale about a black, neo-nazi vigilante group.

If some observers found blaxploitation films indigestible for wholly artistic reasons then other critics of the genre found them unpalatable on moral and political grounds.

Leaders of black communities in the USA regarded nihilistic, foul-mouthed films like *Black Caesar* and *Boss Nigger* with their emphasis on violence and criminal activities as systematically eroding the positive role models that the sixties Civil Rights campaign had strived so hard to

Superfly

achieve. They castigated the blaxploitation film makers for presenting a bad example to impressionable black youth, not only for perpetuating racial stereotypes but also for reinforcing white prejudices about black culture. This critical and cultural backlash sounded the death-knell for blaxploitation entertainment and as the thrill-seeking, hedonistic seventies dissolved into the moral-righteousness of Reagan's eighties, so blaxploitation's profile declined.

But blaxploitation refused to die. Popular, well-attended, nostalgic re-runs at American movie houses sustained the interest in the genre, making an indelible impression on the minds of hero-starved black youngsters.

The advent of hip hop culture in the States as a potent new musical form helped resurrect interest in blaxploitation, as did the burgeoning new video market in the 1980s. Hard-core gangsta rappers like Ice T and Ice Cube with their graphic ghetto tales modelled themselves on the brazen anti-heroes of old blaxploitation flicks. The genre gained a new lease of life via this new generation of admirers, prompting new movies to go into production.

Black actor, Fred Williamson, star of classic movies like *Black Caesar* and *Boss Nigger*, was instrumental in reviving the black action movie, utilising his past experience to direct films such as *The Big Score* (1983) and *Fox Trap* (1986).

Action Jackson (1987) represented another attempt to update the genre while the eighties also witnessed some successful blaxploitation send-ups like the hilarious spoof, *I'm Gonna Git You Sucka* (1988).

The 1990s have witnessed a vigorous resurgence in black cinema not seen since the heady days of the 1970s. Directors like Spike Lee and John Singleton have led the way, acknowledging their debt to the filmmakers of the blaxploitation hey-day. Although black cinema is much more diverse and variegated than it was back in the seventies, there has, nevertheless, been a steady stream of black-made movies that are the direct lineal descendants of movies like *Shaft* and *Superfly*.

Ironically, Melvin Van Peebles's son, Mario, was responsible for this decade's earliest example of a blaxploitation revival movie, *New Jack City* (1990). John Singleton's superlative *Boyz N The Hood* examined the internecine gang warfare of 90's black urban America. *Menace II Society* (1993), directed by the Hughes brothers (Albert and Allen) paints a bleaker picture of 90's ghetto life, as does the directorial duo's later movie, the somewhat pessimistic *Dead Presidents* (1995). The re-awakened interest in blaxploitation culture and its fables of black urban life also resulted in the 1996 movie, *Original Gangstas* (1996), where veteran director Larry Cohen assembled a stellar cast of old-school blaxploitation icons (Pam Grier, Fred Williamson, Jim Brown and Richard Roundtree) to wage war on their Uzi-toting, crack-smoking contemporaries. No bets on who won this battle-royal!

So, that, in a nutshell, is blaxploitation. The legacy it left behind is finally being acknowledged as a positive contribution to Afro-American culture. The term blaxploitation has now been disarmed of the potentially explosive political ramifications it once had. It's a label that defines a genre rather than a political agenda, referring to both white and black produced cinema entertainment that focuses on Afro-American culture.

Trends come and go in the entertainment industry with alarming alacrity and at the moment, blaxploitation is a victim of Sunday supplement hipness and undergoing something of a revival. But at least this re-kindling of interest in the genre has allowed former blaxploitation movie stars like Pam Grier, Richard Roundtree and Fred Williamson to jump-start stalled careers and taste the limelight once more.

Conclusion- The Final Reel

It would be misleading to declare that blaxploitation is back with us: if truth be told, it never really went away. The emergence of young black actors like Eddie Murphy in the early eighties assisted with the assimilation of black

culture into the conventional Hollywood movie. Since then, a succession of black actors (among them Denzel Washington, Samuel L Jackson, Will Smith, Wesley Snipes, Laurence Fishburne, Angela Bassett, Halle Berry) have succeeded in establishing themselves as big box-office draws, confirming that the achievements of their antecedents like Fred Williamson, Richard Roundtree and Pam Grier were not in vain. In this sense, blaxploitation has triumphed. It has not only been thoroughly assimilated but has also, if you will, become the mainstream.

Sold out? No way, José! It's payback time and black actors, (though still vulnerable to Hollywood typecasting and not able to command the fees, say, of Mel Gibson) are at least getting good parts, and, for a change, getting paid, big time. Sho'nuff!

Blaxploitation—The Literature

Although there was no identifiable literary movement running parallel with the blaxploitation movie explosion, it is possible to perceive that the books of black authors, Chester Himes and Iceberg Slim, had a profound influence on the makers of movies which depicted urban American ghetto life.

Chester Himes (1909-1984) was a pioneer of black literature, opting to use the accessible format of the crime novel as a vehicle for exploring the black experience in twentieth century America. Himes was one of the first black novelists to paint an honest portrait of urban black America. His most popular novels were those that constituted the nine book Harlem Cycle, (written between 1957 and 1983) featuring his most memorable characters, the two hard, black Harlem cops, Gravedigger Jones and Coffin Ed Johnson. Three of Himes's novels were translated into Hollywood movies: *Cotton Comes To Harlem* (1970), which anticipated the blaxploitation boom, *Come Back, Charleston Blue* (1972, a re-working of the Harlem Cycle novel, *The Heat's On*) and the more recent *A Rage In Harlem* (1991).

If Himes was a subtle but latent subversive, then the flamboyant Iceberg Slim (aka Robert Beck, 1918-1992) was more brazenly graphic about ghetto life. His autobiography, *Pimp*, painted a vivid picture of a criminal underworld populated by conmen, whores, dope addicts and hard-assed muthafuckers. With the success of *Pimp*, Slim turned his hand to lucrative fictionalised accounts of ghetto lives. Hard-hitting novels saturated with sex, violence and profane language (e.g. *Long White Con*, *Trick Baby* and *Death Wish*) established the Chicago-born hustler turned novelist into an influential black cultural figure in the USA where his work inspired gangsta rappers like Ice-T.

Recommended Viewing:
Most of the major movies mentioned in this article are now available to buy on video. Also check out recent releases by the UK's premier blaxploitation outlet, Superfly Video, whose range of Soul Sister and Soul Brother films include the most important seventies' work by the likes of Pam Grier, Fred Williamson and Jim Brown.

Recommended Listening:
Various Artists: Badmuthas: 18 Original Black Movie Hits, MCI Records MUSCD039 (1997)
This is highly recommended as an introduction to blaxploitation soundtracks
Various Artists: Blaxploitation (Volumes 1-4), Global Records
Various Artists: The Big Score, EMI Records 49326918 (1998)
Curtis Mayfield: Superfly, Curtom/Sequel Records
Marvin Gaye: Trouble Man, Motown
Isaac Hayes: Shaft, Stax/Ace
Willie Hutch; Foxy Brown, Motown
Willie Hutch: The Mack, Motown
James Brown: Black Caesar, Polydor

Recommended Reading:
Chester Himes: The Harlem Cycle Vols 1-3, Payback Press
Iceberg Slim: Pimp, Death Wish, Trick Baby, Payback Press

Blaxploitation—The Music
Perhaps the greatest legacy that blaxploitation films left behind was, somewhat ironically, more to do with sound than visual image. Let's face it, the majority of the movies made under the blaxploitation banner were of little artistic merit. However, the irresistibly funky music that accompanied these films often transcended the narrow parameters of the genre to lodge themselves into the mass consciousness of popular culture.

Nowadays, it is the evocative music that is remembered rather than the often throwaway, forgettable movies. When you hear the taut, syncopated hi-hat rhythms and rasping wah-wah guitar that signifies the distinctive introduction to the Theme From *Shaft*, more often than not, it will be Isaac Hayes who comes to mind rather than the film's star, Richard Roundtree.

The recent resurgence of interest in blaxploitation culture has primarily been due to a re-awakened interest in music rather than the medium of film. In general, the soulful musical accompaniment was inordinately better than the blaxploitation movies themselves. Much of the music has stood the test of time. Unfortunately, the same cannot be said for most of the motion pictures.

Many of the soundtracks commissioned to accompany blaxploitation films were composed by already established, bona fide black soul superstars. By the time he had completed the score for *Shaft* in 1971, Isaac Hayes, the muscle-bound, gravel-voiced shinehead, was one of r'n'b music's hottest stars, with million-selling albums like *Hot Buttered Soul* and a host of songwriting and production credits for many other successful black artists (Hayes also went on to star in the lead role of the blaxploitation movie, *Truck Turner*, 1974).

Likewise, seasoned jazz trumpeter and orchestral arranger, Quincy Jones brought all his musical expertise to films like *In The Heat Of The Night* and *They Call Me Mr. Tibbs*.

Other black soul icons followed Hayes into the more experimental world of soundtrack composition. Curtis Mayfield, one of soul music's most articulate social commentators, contributed songs that enhanced *Superfly*'s bleak fable about ghetto life while the king of erotic soul, Marvin Gaye, expanded his eloquent musical vocabulary with the largely instrumental soundtrack to the film *Trouble Man* (1972).

The self-proclaimed Godfather of Soul, funkmeister extraordinaire, James Brown, contributed songs to a couple of early seventies blaxploitation films in the form of *Black Caesar* and *Slaughter's Big Rip-Off*.

In the wake of rekindled interest in blaxploitation, much of this classic, timeless music has been made available again on several imaginative, attractively priced compilations.

Blaxploitation: The Significant Movies

Sweet Sweetback's Baadasssss Song (1971)

As already mentioned renaissance man Melvin Van Peebles singlehandedly kick-started what was to become blaxploitation.

Disillusioned with Hollywood, Van Peebles decided to make a film in which he had absolute artistic control. With the independently financed *Sweetback*, Van Peebles gave a virtuoso solo performance, not only acting the main role of the eponymous anti-hero but writing, photographing, editing, directing and even supplying the musical score for what was to become his magnum opus.

Although *Sweetback* utilised the crude racial stereotype of the oversexed black buck in trouble with the police (aka white authority), Van Peebles's movie possessed a potent, underlying political agenda. Much of the movie's action scenes were sadistic and brutal but rather than function solely as the kind of mindless violence that became the trademark of later, inferior black movies, Van Peebles's intention was to inflame his viewers sensibilities to the point of militancy. He intended to use the film as a provocative tool to incite anger and rage at black suffering, directing his audience towards the idea of pro-active political revolution. This, of course, didn't happen. What did happen was that Hollywood hijacked the essence of Van Peebles's film and watered it down for popular consumption. The fact that *Sweetback* grossed in excess of $10 million was sufficient evidence to persuade Tinseltown executives to invest in the development of black cinema. Much to the chagrin of Van Peebles, the bastard offspring of *Sweetback* became the brainless, absurd action romps that formed the core of the blaxploitation phenomenon.

The Plot: The film begins with a flashback sequence depicting the film's eponymous hero, *Sweetback*, back in 1944 as a young boy living in a whorehouse. The barely pubescent youngster is encouraged by a naked, Afro-topped black whore to climb aboard her voluptuous body and commence love-making. As the whore writhes in orgasmic ecstasy she exclaims *"You got a Sweetback!"* Van Peebles then cuts back to the present day (1971) where we find an adult Sweetback performing as a sex entertainer in a California brothel. The 'show' is interrupted by two white cops who are visiting on the pretext of investigating a murder. Sweetback is hauled in for routine questioning by the cops who drive him to the station. During the drive, however, the cops are diverted by radio-call to a shooting in South L.A. Arriving on the scene (with Sweetback still in tow), they arrest a black revolutionary called Mo-Mo and begin to beat him. A sense of anger and injustice overcomes Sweetback who attacks the cops, freeing Mo-Mo in the process. Both men are now fugitives and run for their lives with the pigs in hot pursuit. Sweetback remains on the run for the duration of the film.

The Music: The distinctive score was written by Van Peebles who performs in the guise of Brer Soul, backed by an embryonic incarnation of the black supergroup, Earth, Wind and Fire, who perform the raucous, mantra-like theme tune.

Available to buy on video (Xenon/MIA).

Shaft (1971)

Shaft represented the first black movie which could be accurately tagged with the label 'blaxploitation.' It was adapted for the screen from his own novel by the late Ernest Tidyman, the Academy Award winning screenplay writer of *The French Connection*. *Shaft* was the sophomore feature by Gordon Parks, a renowned, veteran still photographer whose penchant for capturing arresting images of ghetto life invested the movie with a vivid authenticity.

Richard Roundtree, a former male model, was chosen for the role of the eponymous action hero (it's hard to believe, but the original part of *Shaft* was written as a white character!)

Shaft is an ice-cool private detective based on the somewhat clichéd template of the traditional hard-boiled dick. Armed to the Afro with a startling array of chic rollneck sweaters, mandatory 70s facial hair and babe-magnet sex appeal, superstud John Shaft turned out to be about as revolutionary as a black James Bond.

The fact that Shaft was portrayed as a private-eye was tantamount to being a cop for many black observers, who consequently regarded the movie with cynical suspicion.

THE PLOT: John Shaft is hired by a Harlem gangster (played by Moses Gunn) to find his kidnapped daughter. Lots of gratuitous violence, sex, black revolutionaries, even more sex, violence and a host of cracker motherfuckers. Antonio Fargas makes his first appearance as the ubiquitous jive-walking pimp figure.

THE MUSIC: An Academy Award winning title song by the shiny-domed mack of soul, Isaac Hayes, whose over-zealous use of the wah-wah pedal becomes a signature sound for all successive black movies. Sho'nuff!

Shaft returned in two inferior sequels *Shaft's Big Score* (1972) and *Shaft In Africa* (1973). It also resulted in a successful spin-off series of made for TV movies in 1973 and 1974. Of these *Shaft: The Capricorn Murders*, *Shaft: The Killing*, *Shaft: The Kidnapping*, *Shaft: Murder Machine*, *Shaft: Hit and Run*, and *Shaft: Cop Killer* had later (limited) theatrical releases.

Available to buy on video (MGM/UA).

Superfly (1972)

Despite the assertion by many critics over the years that Curtis Mayfield's soundtrack was the best thing about this movie, blaxploitation revisionists have begun to see *Superfly* in a new light. It is, in fact, one of the best blaxploitation movies ever made. The film's director was Gordon Parks Jnr (son of *Shaft's* director, Gordon Parks Snr) and starred Ron O'Neal as the movie's ambivalent drug-pushing anti-hero, Youngblood Priest. *Superfly* possesses not only a rare subtle moral ambiguity but a gritty realism not often found in most blaxploitation features (maybe that's because Parks allegedly hired bona fide mobsters as extras in exchange for filming on location in their gangland territory!). Despite its small budget, *Superfly*, with the aid of strong action sequences and Mayfield's evocative soundtrack grossed over $6 million. *Superfly* was a landmark film for black cinema not only because it was financed by a group of Harlem businessmen but also on account of its all-black cast and crew.

The film spawned an ill-judged sequel a year later in the shape of *Superfly TNT*.

The Plot: Youngblood Priest (Ron O'Neal) is a coke dealer hoping to do one last big deal before he quits the ghetto and starts a new life. Naturally, things do not go to plan!

The Music: Curtis Mayfield's seminal soundtrack is one of the best ever blaxploitation scores. The bespectacled soulman with the sweet falsetto voice has made musical contributions to seven movie scores over the years. Mayfield even set up his own film company, Curtom films, which made *Short Eyes*

(1977), a grim tale about paedophiles in prison. The soulman played a small cameo role in Short Eyes. He can also be spotted in *Superfly* as a musician in a night club band.

Available on video.

Foxy Brown (1974)

Jack Hill directed the voluptuous Pam Grier in the title role of 1973's *Coffy*, a tale about a feisty heroine ("*the baddest one-chick hit-squad that ever hit town*") wreaking retribution on those who dealt drugs to her sister. Grier reprised her role a year later as a pugilistic female vigilante in Hill's *Foxy Brown*. Posters for the movie bore the legend "*if you don't treat her nice, she'll put you on ice!*" This was the role that established Grier as a sassy, sexy, soul-cinema icon in the seventies and prompted Tarantino to cast her in the lead role of last year's *Jackie Brown*.

The Plot: Foxy Brown ("*the meanest chick in town*"), revenges the brutal slaying of her boyfriend (an undercover narcotics investigator). After infiltrating a prostitution and drugs racket, Foxy (after enduring rape and torture along the way) takes her retribution by authorising the slicing off of Mr. Big's honky pecker and storing it in a jar for his girlfriend to see! Yes, indeed! Antonio 'Huggy Bear' Fargas turns up in his usual role as a cowardly jive-ass drug dealer.

The Music: The funky score by Motown musician Willie Hutch (who also scored *The Mack*) included the memorable theme song.

Available on video (Orion Home Video/*Superfly*)

Blaxploitation: The Stars

Fred Williamson

With over 50 blaxploitation films to his credit, Williamson is the uncrowned king of the genre. Born in Gary, Indiana in 1938, Williamson began life as a professional footballer nicknamed 'The Hammer' who aspired to be an actor. After making a TV cameo appearance in the original series of *Star Trek* (as Anka in the 74th episode, *The Cloudminders*, from 1968) and a small part in Robert Altman's *M*A*S*H* (1970), Williamson made his starring debut in 1972's *Hammer* (directed by Bruce Clark) about a prizefighter having to take a dive in the ring. He began his own Po'Boy production company soon after and turned his hand to both writing and directing in addition to developing his acting skills. Williamson made a return to the mainstream with an appearance in the Tarantino scripted/Rodriguez directed bloody gore-fest, *From Dusk Til Dawn* (1996).

Significant films: *Hammer* (72), *The Legend Of Nigger Charley*(72), *Black Caesar* (72), *Hell Up In Harlem* (73), *Crazy Joe* (73), *Boss Nigger* (75), *Darktown*(75), *Mr. Mean* (77), *The Big Score* (and director 83), *Foxtrap* (and director 86), *Soda Cracker* (and director 89), *Original Gangstas* (96).

Pam Grier

Grier (born in North Carolina in 1949) is the undisputed queen of blaxploitation entertainment. She actually spent part of her childhood growing up on US military bases in Europe (including some time spent at an airbase near our very own Swindon in Wiltshire) before returning to live in Denver, Colorado. Grier, a striking, curvacious, mixed-race teenage beauty queen, took acting classes after moving to LA at the age of eighteen. She made her debut in a film by renowned female breast aficionado, Russ Meyer, of all people (Beyond *The Valley Of The Dolls* in 1970) but went on to star in prototype female action pictures like *Coffy* and *Foxy Brown*. When the blaxploitation market dried-up at the end of the seventies, Grier continued to find work in the film industry, albeit in an unaccustomed supporting capacity. Despite more recent cameo roles in films like *Mars Attacks* and *Escape From La*, it wasn't until Tarantino's inspirational casting of Grier as the main star in *Jackie Brown* that finally brought her deservedly into the mainstream in a big way.

Significant films: *The Big Doll House* (71), *Blacula* (72), *Coffy* (73), *Foxy Brown* (74), *Black Mama White Mama* (74), *Sheba Baby* (75), *Friday Foster* (75), *Drum* (76), *Fort Apache, The Bronx* (81), *Something Wicked This Way Comes* (83), *Bill And Ted's Bogus Journey* (91), *Posse* (93), *Original Gangstas* (96), *Escape From La* (96), *Mars Attacks* (96), *Jackie Brown* (97).

Jim Brown

Like Fred Williamson, Georgia-born Jim Brown (now sixty three) began life as a footballer. However, Brown's status as a brawny, black sex symbol (who's alleged motto was "*walk softly and carry a big dick*") was firmly established way before the blaxploitation phenomenon came along. Brown made his screen debut in the western *Rio Conchos* way back in 1964, before starring in such Hollywood blockbusters as *The Dirty Dozen* (1967), *Ice Station Zebra* (1968) and *100 Rifles* (1969). In the seventies, Brown's charismatic screen presence

distinguished blaxploitation movies like Slaughter and its sequel, *Slaughter's Big Rip-Off*. Throughout the eighties and the nineties, Brown has continued to find work in Hollywood and more recently appeared in films like *Original Gangstas* (where he teams up with fellow soul-cinema icons, Fred Williamson and Pam Grier).

Significant Movies: *Rio Conchos* (64), *The Dirty Dozen* (67), *Ice Station Zebra* (68), *100 Rifles* (69), *El Condor* (70) *Black Gunn* (72), *Slaughter* (72), *Slaughter's Big Rip-Off* (73), *Three The Hard Way* (74), *Take A Hard Ride* (75), *I'm Gonna Git You Sucka* (88), *Original Gangstas* (96).

Richard Roundtree

Before he turned to acting, Richard Roundtree (born in New York in 1937) was a clothes shop salesman and male model who, at the suggestion of Bill Cosby, began taking acting classes with New York's Negro Ensemble Company. *Shaft* (1971) proved Roundtree's big break. A couple of inferior *Shaft* sequels and a lucrative TV spin-off followed with Roundtree continuing to make a living from his thespian skills, though more often in an ancillary role. More recently, Roundtree could be seen in the crime thriller *Seven* (1996).

Significant films: *Shaft* (710, *Charley One Eye* (72), *Shaft's Big Score* (72), *Shaft In Africa* (73), *Earthquake* (74), *Man Friday* (75), *Escape To Athena* (79), *Q, The Winged Serpent* (82), *The Big Score* (83), *City Heat* (84), *Crack House* (89) *Seven* (96).

Antonio Fargas

Although he never received star-billing in blaxploitation movies, New York-born Antonio Fargas often played memorable supporting roles in films like *Shaft*, *Cleopatra Jones* and *Foxy Brown*. Unfortunately, Fargas (whose family background reveals a shared West Indian and Puerto Rican heritage) quickly became typecast as the quintessential turkey necked, jive walkin' black dude. Often he was cast in the role of smalltime hustlers in loud suits or weak, seedy *Pimp*s. Although his name graced the screen credits of many classic blaxploitation movies, Fargas was almost always required to play the stereotypical role he perfected as the camp figure of Huggy Bear in the Seventies cop show *Starsky And Hutch*.

Significant Films: *The Cool World* (64), *Putney Swope* (69), *Shaft* (71), *Across 110th Street* (72), *Cleopatra Jones* (73), *Foxy Brown* (74), *Car Wash* (76), *I'm Gonna Git You Sucka* (88).

Ron O'Neal

Before his blaxploitation debut in *Superfly* (1972), Cleveland-raised New Yorker, Ron O'Neal, was already a highly regarded Broadway actor who among his many accomplishments included teaching acting up in Harlem. O'Neal was brought to *Superfly* by an old screenwriter friend, Phillip Fenty. The actor went on to direct the film's sequel (*Superfly* TNT, 1973) himself but couldn't inject credibility into Alex Haley's limp script.

Significant Films: *Superfly* (72), *Superfly Tnt* (73), *The Master Gunfighter* (75), *When A Stranger Calls* (79), *The Final Countdown* (80), *Red Dawn* (84), *Mercenary Fighters* (88), *Original Gangstas* (96).

a personal view
mark timlin

IS IT JUST ME or is hard boiled American crime getting nastier and more brutal?

Am I spotting a trend here? I do hope so. I love to be known as a trend-spotter. Not that I'm complaining, but things seem to be getting very weird on the other side of the Atlantic.

Take for example the new Joe Lansdale novel *Rumble Tumble*, in which, Hap and Leonard, normally the most reasonable of souls take on a biker gang and kill them all. Fair enough. But once upon a time they only reacted when in danger. In this one, they just go for it big style. And then there's the latest Lawrence Block. Now I've read all the Matt Scudder novels, and Matt used to be a real pussy cat. Once a boozer, then a confirmed twelve stepper, Matt didn't carry a gun because he'd once accidentally killed a little girl whilst under the influence. But in *Everybody Dies* just published in the US as I write this, Christ, nearly everybody does die, and good old dependable Matt feels undressed without a pistol in his pocket. And when a couple of his best friends, and I *mean* best friends are killed by people trying to kill him, he hardly turns a hair.

Not the Matt Scudder I know. But once again I'm not complaining. The old Matt Scudder could be a trifle po-faced to say the least. But these are not the worst examples. Check out *Beam Me Up Scotty* by Michael Guinzburg just published by Rebel Inc. And whilst I'm on the subject if you're not subscribing to the Canongate catalogue who distribute Rebel Inc as well as several other worthwhile imprints you're missing out. Anyway, I digress. In *Beam Me Up Scotty*, one man, his dog and a 9mm semi-automatic take on the entire New York drug dealing culture and kill as many bad boys as possible whilst also attending the twelve step programme and trying to get his estranged family to come home.

Not convinced? Then get a copy of *Down On Ponce* by Fred Willard on No Exit. This is one cold blooded volume, and it's been shortlisted for the 1998 John Creasey award for best first crime novel.

Not a chance. In fact I'd go as far as to say that in the unlikely event of it actually winning I'll rejoin the CWA and deliver my first years subscription crawling across broken glass with a wad of used fivers between my teeth.

But I digress again.

Next up in the nastiness stakes is a book called *The Speed Queen* by Stewart O'Nan. I've reviewed it elsewhere in this edition and it's brilliant. But extremely nasty and not recommended for those of a nervous disposition or who live in trailer parks. Also reviewed is a the most recent Daniel Woodrell. A charming little volume entitled *Tomato Red*. Another one not for the squeamish. Just like *Bringing Out The Dead* by Joe Connelly on Warner Books which tells the tale of a psychotic paramedic in Manhattan who drowns out the horrors he sees with booze and drugs whilst still submerging himself in them like a drowning man. What the hell is going on in the minds of these writers? Which leads me to the most horrible of the lot. Hailed as the next *Silence Of The Lambs* by a lot of people I listen to, it's

called *Every Dead Thing* and comes out in 1999 on Hodder & Stoughton. It's by a thirty year old Irishman named John Connolly (no relation I think) but set in America, and it's a stinger. A serial killer story that may be slightly too long and confusing for some, nevertheless it's going to be a hot title, and it made my blood run cold.

These books among others that I've read recently are totally amoral. Something I've been accused of myself, but I'd have to get up very early in the morning to keep up with this little lot.

You don't very often read about music in the pages of Crime Time, but recently I came across a CD which is just perfect to have on the Hi-Fi whilst curling up with the latest Crumley or Elmore Leonard paperback. It's called *The Crime Scene* and subtitled *Spies, Thighs And Private Eyes*. It's part of Capitol Records Ultra-Lounge series, volume seven to be precise, and it's available at bigger branches of HMV if nowhere else at about a tenner, although I got mine in a little record shop in Greenwich for £6.99.

There's over twenty tracks including *Dragnet* and *The Peter Gunn Suite*, both by Ray Anthony, *Staccato's Theme* by Elmer Bernstein, *Music To Be Murdered By* with vocal accompaniment by Alfred Hitchcock, and a great version of theme from *The Silencers* by Vikki Carr. Maybe our younger readers won't be totally conversant with the excellent TV series and films that the music came from, but take my word it's worth a punt of anybody's hard earned cash. Excellent and highly recommended.

So that's it for another couple of months. Nothing too controversial I think you'll find. But interesting things are going on in the world of publishing which I love and hate with almost equal intensity, and maybe next time we can delve a little deeper as Alfred Hitchcock himself might have said at the end of one of his shows, and really let the claret flow.

Bye now, and keep the letters and postcards coming.

Timlins Top Tips for Today...

Eleven Days by Donald Harstad, 4th Estate, £9.99

Written in the kind of realistic style that you'd expect an ex-Iowa deputy sheriff to use, *Eleven Days* has no time for frills, as the local police discover a ritualistic mass slaying in the winter Iowa farmland. First one body is discovered, then another three, and finally a fifth, and from the evidence it is clear that a coven of Satanists is active in the district. Told in first person by deputy sheriff Carl Houseman, a good guy who has not been brutalised by his work, this first novel really rocks, and if indeed it was written in eleven days as it has been claimed then it's quite something. I look out for the return of Houseman in future brushes with the bad guys.

Tomato Red by Daniel Woodrell, No Exit Press, £10

Sammy Barlach is a red-neck fuck-up, small time criminal big style. Stuck in Shit City Missouri in a dead-end job

'Woodrell is a marvellous writer' – Roddy Doyle

DANIEL WOODRELL

sweeping up in a dog food factory, when he meets an incestuous brother and sister team with a beautiful whore for a mother. When they offer him the chance to improve himself, he jumps at it. But then the brother is brutally murdered, and when Sammy and his two female companions try to get to the bottom of the case things get out of hand in the worst way. Woodrell's books are stylish and different. Of all the bad boy writers to come out of the southern USA in the last few years he must be the best, and now Hollywood is rushing to pay him big bucks to get in on the act. Of course they'll screw it up as they always do, but at least he'll get something out of it. Take my advice and stick to the novels.

The Speed Queen by Stewart O'Nan, Penguin, £5.99

Imagine if you will that a murderess sells her story to Stephen King to turn into a killer road novel. Imagine that the night before her execution she tapes her story in her own words interrupted only by the minutiae of that situation. Then this book is the transcript of that tape. A great premise and a great book. One of the most frightening I've ever read. Marjorie is the killer, along with her husband Lamont and her lover Natalie. Together they blaze a trail of destruction across south-west America in a 1969 Roadrunner stacked with junk food like a latter day Bonnie and Clyde and er...Bonnie. Marjorie has two major problems: Drugs and the fact that she's been hit on the head too may times. Between them they've turned her into the Speed Queen—A monster who truly believes that everything she's done is alright. This is white trailer trash USA. It's Oprah and Jerry Springer land. And it's coming this way, take my word. Believe me you middle class citizens, this is the future.

Gumshoe by Neville Smith, Slow Dancer Press, £6.99

I met Neville Smith a few years ago and I liked him. He's a sound bloke who seems to have retained some of the socialist ideals that so many people pretended to have in the sixties. He was surprised that I remembered him from his acting days, and that I knew all about *Gumshoe* the movie and *Gumshoe* the novel. I told him that I saw the film, starring Albert Finney as Eddie Ginley, the Buddy Holly, Raymond Chandler obsessed Liverpool bingo caller who just wants to be Philip Marlowe, when it first came out, and I bought the book on the strength of it at the time. The book's gone now like so many other things from then. My Ray Charles vinyl LP's and my Anello & Davide pointy toed Beatle boots, so I'm glad it's been reprinted. You should be glad too.

Rumble Tumble by Joe R Lansdale, Gollancz, £9.99

Joe's back, and a bloody great hurrah for that. The first time we met he said that James Lee Burke was *"Just too damn good."* Well I've got news for you. Joe Lansdale is *"Just too damn good"* too. In fact there's only a few crime writers in the world who make me wonder why I bother. Lansdale, Burke, Woodrell and Crumley. They're all just too damn good. And it's a Hap and Leonard novel which makes everything in this crummy world seem just fine. This time our intrepid heroes, beginning at last to feel the onset of creeping middle age, get involved in rescuing the daughter of Hap's latest squeeze, a red headed tornado named Brett who's previous relationship ended with her setting fire to her husband's head after stoving it in with a shovel. Nice girl. Anyhow, her daughter is a hooker who wants to quit, but has got herself involved with a nasty biker gang who think she's got plenty of mileage left in her yet. The story shifts from East Texas to Mexico, and the trio team up with a motor mouthed midget, an ex-biker turned preacher turned not much at all, an Armadillo named Bob. And why not? Bob's a very nice name. Plus various other eccentrics, and ends in a gun battle and a plane crash. Hell, read the book. It's a cracker.

it's raining violence:
a brief history of british noir
paul duncan

VIOLENT MEN. Femme fatales. Robbery. Seduction. Sadism. Betrayal. Victims.

Sound familiar? Then you've seen film noir and read hard-boiled fiction. And, if you live in Britain, the chances are they've been US imports.

However, it's less well known that, since the Twenties, Britain has been producing its own brand of noir, tinged with class consciousness and regional accents. It's tough. It's grim. It's gritty.

It's raining violence...

DARK HIGHWAY

The popular myth of the American cowboy is as a wanderer, a free spirit. It's hokum, of course, but the myth evolved—the trail turned into the railroad, and later into the highway. The metaphor of travel was used as a device to describe and discover America. In the hands of Jack London and Jim Tully, the cowboy turned into the hobo. Later, during the Depression, socialist writers like John Steinbeck led us down dustbowl roads telling us about the bitter grapes of wrath, telling it like it was.

Writers travelled the highways and byways, going walkabout to discover the world and themselves, to put themselves in touch with the masses, with society. In Britain, writers like George Orwell turned hobo to find out about the world they lived in.

The ultimate aim was freedom—freedom from the crippling poverty of the city, from the dirt and grime, the overcrowding. In Europe, many people suffering from poverty and oppression looked to America, to its mythology of freedom, to its wide open spaces, to its possibilities. It was everyone's manifest destiny to find their own part of heaven and turn it into a utopia.

In Britain, the exotic allure of America was heightened by the importation of pulp culture. After the First World War, a great deal of American popular fiction found itself transported across the Atlantic as ballast. The films showed vast cities and untamed wilderness, as well as the latest fashions. The American voice was beginning to take over the language of books.

At the beginning of this century, in Britain, the novel was seen as a medium where the writer's upper-middle-class moral ideas were explained in story form. It was the writer's role to attain the most elevated of thoughts and ideas, not to indulge in the darker side of human nature or to point out all the horrible things in life which happen.

Britain had the professional and amateur detectives of classic mystery fiction—Sherlock Holmes et al. We didn't have loners. Instead, we had the gentleman hero—Sapper's Bulldog Drummond, Dornford Yates' Berry Pleydell, John Buchan's Hannay—who had a set of ideas/moral values that had to be upheld. This was the retention of Empire—rampant racism, and snobbery with violence.

HARD AS ROCK

It is generally accepted that Dashiell Hammett and other American pulp writers of the Twenties wrote down what they heard on the streets. They used the voices of ordinary people. Also, they reduced descriptions to the minimum, to keep the story line going as quickly as possible, to keep the reader interested. This powerful, direct American style is evident in the work of Ernest Hemingway, William Faulkner, John O'Hara and John Dos Passos.

When some English writers read these books, they started to think the same way, started to use the mystery plots of Hammett, Horace McCoy et al, but working the language on the English streets into their writing. Also, writers imported ideas from Europe, like the psychological notions popular in Vienna, and the naturalistic approach of Emile Zola and his followers.

The influence of the American hard-boiled style increased the pages of sex and violence, and decreased the snobbery and racism. The stories were now about the common man, the man on the street, good or bad, the base emotions that drove him to destruction or—and this is important—to prosperity. Just because someone is evil it doesn't mean they are going to lose.

Certainly the most popular English novelist to emerge at the beginning of this century was Edgar Wallace, who wrote many books, plays, films and essays on many subjects, but returned to crime thrillers time and time again. Not afraid to mix locked-door mysteries with

comedy and terror, Wallace brought a lifetime of experiences living and working on the streets to his characters. One can easily imagine that the lowlife cat burglars and petermen (safecrackers) which fill his books are evocations of the people he met growing up in the slums of southeast London. Written ferociously fast—a play in four days (*On The Spot*, tremendously successful, made a star of Charles Laughton playing an Capone-type character), a novel dictated over a weekend—his work has an energy and snap missing from most of his contemporaries. Not only that, they are relentlessly driven by first person narratives, colloquial slang, obscure diversions—just like the American hard-boiled writers.

There may have been writers using the language of the English streets, but the influence of America was all around. Many of the wittiest New York writers became popular in the UK, not least because of short stories being printed in the London Evening Standard every day by the likes of Dorothy Parker, William Saroyan and, most importantly, Damon Runyon.

It is very easy to stop reading Edgar Wallace and begin one of Peter Cheyney's Lemmy Caution novels without stopping. The reason for this is that both authors wrote in a flowing stream-of-consciousness style which left no room for pause or reflection.

There were major differences, however. Lemmy Caution was American, a G-Man, and was written in the first person. If you open a Caution at any page, you'll recognise the voice immediately. It is a mock American, a bit like the rhythm of James Cagney. It's a language where women are called 'dames', men are 'guys' and victims are 'mugs.' The prose is often surreal in its structure—truly unique. And as for the plot—Lemmy is obviously more interested in how many women he can interrogate, personally you understand, rather than finding the murderer. I don't think there are any ugly women in these novels!

With the publication of Peter Cheyney's

first Lemmy Caution novel, *This Man Is Dangerous* (1936), Cheyney immediately leapt into the limelight he so often craved. However, that limelight had been hard earned. Although Cheyney had tried many kinds of writing previously, he rarely attempted prose. In the Twenties he briefly tried to enter the pages of the *Union Jack*, which published Sexton Blake, and attempted a Blake story called *The Clue Of The Yellow Moccasin*, but Cheyney's style was not deemed acceptable. However, a keen reader of the publication, he did remember a serial character called Lemmy Caution (as in 'Let me caution you'), and stored the name away from future use.

Ex-solider (wounded in the Battle Of The Somme during World War One), ex-special constable, ex-private enquiry agent, ex-newspaperman/editor Peter Cheyney was a noted raconteur and storyteller among his friends and acquaintances. He was a song and dance man, an actor, wrote music hall sketches, and had many songs published. He performed on both stage and radio. At one stage he was even a dressmaker. A keen fencer (he once fenced for England against Scotland), a practitioner of Judo, a regular at shooting galleries, and he played golf. Cheyney was a great maker of friends. He joined every men's club in London, knew people in every profession.

Actively interested in politics, Cheyney was a steward at meetings of the New Party, a right wing group led by Sir Oswald Mosley, which later became the British Union of Fascists. (Cheyney's racism is illustrated by his refusal to have drinks with coloured men, no matter how famous, in any of his clubs.) Accounts differ as to Peter's influence and importance in the party—Sir Oswald Mosley said that he was just a zealous follower, whereas Sir Harold Nicholson maintained Cheyney changed the course of the party from it's Socialist and Liberal beliefs to Fascist thuggery. (Indeed, Cheyney was present at the riot at Birmingham's Bullring.) It has even been suggested that Cheyney later broke with Mosley because he couldn't stand someone else running the show.

Instead, throughout the late Twenties and early Thirties, Cheyney concentrated his efforts on Krasinsky, a Polish Raffles, whose stories appeared in *The Bystander*, as well as other Michael Arlenesque characters like Etienne Macgregor and Alonzo MacTavish. Later, using his connections as a special Constable, he did write about true crime and the latest forensic science developments for Tinker's Notebook in *Union Jack*, and ghosted the police memoirs of Harold Brust. Through his growing connections he eventually got to ghost the memoirs of Princess Paul Troubetskoy for *Tit-Bits*, and then a biography of the Princess Of Wales for *The Sunday Graphic*— a biography given the blessing of St James Palace no less!

The long gap between his first journalistic prose in 1926 and his 1935 success, were hard days living in Shoe Lane, running an editorial service, which became a detective agency—these times were relived, it seems, in his early Slim Callaghan novels, beginning with *The Urgent Hangman* (1938). Written in the third person, these were more typical private eye novels, only set in the UK. Raymond Chandler and Dashiell Hammett were obvious influences, as well as the funnier pulpsters like Jonathan Latimer, Norbert Davis et al. Interestingly, the series begins with Slim down at heel but, as the books progress, he becomes more affluent, employing a cast of characters who would do most of the footwork for him.

Cheyney's novels may have a reputation for violence, but it's unfounded if you make comparisons to the equivalent contemporary novels. His stories rely more on convoluted plots, crosses and double-crosses, family and mob intrigues and in-fighting. There is nothing profound to be found in these pages, but they do have the speed and gusto to keep you reading.

The 'Dark' novels (they all used the word 'Dark' in the title) were the most acclaimed. Cold-blooded spy novels, they were perfectly timed to follow on from the work pioneered by W Somerset Maugham, Eric Ambler and Graham Greene.

Tremendously popular in his lifetime—in 1944 Cheyney published audited figures showing that he sold one and a half million copies that year—since his death in 1951 his work has mostly been ignored. This is probably fair—he was entertaining but derivative—there is nothing new to discover in his work. At his peak, he sold 300,000 copies a year in the US and, amazingly, just under a million in France. Such his fame that Lemmy Caution, as played by Eddie Constantin, appeared in more than eight films, and was eventually borrowed by French film director Jean Luc Godard for his futuristic crime film, *Alphaville* (1965).

It wasn't all flying fists and shooting slugs. Patrick Hamilton provided many moments of suspense in his psychological thrillers. His most famous is probably *Rope* (1929), filmed by Alfred Hitchcock in 1948, which was based on the notorious Leopold-Loeb case. *Rope* is the story of two students who decide to kill someone as an intellectual challenge, to prove their superiority over the rest of the human race. Another play, *Gaslight* (1938), tells of a jewel thief slowly driving his wife to insanity as he desperately searches the house for lost rubies.

Although well known for his plays, Hamilton's novels are of more interest. *Hangover Square* (1941), is the story of a brilliant composer, George Harvey Bone, who also happens to be a schizophrenic. Filmed by John Brahm in 1944, starring Laird Cregar in his final role, the film has a brilliant sequence as, on Guy Fawkes night, Bone carries the lifeless body of a prostitute over his shoulder through the streets and eventually deposits her on top of an enormous bonfire.

Patrick Hamilton began a quartet of novels about Mr Ernest Ralph Gorse in 1951, beginning with *The West Pier*, followed by *Mr Stimpson And Mr Gorse* (1953) (the basis for the 1987 UK TV series *The Charmer*) and *Unknown Assailant* (1955). The fourth book was never completed—Hamilton's drinking and emotional problems over the last years of his life interfered with his muse. Gorse uses his charming and smooth veneer to woo women, seduce them and then take their money. Even though Gorse succeeds in destroying his victims both emotionally and financially, we know he will eventually get his comeuppance—but we never see it. In some ways, these novels have elements that Patricia Highsmith used to great effect in her Tom Ripley novels, begun in 1956.

But he wasn't the only hard-boiled exponent. Whereas Wallace and Cheyney were all fists and fear, Graham Greene opted for a more studied, intellectual approach. His 'entertainments' as he so coyly labelled them, were as hard-boiled as they came. Beginning with *The Man Within* (1929), Greene examined the effects of sin, damnation and redemption, often using the crime and spy worlds as his canvas. His most well-known books like *Brighton Rock* (1938), about juvenile gang boss Pinky, and *The Third Man* (1950), which details the erosion of ideals, are about the betrayal of friendship and trust. Once trust is broken with your lover or closest friends, how can you trust or believe in anyone else? The world becomes uncertain, dark, a dangerous place.

Don't be fooled. Although Greene may be considered a literary writer, his deft agility with words, his wit and timing, and the sheer dexterity of his storytelling put him amongst the best of the hard-boiled school. He was also lucky enough to have his work turned into some excellent films: *This Gun For Hire* (1942) starring Alan Ladd and scripted by the great W R Burnett (*Little Caesar, High Sierra, The Asphalt Jungle*); *Brighton Rock* (1947), starring Richard Attenborough, directed by Roy Boulting; *Ministry Of Fear* (1944) directed by Fritz Lang; and *The Fallen Idol* (1948) and *The Third Man* (1949) directed by Carol Reed.

THERE AIN'T NO JUSTICE

Although many writers have no other purpose than to entertain you, to divert your attention for a few hours as they spin a story, there are some who use the form for different reasons. These are critical writers, people not happy with the world and the way it is.

One of the most interesting writers of the Thirties, now all but forgotten, is James Curtis. Whilst Wallace, Cheyney and Chase followed the American language into the Hardboiled school, Curtis used the language of the streets and slums (like Theodore Dreiser and Upton Sinclair in America) to comment on social conditions. He wrote about people in the hard parts of London, where it was accepted that you resorted to crime to survive. They had no other way out of their lives. They were confronted with situations, reacted to them, and were then confronted with even more problems. His characters did not have time to reflect on their lives, and only just enough time to live them.

James Curtis was a pseudonym, but I don't know why he used it. As it is made obvious in the books, he was very active in the communist and socialist movements of the Thirties. According to a very sparse biography, he had a conventional upbringing, then a very unconventional life which, apparently, has been incorporated into his novels. He married, had a daughter, and in later life worked as a school caretaker before his anonymous and unheralded death. I've listed his books here because I've never seen anyone else do it, and they are well worth tracking down.

The Gilt Kid (1936)—set in working class London, among people who have to think first about surviving in the world before thinking about the possibilities this world has to offer, this is the story of a man, who has no name, who gets out of jail and tries to make his way in a world of conmen, gangsters, prostitutes, burglars, and pimps. A failure at everything, frustrated at the lack of opportunity in the world, he thinks the world is against him. By the end of the book, you think he's probably right.

You're In The Racket Too (1937)—Curtis compares the crimes of middle and working

class people. Dickie Lambert, the clerk, is engaged to the boss's daughter in the hope that after the marriage he'll be on easy street, but he's also having an affair with a prostitute, Pidgy. Snowy, a petty thief just out of jail, persuades Pidgy into blackmailing Dickie, and does a bit of burglary himself.

There Ain't No Justice (1937), filmed—set in the cutthroat boxing world were the safest place to be is probably in the ring. Tommy is an up and coming fighter, recently turned pro, looking for easy money, who gets embroiled with a dodgy fight promoter, a parasite, who wants to suck Tommy dry as quickly as possible.

They Drive By Night (1938), filmed the same year (brilliantly) and then in 1958 as *Hell Drivers* (also powerful)—The story of Shorty, just out of jail, who finds the murdered body of a prostitute, is blamed for it, and goes on the run, hiding in a job driving all-night, long-distance, and finds that the people on the outside, the ordinary people, the capitalists, are just as dirty and crooked as the people inside.

What Immortal Hand (1939)—Jacky is a gifted student, forced to leave school to support the family, and when his mother dies, he leaves with his sister, Peggy, to build a life. They fail. Jacky ends up in and out of jail, Peggy in one faithless affair after another.

Look Long Upon A Monkey (1956)—three men break out of jail, an honest burglar, a Teddy boy and an IRA man. On the run they discover things about life from the people they meet.

These are books about victims, about people who will never ever succeed because the whole world is against them. They are not romantic or sentimental. There are no easy endings. There certainly isn't any justice that Curtis' books remain out of print and forgotten.

Another author out of print, but not out of memory, is Gerald Kersh. Harlan Ellison, Michael Moorcock and Bill Pronzini, among many others, are great fans of Kersh, and he is most well known in America for his science fiction and war novels, but he wrote crime novels and short stories as well. Although he wrote *Night And The City* (1938) about loser Harry Fabian, (and Fabian appeared as a supporting character in a later novel *The Song Of The Flea* (1950), ending the book a rich man in the South of France—crime DOES pay) long-standing readers of *Ellery Queen Mystery Magazine* will recall Kersh's masterraconteur Karmesin—either the world's greatest criminal or most outrageous liar. The format of each short story involves Kersh talking to this old rogue in various cafes and bars around London. As Karmesin tells his tales of robbery, blackmail, deceit and murder, he offhandedly cadges cigarettes off Kersh or surreptitiously fills his pockets with sachets of sugar. Written from as early as 1936, so far I've found 17 stories, of which only 3 have been collected in Kersh anthologies.

Kersh's greatest crime book is undoubtedly *Prelude To A Certain Midnight* (1947), which lifts the lid off crime fiction, stirs the can of worms and pronounces it foetid. It concerns the hunt for a child-murderer in Soho. Technically, it is a critique of the whole crime and mystery genre. There is the Laura Ashley School of crime writing in the presence of the formidable do-gooder Miss Asta Thundersley, who pokes her nose into the case of a murdered little girl. She gathers everyone she suspects at a party, and the only thing she learns is how to mix punch. The police procedural is in the hands of Detective-Inspector Turpin, whose hands find nothing but walls as each clue leads to a dead end. The innocent in fear of her life is Catchy, the woman who knows everything. She is one of life's natural victims who gave the murderer confidence because she took all the abuse he could give. She was his training ground, and Catchy has to live with that. The little girl's family, the Sabitinis, is effectively destroyed by the murder. They never recover. Emotionally, the book is about the realisation that life is not always what you want it to be, that there are many

losers for every winner. And in this story, the only winner is the murderer. I always recommend people to read this Kersh novel first.

KISS THE BLOOD OFF THEIR HANDS

The socialist novel comes and goes, but the bloody pulp thunderers continue relentlessly. Edgar Wallace may have picked up on the American slang and clipped style for some of his work, but Peter Cheyney, James Hadley Chase and their ilk churned them out in the hundreds. They upped the ante regarding sex and violence, and were often banned as obscene, withdrawn from sale and pulped—I'm sure the irony of pulps being pulped was not lost on these writers.

James Hadley Chase was born René Raymond in London. Aged 18, after a disagreement with his father, he left home, ending up selling children's encyclopaedias door-to-door. Two years later he joined Simkin Marshall, the famous London wholesale booksellers. Seeing the likes of Chandler, Hammett and James M Cain fly out the door, he decided to try likewise over six week-ends in the late Summer of 1938. The result? *No Orchids For Miss Blandish* (1939), one of the world's best-selling crime books, racking up 1 million copies sold over five years in America alone. He eventually totalled over 500,000 hardback sales, selling particularly well in France and Italy.

Orchids was banned, pilloried by George Orwell, is full of sadistic, amoral, unsympathetic characters, and is thoroughly enjoyable. The story is about a gangster, Slim Grisson, who falls in lust with the rich girl his gang has kidnapped from another gang. During the book, you have to ask the question 'Is Miss Blandish worth rescuing?' and at the end, 'Has she been rescued?' The sadistic, perverse nature of the book is truly shocking, even today. Many critics dismiss it, but it must be connecting with people in some way to be so successful.

There has been a suggestion that *No Orchids* is loosely based on William Faulkner's

Sanctuary (1929)—both tell the story of an impotent gunman kidnapping an unattainable girl. This allegation, and others (*Blonde's Requiem* (1945), written as Raymond Marshall has passages copied from Hammett's *Red Harvest*; Mickey Spillane sued for similar infringements), dogged Chase to the point that he went to court—it meant some titles are very difficult to pick up nowadays. In our post modern age, Quentin Tarantino and others call it homage, or sampling, to make something new out of the old.

The furore over the book also dogged the British film version of *No Orchids* in 1951. Although it was passed by the British Boards of Film Censors, it was banned by local councils under pressure from do-gooder groups. There were three film adaptations of Chase books in the late fifties, when Truffaut and other directors or the French New Wave were adapting the popular Serie Noir book imprint. Over 20 adaptations have made it to the silver screen. I've also noticed that films and TV adaptations have started to reappear—certainly, he is still in print in France, on sale in all the major supermarkets.

Chase himself was supposed to be a quiet man, typically British even though he lived in France, then Switzerland. He loved being at home, looking after the flowers, listening to a bit of classical music. Yet he almost exclusively wrote about hard-boiled characters, set in America, having only made a couple of trips to Florida and New Orleans in later life. Chase got his information by making extensive use of slang dictionaries, police reports and maps for research. Although influenced by the American hard-boiled style, he is closer to the violence and misogyny of Mickey Spillane than the control and righteousness of Hammett.

Unusually, Chase generally didn't use series characters. David Fenner, the reporter turned detective of *No Orchids*, only appeared in a subsequent novel, *Twelve Chinks And A Woman* (1940). Other characters who turned up twice include: Vic Malloy, a Californian

private eye; Mark Girland, a former spy working in Paris; Brick-Top Corrigan, a former commando who is likely as not to demand his fee up front and leg it without doing a stroke of work; and Don Micklem, a millionaire playboy involved in international intrigue.

Even though he wrote 74 novels under his own name, 21 as Raymond Marshall, in 45 years, they all feel like Thirties and Forties characters and locations—and the last novel was published in 1980! They all follow the same formula of speed, violence, women and America. There is a fast and furious style, which transcends common sense—once in the Chase world, you're in. And unlike Cheyney, they are full of very horrible people who do nasty things to get what they want.

Very little is known about Gerald Butler, except that for many years he wrote advertising copy in the same agency as Eric Ambler, then wrote 6 novels, starting with *Kiss The Blood Off My Hands* (1940), an enormous bestseller, over 250,000 sales in hardback. The story is simple—an American conman in London gets into a rage, kills a man, and goes on the run, finds refuge in a woman's room, holds her hostage, they fall in love, he tries to reform, circumstances conspire against them, they both go on the run. It was banned for obscenity, and filmed as *The Unafraid* (1948, starring Joan Fontaine and Burt Lancaster, directed by Norman Foster). When I read the novel I found it incredibly hard-boiled, a fever dream—it reminded me of Steve Fisher's *I Wake Up Screaming*, published a year later in America. The most shocking thing about it, like *No Orchids For Miss Blandish*, was the ending—something they changed for the film, the wimps.

Butler's other novels are well worth searching out: All these books deal with obsession—men for women and women for men. When people are in love, to what lengths will they go? These books get darker and darker. The violence becomes more psychological. Hard choices have to be made. There are no easy solutions.

For the record, the books are: *They Cracked Her Glass Slipper* (filmed as *Third Time Lucky* starring Glynis Johns); *Their Rainbow Had Black Edges* (1943); *Mad With Much Heart* (filmed by Nicholas Ray as *On Dangerous Ground/Dark Highway*); *Slippery Hitch* (1949); *Choice Of Two Women/Blow Hot, Blow Cold* (1951); and *There Is A Death, Elizabeth* (1972).

The writing is deceptively simple, as though within everything there is *something* to fear, I have to say that these are some of the best written pulps I've read in a while. The sweep of emotion is mixed with a hammer-like violence to brew a stunning cocktail of love and doom. One novel ends: *"I love you. I love you. I'll smash the guts out of anyone who looks at you!"*

DANGEROUS CURVES

With the proliferation of American GIs in the UK during the war, who brought pulps and other cultural attitudes with them, the lure of America created a post-war demand for all things from across the Atlantic. In Britain, the restrictions on food, luxuries and imports meant that people couldn't get what they wanted. In fact, All-American periodicals were banned because of the dollar balance of payments problem. Also, there was very little paper in Britain, everything having been pulped to help the war effort. Publishers were even printing new covers on the backs of dust wrappers from leftover hardbacks. So, when printers got a supply of paper stock they formed publishing companies and printed brand new American-type crime, science fiction, horror and western digests wrapped in lurid covers. The page size of the digests was slightly bigger than a paperback, but the page count was less. Each novel was about 40,000 words. Steve Holland, paraphrasing pulpster John Russell Fearn, called it *The Mushroom Jungle*, because these publishers sprouted up overnight, and disappeared just as quickly.

Publishers could print and sell anything

for any price, because reading materials were in such short supply. There were ruthless, mean, opportunistic businessmen who exploited writers and artists alike. One publisher had a writer chained to a typewriter in their cellar. Another publisher used to break into his own warehouse at night via a ladder from window to window then sell the books to a friend for a bit of extra cash in his pocket—all so that his wife didn't find out.

The writers, like the American pulp writers, wrote a lot of words on any subject for very little money. Norman Lazenby, who mostly penned western, gangster (he was told to copy *No Orchids For Miss Blandish*) and science fiction digests, recalled his ten years of toil between 1941 and 1951, earning £1 per thousand words. This meant that a writer would have to type 3,000 words a day, five days a week to earn a living wage. Lazenby's top word count was 12,000 in a day, and 80,000 over eight days.

Once the printer was allocated paper stock, there was a need for speed, to turn the paper into paper money. Lazenby recalled how, for publishers Muir-Watson, he wrote and sent 4,000 words a day, so they were printing the first chapter whilst he was still writing the last few.

There were many authors writing under various evocative pseudonyms (Griff, Brett Vane, Jeff Bogar, William J Elliott, Michael Storme, Dail Ambler et al), and there were some good writers (Darcy Glinto,—*Lady-Don't Turn Over* (1940); Ben Sarto—*Miss Otis Comes To Piccadilly* (1946)), but the undisputed king was Hank Janson.

One Friday in 1946, Stephen D Frances, co-publisher of Pendulum Books, got a phone call from a printer saying he had enough paper for a 25,000 print run on a 24 page book, but he needed the manuscript Monday. Frances didn't have a suitable manuscript, and neither did any of the writers he rang. There was no other solution but for Frances to dictate it to his secretary over a weekend. The resulting book was *When Dames Get Tough*, and

Frances used the name of the narrator Hank Janson, as the author of the book.

It was a moderate success, followed by some shorter books and novels, which he published himself. Soon the distributor was requesting first printings of 35,000 copies as well as reprints of the earlier books. The Hank Janson books were taking off! Within two years, a million copies had been sold and the average was 60,000 per book.

The official biography was that Hank Janson was born in Britain, ran away from home and had many adventures on the high seas, before eventually landing in America, where he was a truck driver, crime reporter for a Chicago newspaper and assistant to a private detective agency. During the Second World War he served in Burma, before returning to England and settling down in Surrey with his wife and children. His books were based on his experiences. Such was the intensity of the writing that many people believed Janson to be a real person—the fan clubs set up around Britain used to write regularly asking for Hank to pay a personal visit. In fact, a TV program about success stories persuaded Hank Janson to appear live—i.e. Stephen Frances, dressed in a fedora, two overcoats (to bulk up his shoulders) and a mask.

The books were very stream of consciousness, but successful enough for Frances to be offered work for other publishers. He wrote under pseudonyms like Ace Capelli, Johnny Grecco, Duke Linton, Steve Markham etc. Even when paper deregulation came into effect in 1951, Hank Janson continued selling more and more. The biggest problem Hank faced was that an increasing number of newsagents and publishers were being prosecuted by the police for obscenity. When the police raided shops, they just picked up anything that looked sexy. It must be said that the Hank Janson covers had some of the sexiest women ever drawn on a gangster digest, courtesy of the master of the menaced dame, Reginald Heade. To combat this, some of the novels were published with just a solid outline of Hank Janson on the cover. Certainly, there was nothing in the writing that was even remotely obscene.

Eventually, Frances got tired of the responsibility and hassle of publishing and sold Janson to co-publisher, Reginald Carter. Immediately, there was a celebrated obscenity trial against seven of the books, allegedly written by another writer, Geoffrey Pardoe, but it could very well have been Frances. The publishers went to jail, but Frances and Heade didn't. Heade found it difficult to find work under his own name, so used his middle names to continue painting covers for bigger paperback publishers as Cy Webb. Frances continued writing stories under many pseudonyms, eventually selling over 20 million copies between 1946 and 1971. He spent his last days in his beloved Spain, dying in 1989.

VERY ANGRY YOUNG MEN

The late fifties and early sixties saw the emergence of the emotional soap operas of the angry young men—working class men driven to be more successful, finding out they loved middle-class older women but were unable to articulate their feelings. Also they felt equally out of place in their working-class haunts (pubs, betting shops, working mens' clubs) or the upwardly mobile social gatherings of the financially advantaged. John Osborne, Stan Barstow, David Storey (*This Sporting Life*), Alan Sillitoe (*Saturday Night And Sunday Morning, The Loneliness Of The Long-Distance Runner*) et al wrote the books and plays. Lindsay Anderson, Karel Reisz and Tony Richardson directed the films.

The great thing about this movement was that the regional accents and slang became more prevalent in films, on TV, in books, giving the elbow to the BBC proper-English school of elocution.

This was most apparent on TV with cop show, *Z-Cars*, which ran from 1962 to 1978 and spawned many spin-offs. It's free format allowed switching between different characters and storylines. It's concentration on the cops as people meant we often saw the cops out of uniform, drinking, betting and venting their frustrations on their wives. Set in the North of England, on the fictitious Newtown estate, the cases were often based on true stories, told with grit and immediacy by a team of the best young writers and directors. Writers included creator Troy Kennedy Martin (later to work on TV series *The Sweeney, Reilly-Ace Of Spies, Edge Of Darkness*), John Hopkins (*Campion, Smiley's People*), Allan Prior (*Thorndyke, The Charmer*) and Alan Plater (*The Beiderbecke Affair, Frost, Dalziel & Pascoe*). Directors included Ken Loach, who went on to direct films like *Kes* and *Hidden Agenda*. This series spawned many imitators on both sides of the Atlantic, not least of which were the American multi-storyline shows like *Hill Street Blues* and *Homicide: Life On The Street*. Unfortunately, *Z-Cars* degenerated into a twee, formulaic *Dixon Of Dock Green* up North.

On British TV and, indeed, in books, there is a tendency for everyone to sit around discussing things like reasonable human beings before admitting that, *"yes, actually, you are perfectly correct—I did it. Terribly sorry about that."* The cops are trustworthy. The lone detective is usually some upper middle class busy body who has nothing better to do but play amateur detective. In Britain disputes are settled by talking rather than by violence.

To disprove this, the first authentic British hard-boiled private eye on TV was Frank Marker, played by Alfred Burke, the violent anti-hero of *Public Eye* (1965-1975). Each week, he would delve into the seedy underworld, get his hands dirty, yet retain a clearly defined moral standpoint. *Callan* (1967-1972), where Edward Woodward played the very reluctant secret service hitman of the title, was also about moral questions of right and wrong. Created and written by James Mitchell, the show worked because of the vulnerability and self-dis-

gust so ably portrayed by Woodward. *The Equaliser*, also starring Woodward, an American rip-off of *Callan*, copied the format but forgot to retain the sharp and subtle characterisations. However, it did point up the differences in the cultures—in Britain killing people is bad no-matter the reason, in America it's acceptable and sometimes preferable.

The criminal had always been a bad guy but, underneath it all, we believed he was a gentleman—there was something admirable about a man who had the nerve to steal from others. Like heck there was! The sixties saw the audacious Great Train Robbery, the politically ruinous Profumo affair, the superhuman Krays sent down and allegations of police corruption proven.

The cynicism began to set in. Criminals were violent. The police were corrupt. Good cops had to be as corrupt and violent as the criminals. There were many films showing this attitude like *Hell Is A City* (1960, directed by Val Guest) based on the book by Maurice Procter, an ex-Constable from the North of England who wrote a series of novels about the police. The film starred Stanley Baker, a mainstay of tough, crime films in the Sixties—he was much like Robert Ryan in the way you could both hate and respect him at the same time, the tough guy with a heart beating inside him. Baker excelled in *The Criminal* (1960, directed by Joseph Losey), playing the title character just out of jail and wanting to take over his old gang. Baker later starred in *Robbery* (1967), a pretty good retelling of the Great Train Robbery. It was so good that director Peter Yates got called over to America to direct *Bullitt* (1968) (and later much undervalued films like *The Friends Of Eddie Coyle*, and *The Hot Rock*).

Allan Prior, a writer from *Z-Cars*, and a prolific TV writer, also wrote some informed and exciting novels that highlighted the ambiguity of the policemen who enforced the law: *One Away* (1961) is about a jail escape; *The Interrogators* (1965) is about a retiring Detective Inspector Savage living up to his name trying to solve a murder; *The Operators* (1966) is a heist novel which delineates the class system within London's underworld.

If you wanted a big juicy read, look no further than James Barlow, who wrote a trio of pot-boiler novels: *The Protagonists* (1956) about a sex murder; *The Patriots* (1960) where ex-paratroopers execute a *Robbery*; and the best of the lot *The Burden Of Proof* (1968), filmed as *Villain* (1971), about a tough, drug-crazed, homosexual London gangster.

The most bizarre novels of this period probably came from the pen of Mark McShane. As a teenager, he read Gerald Kersh's *Prelude To A Certain Midnight*, realised that books didn't have to follow any rules, and so when he began writing, McShane ensured his books didn't have any either. He started with fairly conventional stories: *The Straight And The Crooked* (1960) is about a robbery going wrong; *Seance On A Wet Afternoon* (1961) is about a kidnapped child, a woman with second sight; *The Passing Of Evil* (1961) is the most Kershian, dealing with the boxing fraternity in seedy side of London. From then on, his books are full of characters who would have no trouble starring in the films of David Lynch. The quaint little English villages, variously called Little Doom, Greyton or Purity, hide cesspools of sex, death and depravity. Mass murderers, serial killers, mad preachers, Lolitas, farmers in love with their bulls—his books are full of them.

More conventional in some ways was Arthur La Bern, who presented the streets of post-war London as a breeding ground of failed ambitions, under-achievers and self-deceivers. His most well known novel *Is It Always Rains On Sunday*. A typical novel begins with a man coming back from the Second World War to find out what he was fighting for—a pack of vultures, living off the slim pickings of a country sucked dry by the war. Having no other options before him, the man turns to petty crime, just to survive, to provide food for his wife. So begins *Pennygreen Street* (1950). Against this social background La Bern weaves tales of suspense and low-life killers, of pimps, prostitutes and racketeers, like: *It Was Christmas Every Day* (1952), where a writer finds his wife with another man and takes the law into his own hands; *The Big Money Box* (1960), a heist book; *Brighton Belle* (1963), based in and around the Brighton races; and *Goodbye Piccadilly, Farewell Leicester Square* (1966), about a serial killer terrorising the streets of London, famously filmed as *Frenzy* (1972) by Alfred Hitchcock, although the book is so much better.

While some writers looked at the social conditions that affect the actions of citizens who would be law-abiding given half a chance, others decided to go inside the people. After the war, everybody realised that man had the capacity to kill, to torture, to degrade their fellow human beings. It was a shock that led to the post-war noir masterpieces.

GBH

With the austerity of the Fifties making way for the prosperity of the Sixties, the generally comfortable masses began to clasp middle-class values to their bosom. Now killers were a 'problem' and we had to find out why they killed. Was it the low-life society they were brought up in? Or was it their nature to kill?

Always the outsider, the crime novels of Colin Wilson stand alone. They are about intelligent men who rip and defile people for reasons which are beyond the understanding of society. Their lucid ideas are drowned by their repulsive actions. Beginning with *Ritual In The Dark* (1960), the focus of the books is the killers and their hunters. Both are treated as artists, as intellectuals. The victims are forgotten. These novels are at least twenty years ahead of their time but, once an intellectual puzzle is solved, one wonders whatever happened to the emotions of the characters. These stories are a way for Wilson to explain his philosophy of life. Consequently, the quest for truth is not the truth society is looking for, but the truth an individual finds. At the time of publication, these books were available from the library, but were on the restricted list—so you had to ask for it, the library ensured you were over 18, the book was retrieved from a locked storage area, and you read until you bled.

Roman Polanski also explored a damaged mind in his excellent *Repulsion* (1965). Rather than travel the highways and byways of thought processes (easy in books), he took the motorway to the senses. In the story, a French woman in an English city (already feeling alienated), goes quietly mad in her flat. The sounds are too loud, the texture of objects change all the time, the world looks and feels different. We don't know what is going on in her mind, but we feel it—and it is repulsive.

For all the organised thinking going on in the minds of these criminals, they are always prone to emotional outbursts—they are disorganised criminals. The organised criminal builds a structure of middlemen and companies between the crime and himself.

It is at this stage that the upwardly mobile, financially successful businessman and the professional criminal often seemed interchangeable. The crime boss went to social functions, was friendly with the mayor, the political leaders, the local celebrities, the police, donated money to charity, had a smart house and a dumb wife, and, most importantly, got other people to do his dirty work for him.

The transition of the criminal as violent punk to the criminal as tough businessman is best encapsulated by *Performance* (1970), directed by Nic Roeg and Donald Cammell. This is the story of sadistic, puritan James

Fox, enforcer for Kray-like protection racket who, being a little over-zealous, kills, runs for cover, and holes up in a flat with sexually ambiguous rock star Turner, played by Mick Jagger. They recognise each other as performers, artists if you like, in their own fields, their unique skills being exploited by big business.

Get Carter! (1971), directed by Mike Hodges, starred Michael Caine as a smartly dressed professional hitman, based in London, returning to his Newcastle roots to investigate the death of his brother. He meets a succession of lowlife characters, which include angry young man John Osborne as a powerful local crime boss, gradually gets angrier and angrier, before the violence starts to crank up.

Get Carter was based on the novel *Jack's Return Home* by Ted Lewis, a former animator who worked on *The Yellow Submarine* (1968). The novel is surprisingly subtle, filling in telling background details of Jack's childhood, showing just how thick blood is compared to water. After the success of *Get Carter*, Lewis tried to write tough British-based crime novels but they didn't gel with the readers, who only wanted more of super bastard hitman Jack Carter. Lewis relented with two outrageously violent Jack Carter novels, *Jack Carter's Law* and *Jack Carter And The Mafia Pigeon*.

However, both of these films were prefigured by a pair of TV serials written and produced by Robin Chapman. *Spindoe* (1968) was a six-part thriller about old gangster Ray McAnally just out after a seven year stretch (shown an the earlier TV Series *The Fellows (Late Of Room 17)* (1967)) trying to regain his former position and territory. It is a tough and violent study of a struggle for power—mixing the old gangster, his unfaithful wife, the rival ganglord and a vengeful private detective who ain't very nice. This led directly to *Big Breadwinner Hog* (1969), by the same production team—about the utterly merciless and ruthlessly ambitious

Hog (played by young, debonair Peter Egan). Because of his vicious and violent methods, he becomes a threat to the established criminal fraternity. As directed by Mike Newell (*Dance With A Stranger*, *Donnie Brasco*) and Michael Apted (*Agatha*, *Gorky Park*, *Blink*) these eight hour-long episodes caused a lot of controversy at the time because of their explicit violence.

Still gritty, but in a lighter vein, other films of this period include: *Otley* (1968), directed by TV scribe Dick Clement, starring Tom Courtenay in the title role, and based on the novels of Martin Waddell, this is a hugely entertaining comedy thriller, which has Otley as a born loser, a small-time thief, who is used and abused time and time again by bigger-time thieves and murders; *Gumshoe* (1971), directed by Stephen Frears (who later directed *The Hit* (1984) and *The Grifters* (1990)), starring Albert Finney, based on the novel by Neville Smith, is a comedy-thriller about a bingo caller in Liverpool who dreams of writing and starring in *The Thin Man*, and ends involved in a real-life murder mystery; and *Pulp* (1972), written and directed by Mike Hodges, starring Michael Caine, about a pulp writer in the Mediterranean who is asked to ghost-write the memoirs of a rich, powerful fan, who also happens to be on the fringes of the Mafia.

And while we're talking about the British underworld, you must never forget *Gangsters*, a TV event is ever there was one. A TV play in 1975, followed by two series in 1976 and 1978, this was the hardest of all the hard TV series. Set in Birmingham, and using a very famous and then still-active, gang of Asian gangsters, as the basis of the story, *Gangsters* concerned Maurice Colbourne, playing London villain John Kline, and his attempts to remain alive amongst drug pushing, prostitution, immigrant smuggling, and gang wars. Filmed on the streets of Brum, utilising a wise script from Philip Martin, this remains one of the forgotten highlights of Brit noir TV.

Taking the villain's point of view, trying to find out what makes things tick, can be done in two ways—either you enter the under world, understand there are rules and follow them (i.e. the villain essentially becomes the hero), or you try to relate the villain to the real world. Now, for the former, you're talking about a TV series like *Out* (1978). Like *Spindoe*, it is about hard man Tom Bell playing bank robber Frank Ross, released from stir, obsessed with finding the pigeon who put him away. Written by Trevor Preston and directed by Jim Goddard, who worked together on The Sweeney among others, Ross becomes the wandering samurai, like Carter in *Get Carter*, or Walker in *Point Blank* (1967), best exemplified by Alain Delon's portrayal of Jef Costello in Jean-Pierre Melville's *Le Samourai* (1967), and more recently Robert De Niro in Michael Mann's *Heat* (1995). For these people there is honour among thieves, and everyone knows their place—every morning they get up and go to work.

There is a subtle, but an important difference between these masterless warriors, who pretend to have some personal code of honour (one which is selfish rather than selfless), and the villain who has to live in the real world. The criminal in the real world can be found in the novels of American writers like Ed Bunker (*No Beast So Fierce* (1972) and Dannie M Martin (*The Dishwasher* (1995)), but in Britain the same cannot be said. We have seen Donald Mac-Kenzie write about his life in *Nowhere To Go*, and Ted Lewis used John McVicar's life story as the basis for the excellent *Billy Rags* (1973). *Billy Rags* is about Billy Cracken, who has a reputation for violence. He is a professional criminal with eight of the past ten years spent in the nick. Now he is serving a twenty-five year stretch in maximum security. But Billy doesn't intend to stay. While his wife is on the outside, Billy fights for supremacy inside—having to keep top con Walter Colman at bay. So Billy breaks out. And on the outside he's a hunted man. The law is looking for him and Colman has put a private army of thugs on his tail. To stay free, Billy has to work another job—the last big robbery that will provide his getaway money.

In 1972, there was also a realistic portrayal of the criminal fraternity in the TV series *Villains*—the story of nine bank robbers, beginning at the moment of their escape from prison. Over the thirteen hour-long episodes, we get to see the men, their accomplices, their women, the original robbery—a sort of *Reservoir Dogs* for the Seventies. Featuring the cream of London character actors (Bob Hoskins, Martin Shaw, Alun Armstrong et al), I doubt we'll ever see this one again.

THEY LIVE WITH THEIR EYES SHUT

Although the cops were often portrayed as tough, no-nonsense types, they were always honourable, honest, trusted. The British legal and law-enforcement system relies on the general public having confidence in the authorities. In America, people are taught to discuss their problems over an exchange of bullets because there is little confidence in the villains being punished, whereas in Britain they are taught to solve disputes by exchanging words because the authorities are sure to deal out justice accordingly.

Towards the end of the sixties, beginning with the Profumo affair, and into the seventies, this belief was shattered. Commander Drury, head of Scotland Yard's Flying Squad, was caught with his hand in the back pocket of the underworld, the first high-ranking police officer to be jailed. More cases followed. We began to see corrupt cops, or cops as villains.

One of the first novelists to mine this rich vein was G F Newman, with his Terry Sneed trilogy: *Sir, You Bastard* (1970), *You Nice Bastard* (1972) and *You Flash Bastard*

(1974). Detective Inspector Sneed has spent seven years taking bribes, using lies, deceit and violence to get where he is, and it's all going to be taken from him. He's got 36 hours to straighten it out. It's a race against the clock to save himself. The second novel shows the workings of criminals based on the Krays and the Richardsons, and how they use policemen like Sneed. The third novel sees Sneed work his way up to Detective Chief Inspector, off the streets and into the cut-throat world of office politics. At the time, they were a turning point in the way we perceive authority—a perception many people now share—Newman has been a constant thorn in the side of authority figures ever since. His other well-known trilogy is *Law And Order* (1977), comprising: *A Detective's Tale*, *A Villain's Tale* and *A Prisoner's Tale*.

Earlier, in the film *The Offence* (1971), directed by American Sidney Lumet in London, Sean Connery plays a cop obsessed with his belief that suspect Ian Bannen is a child molester. This is one long interrogation where the power shifts back and forth between the protagonists. Originally written by noted TV writer John Hopkins, for the stage, it points out the moral ambiguities in the relationship between cop and suspect. The word intense comes to mind whenever I remember watching the film.

The theme of the cop as anti-hero, using criminal tactics to catch the baddies, was prevalent throughout the Seventies. The best exponent of the art was *The Sweeney* (1975-8), a TV series created by Ian Kennedy Martin. His idea was that, after the embarrassment of Commander Drury and other much-publicised police corruption cases, a tough, street-smart cop was becoming obsolete in the new whiter-than-white, University-educated Metropolitan police force. Specifically, Kennedy Martin had a friend on the force, the prototype for lead character Regan, who had a few choice things to say about Robert Mark, who had just come in to head the force and had totally reorganised it. Afraid of more corruption allegations, Mark had said, effectively, that Flying Squad officers couldn't go into a pub and get information out of a snout—they had to do it from their desks. (The Flying Squad were called *The Sweeney* from the Cockney rhyming slang Sweeney Todd)

The idea was to show what it was like to be on the streets day-in, day-out, and the effects the job had on your home life. For good coppers like Regan that meant that you had to be as mean and dirty as the villains, but you didn't have as much money. Also, Regan was work-obsessed, had a broken marriage behind him, and a string of intelligent, independent women for company on those occasional nights when there was no oppo on. By way of contrast, the villains' wives waited years whilst their blokes were banged up or sunning themselves in some sunny clime until things cooled down.

Regan, is a loud, temperamental, foul-mouthed, below-the-belt, street fighter, who lies through his teeth to get the villains. Sometimes, he goes too far, people get hurt. Regan's reputation was such that in one episode, *Big Brother*, when a suspect collapsed whilst under arrest, Jack was publicly accused of beating him to within an inch of death. In another, *Sweet Smell of Succession*, when a boss unexpectedly dies and the University-educated son is caught between the two rival gangsters, Regan has no hesitation in using the son as bait.

The rogue policeman was in vogue throughout the late Sixties and early Seventies. Film director Don Siegel virtually had a monopoly on the genre with *Madigan* (1968), *Coogan's Bluff* (1968), and, most significantly, *Dirty Harry* (1971) serving as role models for those ever-so-nice Sweeney boys. 1971 also saw *The French Connection* on the silver screen—another major influence on the style and attitude of *The Sweeney* producers and directors. In fact,

one scene where Popeye Doyle, played by Gene Hackman, stands out in the freezing cold drinking a cup of coffee, whilst the drug pushers sit in the nice warmth of a posh restaurant enjoying slap-up nosh, was often quoted by the team.

On the writing side of *The Sweeney*, there was the reassuring presence of Roger Marshall, the creator of *Public Eye* (1965-1975), with eight episodes to his credit, bringing a dogged realism to the series. However, the most influential writer was Trevor Preston, who contributed 11 of the 53 episodes. Another writer was Murray Smith, master-writer of the *Xyy Man—Strangers—Bulman* strand of related series about cops who always seem to lose more than they succeed, and more recently 99-1, an effective and darker reworking of the *Callan/Equaliser* formula.

In 1977, *Laidlaw* by William McIllvanney was published, followed *By The Papers Of Tony Veitch* in 1983. McIllvanney is a poet and writer of some distinction who uses the crime format as a showcase for his ideas. Jack Laidlaw uses a lot of violence to find out who did what. The moral ambiguity of the character and his actions are pointed and counterpointed by all the characters in the books. In the first book, a girl is killed, and it's a race between the criminal fraternity, who want to catch and kill the murderer, and the bastions of law and order, who want to bring him to justice. In the second book, a tramp on his deathbed summons for Laidlaw and, in his cryptic last message, Laidlaw sees a clue to a gangland killing. Laidlaw then doggedly follows this clue through every layer of society. Basically, McIllvanney says that in a tough, masculine world, in an urban landscape of iron and metal, you have to be as hard as rivets to survive. Having said that, McIllvanney uses some of the most poetic language and nuance to express these ideas. In the end, Laidlaw is seeking not only the truth about the criminal events, but also the moral truth surrounding those events. The result is mesmeric and not that dissimilar to the Factory series of Derek Raymond.

In the sixties, as Robin Cook (Derek Raymond's real name), he wrote about wideboy chancers and conmen as heroes, or about seedy Soho pornographers and their friendly priests. Crime was fun in the swinging sixties, especially since Robin Cook was a criminal and making a good living out of it.

However, years of hard labour in Italian and French vineyards, and a sober face-to-face with reality, resulted in a remarkable series of books where the dead victims had names and the police detective investigating their death didn't. The Factory novels, as they are known, dance on the abyss of death, destruction and failure, jump in, wallow in it, and somehow manage to retain their humanity when all about them lose theirs. The heart of darkness beats. Thus are the Factory novels of Derek Raymond beginning with *He Died With His Eyes Open* (1984), and ending *With Dead Man Upright* (1993).

The mid-Eighties were a great time for noirish TV. *Edge Of Darkness* (1985), the story of Craven (Bob Peck), a police detective whose daughter is murdered in front of him, provided high-voltage tension over six weeks. Written by Troy Kennedy Martin, Craven leaves the force, breaks into an underground Government nuclear establishment, joins up with a maverick CIA agent (Joe Don Baker), and eventually barges into a top level conference. All the while, Craven carries on conversations with the ghost of his daughter. *Deadhead* (1986), imaginatively directed by Rob Walker from a Howard Brenton script, was a four part series following small-time sarf London crook Eddie Cass (played by Denis Lawson), who is innocently roped into a gruesome crime (featuring the dead head of the title) and henceforth used as a pawn of the state. *The Singing Detective* (1986), is a phenomenal piece of writing by Dennis Potter—a musical thriller featuring a pulp writer in hospital suffering from a severe bout of psoriasis, constructing a fantastic thriller around the death of his wife and her lover, interspersed with real events from the writer's childhood and life. Superb in every respect.

The times weren't too bad for films either. The eighties started with a bang: *The Long Good Friday* (1980), directed by John MacKenzie, recently voted by one film magazine as the best British film ever! London gangster Bob Hoskins is worried because someone is invading his patch and taking over—they're blowing up and blowing away everything and everyone. Emphatic filmmaking. For a more subtle approach to the genre look to Neil Jordan and *Angel* (1982), about a saxophone played (Stephen Rea) who ends up protecting a witness to a killing—the film is about personal responsibility. Another excellent Neil Jordan film (Jordan started out as a promising novelist by-the-by) is *Mona Lisa* (1986), which shows the growing relationship between minder Bob Hoskins and prostitute Cathy Tyson. *Defence of the Realm* (1985) has Gabriel Byrne as a London hack who accidentally comes across an important story and is stalked by the state as a result. *The McGuffin* (1985) was a Hitchcockian thriller, starring Charles Dance, which ends up at a porn film festival. Director Mike Figgis presented Newcastle as a 50s film noir set in *Stormy Monday* (1987), and went on to direct the excellent *Internal Affairs* in America. *The Cook, The Thief, His Wife And Her Lover* (1989) is another bizarre tale of sex, eating, love and death from Peter Greenaway—a gangland thug loves eating, his wife loves sex, they all eat/meet in a restaurant, and the result is much death on the menu. The decade was finished off with *The Krays* (1990), Peter Medak's biopic of London's favourite kneecappers.

TOOLED UP

The spirit of Mickey Spillane is alive and well and living in South London under the nom-de-plume of Mark Timlin. Timlin, ex-roadie for The Who, writes about ex-cop private eye Nick Sharman—honourable rogue, drunk no-hoper, self-defeating desperado. There have been 16 books since the first, *A Good Year For The Roses*, appeared in 1987. They are full of drugs, sex, violence and rock'n'roll, heaped together in glorious chunks of over-emotional prose.

The series is now sadly prone to repetition—the death of a friend, a lover, a wife or child invariably unleashes Nick's anger on the underworld. In nineties Britain, this means he can tool up with mortars, bazookas, armour-piercing shells and the Uzi 9mm of his choice. The result is fluorescent red walls and ceilings. This is not in yer face, more through it.

Mention here should be made of P B Yuill, a sure-fire influence on Mr Timlin. Gordon M Williams (writer of *The Siege Of Trencher's Farm*, filmed by Sam Peckinpah as *Straw Dogs*) and soccer manager Terry Venables wrote three Hazell novels under the pseudonym P B Yuill. The first *Hazell Plays Solomon* (1974), opens with our heroic private eye resting his ankle, recently broken when some clients slammed a door on it three or four times. Very obviously a British Marlowe, hobbling down the lean streets of Cockneyshire, it's a pity so few books were written. A TV series of 22 episodes, starring Nicholas Ball as the eponymous hero Hazell found it's way into UK homes in 1978.

Although Mark Timlin takes his lineage directly from Ted Lewis, P B Yuill, Derek Raymond and the bloody thunderers of the past, a new mutated breed has followed him. These are hip, with-it, druggie, writers who portray a different view of Britishness. It's based around youth culture, teenagers. Again, instead of the authority figure, or the errant knight, we have come back to the reckless youth, the amoral criminals on the streets—taking a lead from the films of Quentin Tarantino—pastiche, ultra-violence, homage, cut-up narratives—and the books of American hardboiled writers Jim Thompson, Elmore Leonard and Charles Willeford.

Nicholas Blincoe shows the transsexual club world of Manchester. Irvine Walsh immerses himself in the world of drugs (and good luck to him). Victor Headley writes about the Yardies—the vicious Jamaican gangsters who roam the streets of Londonshire, cocking their guns at authority. Christopher Brookmyre, the Hiassen of the Highlands, seems to have his gun firmly inserted into his cheek.

The lack of respect for the old, shown by the young, as we hit the millennium.

FADE TO BLACK

The modern Noir novel seems to emulate the style and sensational aspects of the genre, rather than the real concerns for humanity that the best writing talks about. Where are our Derek Raymonds and Patrick Hamiltons and James Curtises? On TV we have seen the brief glimmer of *Edge Of Darkness* and *The Singing Detective*, the moral maze of *Callan*, but nothing since. The film world gave us *Performance*, and we are most grateful.

The thing is that good writers only turn up once in a blue moon. The trick is recognising them, and once you do that, holding on to them. If you haven't heard of some of these writers before, perhaps this article will give you a few clues of where to go for more sustenance until the next great Brit noir writer emerges.

Paul Duncan, co-founder of CT, has been writing about British Noir in CT for some time. His interview with Derek Raymond, probably the most authoritative interview ever done with him, is available in **The Third Degree** *(No Exit Press, 1997), and there are articles about Gerald Kersh, Ted Lewis and* **The Sweeney** *in CT8, 9 and 11 respectively. He is presently writing a biography of Gerald Kersh. Next issue Paul starts a full history of Noir fiction in CT.*

fiction

the dark path

jason starr

One of Crime Time*'s favourite
authors, with a chilling tale about
responsibility...*

IT WAS ALMOST twilight in October
Mountain State Park in the Berkshires and
Susan and I were walking along the dark
wooded path in silence. We hadn't been
getting along all day and there was no
sign things would get any better. Later
on, back in our room at the B&B, I was
going to tell her it was time to start seeing
other people. "We both know this isn't
working out," I'd say. "Isn't it better that
we end it now?" Naturally, she'd be very
upset. I'd probably be upset too—after
all, two and a half years is a long time for
two thirty-something people to be
together—but this "Let's-find-out-
where-the-relationship-is-going"
weekend had been a major disaster. So
far there had been non-stop arguing,
proving that we weren't meant for each
other. After we cried all night and drove
back to New York where we'd have
another tearful goodbye, it might take a
few weeks, or even months, to get over
her, but eventually I would, and I'd
probably thank God for it too.

After about fifteen more minutes of
walking in silence, wishing I was alone, I
realized how it was suddenly noticeably
cooler and darker, and I said, "Do you
remember how to get out of here?"

"You're the one who's supposed to
have the brilliant sense of direction."

"I'll take that as a no."

We continued to walk along an unfamiliar-looking path. Occasionally Susan grunted in frustration or disgust, as if it was *my* fault that we had gotten lost. This only angered me even more. I started walking faster, keeping a few paces ahead of her.

"What's wrong with you?" she said. "Why are you acting this way?"

I didn't answer her, knowing it would only lead to more arguing. I wished I'd broken up with her before we'd taken this trip. I wished I was back home at my apartment in Manhattan, alone, drinking a beer and relaxing on my couch watching a baseball game.

"Great," she said. "So now you're ignoring me. That's really intelligent, Robert. Will you please stop walking and wait for me?"

I walked a few more steps and then stopped, waiting for her to catch up with me.

She said, "So did you figure out where we're going yet?"

"What do you think?"

"You don't have to snap at me."

"Will you stop trying to start an argument every two seconds?"

"You're the one who's arguing."

"When we find our way out of here that's it."

"What's that supposed to mean?"

I didn't answer her—figuring, at this point, it was best to be ambiguous.

We veered right along another rocky, root-covered, path, walking for about a minute longer without speaking, then Susan said, "It's getting dark. What happens if we can't find our way out of here?"

"We will."

"But what if we don't? I'm not going to spend a night in the woods."

"Can you just stop it?"

We walked for about another minute without talking. I was getting bitten up by mosquitoes and gnats were swarming around my head.

Susan said, "I told you this was a stupid idea."

"*You* wanted to come."

"You didn't tell me what it was like. You didn't say it would just be a forest."

"What did you expect it to be like?"

"You know there are bears in these woods."

"Who told you that?"

"The woman who runs the B&B. She told me a story—how one time a bear came into the town or something and they had to call in somebody from the gaming commission."

"We won't see any bears."

"How do you know?"

"I think I see a road."

We walked faster toward an opening in the woods. When I saw that it was indeed a road and not a mirage, I felt the sudden exhilaration that people in the desert must feel when the come up a river or a stream.

"Thank God," Susan said. "This is the last time I ever go hiking with you."

It sure will be, I thought, hearing myself later saying, "I think we should break up." It was going to be so liberating to finally say that simple sentence, to suddenly be released from the burden of a bad relationship. I'd probably realize how much stress I'd been under lately.

"I want to be engaged by Christmas."

It was the fourth anniversary of the night we'd met. We had gone out to dinner at a nice Portuguese restaurant on Restaurant Row and then we had theater tickets to see *Les Miserables*. But in the cab ride back to my place she had to put a downer on the whole night by trying to get me to make a commitment to her.

"Come on," I said. "Let's not talk about that tonight."

"Why not?" she said. "It's been two years you know."

As if I was such a louse I didn't know what anniversary we were celebrating.

"Why do you have to put this kind of pressure on me?"

"I want to know where this is going—if you're serious about me or not."

Staring out the cab window I didn't answer her right away. Then, still looking out the window, I said, "I really don't think this is the time to discuss this.

After that night, the flaws in Susan's personality, which I had overlooked until then, started to take on new prominence. She was too controlling, too demanding, too uptight, too stuffy. I began to forget why I'd started dating her in the first place. True, she was very attractive. She was thin with small toned muscles and short stylish brown hair and she always dressed well and took good care of herself—dieting constantly and going to the gym fanatically, five or six times a week. But there was nothing very unusual about her looks either. What I mean is there were thousands of woman in New York who were attractive and in-shape—why did I necessarily have to marry Susan?

I decided that the only reason she was interested in me at all was because I was a successful lawyer. She often talked about how she had broken up with previous boyfriends because they weren't on "a

career track"—i.e., they weren't earning enough for her to retire at forty. Outside of having similar backgrounds—we grew up in adjacent towns on Long Island—we didn't have much in common. She worked in advertising and always seemed bored when I talked about something that was going on at my job, and I was the same way about her career.

I knew that our relationship was Susan's main topic of conversation with her friends. "Did Robert get you ring yet?" "Do you think he'll pop the question soon?" "How much more time are you going to give him? "Getting a ring" from me seemed to be becoming her true M.O. It had nothing to do with me anymore or getting married. I felt like it was all a game to her and that I was the prize. Once she got a ring from me the game would be over and then it would be on to a new game—having children. I felt like I was being manipulated, used. I was a good-looking, successful, extremely eligible bachelor with a lot to offer, and if I wanted to marry a woman I wanted it to be my choice and my choice alone.

"Where do you think this road leads?" Susan asked.

I had been so distracted by my own thoughts I realized that Susan had asked the question a few seconds ago and that it took awhile to register.

"I have no idea," I said, "but it's going downhill. It probably leads to the parking lot where we left the car."

"It's going to be pitch dark in like two minutes."

"Let's just keep walking."

Just then I heard the sound of an engine, probably a truck, and then headlights appeared on the road. The driver had the vehicle's brights on and Susan and I both squinted, shielding our eyes. The vehicle stopped above the road, about fifty yards ahead of us.

"Let's ask for a lift," Susan said.

Usually, as a paranoid New Yorker, I never would have even considered such an idea. At home, I didn't even know the names of the people who lived in the apartments on my floor in the building, and, like my mother taught me, I never spoke to strangers. But now getting a lift down the mountain didn't seem like such a bad idea. It was going to be dark soon and I was tired and I was sick of fighting with Susan. The idea of getting back to the room at the B&B sooner, rather than later, was appealing.

"All right," I said.

We started walking faster, toward the vehicle, when headlights went off. It was still bright enough to see a silhouette taking something off the back of the truck and carrying it into the woods.

I squeezed Susan's hand and stopped walking.

"What's wrong?"

"Sshh," I said.

I pulled her off the road, toward the woods. We were still at least twenty yards away and I didn't think whoever was in the truck had seen us.

"What are—"

I put my hand over Susan's mouth and whispered, "Be quiet. I think I saw that guy carrying a body off that truck."

I moved my hand away and Susan said in a quieter voice, but not whispering, "Are you crazy?"

"I'm telling you it looked like a body," I said. "And keep your voice down."

I heard a door slam—the guy getting

back in the truck—and then the engine and headlights went on and the truck started moving slowly in our direction. I pulled Susan back into the woods and we knelt down as the truck—it was red, probably a flat-bed Ford—sped by.

"You idiot," Susan said. "Thanks to you we're going to have to walk in the dark."

"And I suppose you'd rather get a lift from a killer."

"What killer? You're always so paranoid, it drives me crazy. He was probably dumping something else out— a bag of garbage or something."

"I'm telling you it was body."

"You wanna go look at it?"

The sound of the truck had almost faded completely. Now there was only the loud country noise of crickets.

"Fine," I said.

Susan let out a deep frustrated breath down the road toward where the truck had been parked. I hoped that she was right—I could have lived with her saying "I told you so" and being angry at me for blowing our chance for getting a lift down the mountain—but I'd had my eyes checked recently and my vision was 20-15 and I knew what I had seen. Still, as we approached the spot, I was praying that I was mistaken.

"There's nothing here," Susan said.

"Farther," I said. "Toward the woods."

As we walked through the tall grass Susan whined, "Great, now I'm going to catch Lime Disease," then she screamed when we came upon a site I will never forget. There was just enough pale light to see the wide open eyes, the huge gash across the neck of the young woman who had been nearly decapitated.

Susan started to scream again. I put my hand over her mouth quickly, terrified that the man in the truck had heard her and would come back. I was pretty shaken up myself, and if I hadn't witnessed a traffic accident in New York a few years ago and seen two mangled bodies removed from the back of a taxi cab, the site of the dead bloody body probably would disturbed me even more.

"Relax," I said, pulling her away, back through the grass. "Just relax, all right?"

On the road, I could barely see Susan's face.

"Oh my God," she said. "What are we going to do?"

"Come on," I said, "we have to get out of here."

Walking along the road, I was holding Susan's hand. Then, realizing what I was doing, I let go.

While Susan was showering I lay in bed staring at the muted television. The walk back to our car along the dark road had taken almost an hour. The plan was to get back to our room as quick as possible and then call the police, but the most important thing on my mind was still how I was going to break up with Susan.

She came out of the bathroom, her bony body wrapped in a towel.

"Did you call the police yet?" Susan asked.

I stared at her for a moment, confused, then I said, "No."

"What do you mean?" she said. "Why not?"

"I was thinking—it might not be such a good idea."

"What are you talking about? Call them—right this instant."

She reached for the phone but I already had my hand on the receiver.

"Think about it," I said. "This is a very delicate situation. We don't want to do anything rash."

"Rash? It's been at least an hour since we saw the body."

"Exactly. Don't you think that's the first thing a detective is going to want to know—why did we wait so long to report it?"

"We had to get down the mountain, didn't we?"

"But we could've gone right to the nearest phone booth, but we didn't—we came back here."

"That's because we were going to call them from here."

"I know that and you know that, but a detective might see it differently. Then what if they find our footprints in the grass or one of our hairs on the body."

"But we discovered the body."

"That's the truth but to them it'll be just a story. We'll wind up being suspects or witnesses and we'll be stuck up here for weeks together."

"I knew you were paranoid," she said, "but this is unbelievable. Will you please give me that phone?"

I still had my hand over the receiver.

"Trust me," I said. "I'm an attorney."

"You're a *tax* attorney."

I decided to ignore the obvious dig. Sometimes Susan just annoyed me—other times she was a flat-out bitch.

"I know what I'm talking about," I said. "Can you afford to miss the next two or three weeks of work while the police are investigating? Do you want to have to schlep back up here for the grand jury hearing, then for a trial?"

"A woman is dead in the woods."

"I'm aware of that, but nothing we

do is going to bring her back to life. It's better not to get involved.

"But there's a killer loose out there. What if somebody else gets killed?"

"That's not our problem—that's the police's problem."

"But we saw him—"

"We saw nothing. Can you describe him?"

"I can describe the truck."

"Just forget about it. Believe me, calling the police won't do anything except create a big hassle for both of us."

Susan was quiet for a moment then she said, "What if the time is important? What if they need to know when the body was dumped?"

"We'll just forget about it," I said. "The body wasn't far from the road—it'll be discovered eventually. We were never there and we never saw anything. It's better that way."

"I don't know," she said drowsily. "My head hurts so much I can't think anymore."

"Did you take any Tylenols?"

"Four," she said rubbing the back of her neck.

Susan tossed her towel onto the chair and took her nightgown out of her suitcase.

"I wanted to ask you something," she said, putting on her nightgown. "Not about the body—about what you said before in the woods."

"What did I say?"

"About how if we find our way out of there that's it. What exactly did you mean by that?"

Get it over with, I thought. Here's your entree.

"I don't know," I said. "Nothing probably."

"Probably?"

"Definitely."

"Then why did you say it?"

"We were fighting."

"You sounded serious."

"Please don't get melodramatic," I said. "You know how much I hate that."

She lay down on the bed next to on her back. There was space between us.

We had planned to go to Tanglewood tonight to hear The Boston Symphony, but now that was out of the question. After awhile, I turned out the light on the night table, but I left the muted television on. Blue flickering TV light shone across the bed.

I still wanted to break up with Susan, but I was tired I and decided to wait until morning.

"I know I won't be able to sleep," Susan said.

"Try."

"I keep seeing that poor girl."

"Forget about it."

"I can't."

"You will."

"How?"

"Just don't worry so much."

I have no idea how long it took Susan to fall asleep or if she slept at all. Within a few minutes I was out cold.

The next morning when I opened my eyes Susan was dressed. She was wearing khaki shorts, a black tank top, and dark sunglasses.

"What time is it?" I asked groggily.

"Early," she replied.

"Where are you going?"

This time she didn't say anything.

Another wave of wakefulness overcame me and I said, "You didn't call the police, did you?"

"No."

"Good," I said yawning. "So where are you going?"

"Home," she said, zipping up her suitcase.

"What the hell are you talking about?" I said, sitting up. "What's going on?"

She turned toward me, looking embittered, as if we were in the middle of a long argument.

"I can't believe I let you talk me into that last night. A woman was killed, murdered, and we did nothing about it."

"I thought we already discussed this."

"And then," she went on, "you just fall asleep, snoring, like you don't have a worry in the world. What kind of person are you?"

"What the hell are you talking about?"

"Look, I think we both know this isn't working," she said.

"What isn't working?"

"*This*...us...everything. This whole weekend has pretty much proved that weren't meant for each other, and it's obvious things aren't going to change."

I wondered if I was dreaming. Could it be true? Was *she* really dumping *me*?

"What's so funny?"

"Nothing," I said.

"Then why were you smiling?"

"I wasn't."

"I'm glad you're so amused by this." She picked up her suitcase. "If you want some advice, you should grow up. You're thirty-four years old and you go around, acting like you're twenty. I think we should have a clean break—no phone calls, no lunches—it'll be easier that way."

I asked Susan if she wanted to wait and drive back to the city together, but she insisted on taking a bus from town.

"Whatever you do, don't call the police now," I said. "I'm serious. They'll ask all kinds of questions and it'll lead to big trouble for both of us."

She looked at me for a couple of seconds, her hands on her hips, then she said, "Goodbye, Robert," and closed the door behind her.

I listened to the silence for a while, letting it soak in. I still couldn't believe I was alone again. Susan, the burden I'd been carrying around for months, was out of my life for good, and the feeling was better than I'd expected.

I checked out of the hotel around noon and headed back to the city. It was great being single again—driving in the rental car with the windows open, listening to loud rock music.

During a newsbreak, an anchorman reported that the sodomized body of a young woman had been discovered this morning by a park ranger on a road in October Mountain State Park. Police believed that the murder could be related to four other rape-murders in the Berkshire County area over the past several months. Anyone with any information about the case was urged to contact the police immediately.

I was driving through a small town and spotted a telephone on the corner. I thought about the girl's grieving family, praying for the attacker to be caught.

I stopped at a crosswalk, letting a man cross the street, then I sped away.

Jason Starr is the author of Cold Caller *and* Nothing Personal, *two excellent novels published by No Exit Press - you should try them...*

OXFORD UNIVERSITY PRESS: BOOK OFFER

The Oxford Book of American Detective Stories, RRP: £9.99 Offer Price:£6.00
Edited by Tony Hillerman and Rosemary Herbert
Includes work by Raymond Chandler, Erle Stanley Gardner, Ellery Queen and Sara Paretsky. The editors bring us a gold mine of glorious stories.

ISBN: 0-19-511792-1

**Murder on Deck!
RRP: £18.99 Offer Price: £11.00**
Shipboard and Shoreline Mystery Stories Edited by Rosemary Herbert
Features stories by John Mortimer, Agatha Christie and Gabriel García Márquez. This is an intriguing new selection.
ISBN: 0-19-508603-1

Hard-Boiled, RRP: £9.99 Offer Price:£6.00
An Anthology of American Crime Stories
Edited by Bill Pronzini and Jack Adrian
From Dashiell Hammett and Raymond Chandler to Ed McBain and James Ellroy. Included are 36 sublimely suspenseful stories that chronicle the evolution of this quintessentially American art form.
ISBN: 0-19-510353-X

ORDERING INFORMATION

CREDIT CARD HOTLINE: Phone our Credit Card Hotline, open 24 hours a day
Tel: +44 (0) 1536 454 534
BY EMAIL: email: orders@oup.co.uk
BY POST: CWO Department, OUP, FREEPOST, NH 4051, Corby, Northants, NN18 9BR
Please Quote the following Code for all telephone or Email orders: CODE:CBCRIME

murder at suicide oak
o'neil de noux

DETECTIVE DINO LASTANZA stepped aside to let a heavy-set crime lab technician take pictures of the two bodies. Backpedaling, he slipped his portable radio into the left rear pocket of his dress black pants. He backed all the way to his unmarked white Ford and leaned against its front fender. Removing his blue sport coat, LaStanza tossed it into the open window of his car. Instinctively, he ran his left hand over the gold star-and-crescent badge clipped to the front of his belt, then rested his right hand on the black rubber grip of his stainless-steel Smith & Wesson two-and-a-half inch barrel .357 magnum holstered on his right hip.

LaStanza studied the crime scene beneath the towering branches of an ancient oak tree at the edge of New Orleans' City Park. The strobe light from the technician's camera bathed the grisly scene in front of him in ultra-white flashes, illuminating the bodies, like surreal snapshots from an R rated gore movie.

Sweat worked its way down LaStanza's arm pits. It streaked his dress blue shirt. He fanned his shirt. Reaching back into the car for the note pad and pen in his coat pocket, he noted the time: 11:41 p.m. He wiped perspiration from his brow.

Snakebitten, he thought, *less than twenty minutes from getting off and we catch two bodies. We're snakebitten!* He looked around for a cottonmouth to step on, just to complete the evening.

LaStanza ran the fingers of his left hand down his moustache and watched the crime lab technician, whose name was Williams, move carefully over the wet leaves. Until an hour ago it had rained in New Orleans, rained a typical summer semi-tropical rainstorm that lasted for hours. As soon as LaStanza arrived at the scene, he took a roundabout way to the bodies and checked the one on the ground. She was dry and still warm.

Fresh kill.

His rookie partner checked the body of the woman in the Thunderbird. Detective Jodie Kintyre, pristine in her white blouse and fitted black skirt, her badge clipped to the front of her skirt, told LaStanza, "She's still warm."

Jodie was now supervising the crime lab technician, following a few steps behind Williams as the photos were taken. With her large flashlight in hand, Jodie carefully examined the ground as she walked. Her blonde hair stood out white hot in the headlights from the police cars.

LaStanza went back to his notes, describing the scene in front of him. The damp air was musty with the scent of dead leaves and the faint coppery odor of blood. The humidity felt like steam on his face.

LaStanza wrote:

Victim #1: White female, 20 to 22 years, about 5'2", 105 pounds, brown shoulder-length hair, small mole on right cheek. Wearing a dark green pull-over shirt with short sleeves, a black skirt, stockings and black high heels.

"Hey, Wyatt," a familiar voice called out behind LaStanza. Turning, he spotted his old partner Paul Snowood walking between the marked police cars. Decked out in a white Stetson, a rawhide colored western suit and dark brown cowboy boots, Snowood pointed a finger at LaStanza and said, "What in the name of Son of Sam is goin' on here?"

LaStanza went back to his notes, adding to the description of Victim #1:

A gold colored ring with a red stone on her right ring finger, a gold ankle chain around her left ankle.

Snowood put a heavy hand on LaStanza's right shoulder and said, "So, what we got?"

LaStanza turned and focused his light green Sicilian eyes on Snowood and said, "Quit calling me Wyatt, all right?"

"Quit shooting people," Snowood said, tapping LaStanza's shoulder with a fist before stepping away.

"Say, Calamity," he called out to Jodie, "this one's yours ain't it?"

Snowood knew damn well Jodie was up for the next murder. This was her's all right. LaStanza closed his note pad and poked Snowood in the back with his pen.

"Why don't you make yourself useful and canvass."

Snowood craned his neck around and said, "Canvass what?"

LaStanza pointed to a nervous looking City Park patrolmen leaning against one of the marked units. "He found them. Talk to him. Then walk the perimeter. You know. Stop all the pain-in-the-ass citizens passing by gaping at us."

"All right. All right." Snowood tilted his Stetson back on his head. "Just tell me what we got here!"

LaStanza pointed with his pen to the body of Victim #1 as she lay on the ground at the base of the oak. "Two bodies. One in her twenties. One about forty. Both shot in the head. The older one's in the T-Bird."

Snowood nodded, giving Victim #1 a good stare as he eased away.

"They're both fresh kills," LaStanza added.

"Damn!" Snowood looked at his watch and said, "Boy are we snakebitten or what?"

As Williams took pictures of the T-Bird and its contents, LaStanza reached back into his car for his black flashlight, then took the same roundabout path back to Victim #1. He went down on his haunches and studied her. Brightly lit by the headlights from the police cars, she lay on her back at the base of the tree, her right arm draped across one of the exposed roots of the huge tree, her left arm limp at her side. Her legs were twisted in a strange angle, as if she'd been dropped from the branches above.

LaStanza looked up at the dark branches. They looked darker than the sky above them. The enormous tree, with its wide spread branches that dipped almost to the ground looked like an inverted black tarantula lying belly-up at the edge of the park.

A drop of rain smacked LaStanza on the left cheek. He wiped it away and looked back at the body. Flipping on his flashlight, he pointed it at the girl's head, which lay in shadow away from the lights. Globs of blackish blood matted her long hair. The back of her head rested in a large pool of blood.

Head shot.

Her face looked like porcelain, her cheeks smooth and young, her lips covered in dark red lipstick. Her eyelids, blackened from the shock of the head wound, were nearly closed. Her eyes looked brown.

In movies and in bad detective novels the faces of the dead were often described as being masked in terror or even smiling. In LaStanza's four years in Homicide, he'd never seen a dead face that wasn't dull and unfocused, totally without expression. The dead were unable to express anything. They were gone.

On his way back to his car, LaStanza jotted another note next to the description of Victim #1. He wrote the word "pretty."

Finished with the photos for the moment, Williams took measurements with Jodie's help, triangulating the location of the bodies in reference to the base of the oak, to the curb of Victory Avenue where the police cars were parked, to a concrete light pole next to the cracked sidewalk that ran along the avenue.

A faint, hot breeze rustled through the trees, as the meat wagon arrived. LaStanza watched two skinny white boys in white attendant's uniforms step out of the wagon that was actually a Dodge van. At the same moment, another car pulled up behind the van. A tall burly black man with a thick black moustache exited the car and looked toward LaStanza.

LaStanza waved Johnny Prejean over. Prejean, a veteran coroner's investigator, was in his shirt sleeves and a pair of khaki pants. A clipboard under his arm, Prejean pulled on a pair of rubber medical gloves as he approached.

"A double, huh?" he said when he arrived.

LaStanza nodded and led the way to the first body. Williams followed them over, pulling on his own plastic gloves. Williams bagged the girl's hands in brown paper bags after Prejean examined the hands carefully. Jodie searched the ground around them with her flashlight.

After a cursory examination of the corpse and the immediate area, Prejean rolled her over so Williams could take a photo of the wound. LaStanza stood back. The wound was in the center of the back of the head. Tiny fragments of skull were embedding in the girl's bloody hair.

"No exit wound," Prejean said, rolling her back over. He stood and motioned to the attendants to come get her. After the body was zipped into a black plastic body bag and hauled up on an aluminum stretcher, LaStanza carefully examined where the victim had laid.

"You got anymore of those gloves?" he asked Prejean.

"Sure."

LaStanza pulled a glove on his left hand. His sweaty palm turned the talcum powder in the glove into a chalky mud. With his flashlight in his right hand, LaStanza fished through the thick pool of blood that had amassed beneath the victim's head. He found nothing.

With the bloody glove still on his left hand, he joined Jodie and Prejean and

Williams at the T-Bird. Both doors of the two-door dark blue car were opened wide when they first arrived. Jodie stood just inside the passenger door, while Prejean and Williams went to the driver's side. Jodie looked tired. A blonde strand of her perfect page boy hair lay across her nose. She blew it away.

Putting a hand on her hip, she told LaStanza, "Snowood says the City Park cop found them at 11:15. He passed here at 11:00 and they weren't here."

LaStanza nodded, watching Prejean reach into the front seat of the T-Bird where the body of Victim #2 lay face down. Her hair wasn't as dark as the other woman's and her body a little thicker. She wore a pink blouse with a lacy collar and black slacks and white sandals.

LaStanza could see a large wound in the woman's right temple and a great deal of blood on the front floorboard of the car. Prejean pulled back out of the driver's side, so Williams could bag the woman's hands. LaStanza leaned in the passenger side. He caught a whiff of burnt gunpowder, along with the acrid smell of blood.

"We have two purses on the back seat," he told Jodie.

"I saw." Jodie let out a long sigh and then said, "They look like sisters. Or mother and daughter."

LaStanza shrugged. He knew better than to even guess. Guessing was for amateurs. They'd learn soon enough from the purses.

Williams finished bagging the woman's hands. He stood back and told Prejean, "I'll dust after you get her out."

Both men moved aside. The skinny white attendants pulled the woman out, leaving the revolver that was under her body there on the seat. LaStanza put his clean hand on his partner's shoulder and said, "This is why we work suicides just like murders."

Jodie stared slack-jawed at the snub-nosed, blue steel revolver. She swallowed so hard, LaStanza heard her gulp.

"It's a murder—suicide?"

"This is Suicide Oak."

"What?" Jodie turned her wide-set cat eyes to him. They were hazel and grew dark sometimes, when her Scot temper flared. Tonight he could barely see her irises.

He pulled his hand off her shoulder and pointed with his bloody hand up at the huge tarantula oak overhead.

"That's Suicide Oak."

Jodie's shoulders sank. "Come on. You're messing with me now."

"Ever hear of Dueling Oak?"

Jodie looked back at the gun and nodded her head. He patted her on the back with his clean hand.

"I'll tell you about it later."

Williams took pictures of the snub-nosed revolver from both doors before leaning in to carefully dust it for fingerprints. He found a good print on the left side of the gun and a partial on the right side. After lifting the latent prints, he opened the cylinder of the six shot revolver. There were three spent casings and three live rounds, all .22 magnums.

While LaStanza held the revolver by its checkered walnut wooden grip, Williams took photos of the position of the spent casings and the three live rounds. Even more carefully, Williams emptied the revolver, dusting each casing and cartridge for prints. He lifted

two partial prints from them before leaning back in the car to dust the interior for prints.

"Three shots," Jodie said aloud. "First could have been a hesitation shot."

LaStanza had taught her that. Many times, before firing a weapon, the shooter will fire a round to make sure it worked.

"Better check those bodies careful at the autopsies," Snowood said. He had come up behind LaStanza, who was noting the serial number of the Charter Arms "Pathfinder" .22 magnum revolver in his notes.

A huge drop of rain slapped LaStanza on the back of the neck as the three detectives waited for Williams to carefully search the purses. He pulled the driver's license from each purse and put them on the hood. The older woman was named Joan Cooper. She was forty-two and lived at 4799 Cleveland Street.

"Same last name," Jodie said, as LaStanza moved his flashlight to the girl's driver's license. She was twenty-two and lived at the same address on Cleveland. Her first name was Alice.

"Poor kid," Snowood said. "Named after a burned out hippie transvestite."

"I got a receipt for a Charter Arms 'Pathfinder' here in the older one's purse," Williams said, holding up a piece of white paper in his gloved left hand. "It was bought yesterday."

"Damn," Snowood said.

"Is it in her name, Joan Cooper?" Jodie asked, her eyes closed.

Williams told her yes. "And I got what looks like a paycheck in the young one's purse." He laid a green check with a matching stub on the hood next to the licenses. LaStanza trained his light on the check which was dated with today's date. Alice worked at La Piazza Bra Italian Restaurant on Canal Street.

"Look at this," Williams said, holding up a white business card.

"Dammit!" LaStanza said. It was a New Orleans Police business card with the name Sergeant Frank Cooper, Third District Patrol.

Stepping back, LaStanza swung his flashlight around and looked real hard for the goddam cottonmouth.

"You mean to tell me there's a Suicide Oak?" Snowood said as LaStanza rolled a daily report form into the tired Smith Corona typewriter they shared between their beat-up city-government issue gray metal desks, which faced each other.

"Notice any moss on that oak last night?"

"Now that you mention it ..." Snowood had his gray snakeskin boots up on his desk as he read the sport section of the *Times-Picayune*.

LaStanza started typing the daily on the autopsies from that morning, beginning with the older woman, Joan Cooper.

"A long time ago," he said as he typed, "back in Creole days, a pair of star-crossed lovers killed themselves under that oak."

He put in a detailed description of the wound to Joan's right temple, the obvious markings of a contact wound, the burn mark, the soot and gunpowder tattooed in the skin, the unmistakable bevel of the skull made by an entry wound. They found the .22 projectile in the left side of the cerebrum. The trajectory of the bullet was right to left, ten degrees upward angle.

"You mean like a New Orleans Romeo and Juliet?" Snowood said from the other side of the sports section.

"Yeah. Then during the Great Depression, when the stock market crashed, a banker killed himself under the tree."

"No shit?"

LaStanza reached into his desk drawer, pulled out his Rand McNally Street Finder and tossed it over the sports section. "Look up City Park," he said.

He went back to the daily. A minute later, Snowood said, "Well I'll be. It's on the map all right. Suicide Oak."

No shit! LaStanza grew up a few blocks from City Park. He used to ride his bike with his big brother, racing up and down Victory Avenue to Lelong Avenue, from Suicide Oak to Dueling Oak and back again. He knew every inch of the park. Even as a boy, he noticed how Suicide Oak, that inverted tarantula, was the only tree in the entire park without any gray-ghost Spanish moss hanging from it.

"You sure about those suicide stories?" Snowood said, tossing the Street Finder back."

"They don't call it Suicide Oak for nothing."

LaStanza wasn't sure about the stories at all. His brother told him. His brother also told him about the werewolves of City Park and the vampires of the Canal Cemeteries.

Finishing the daily as quickly as he could, before the Smith Corona sputtered and died, as it did after about twenty minutes of constant use, LaStanza put in a description of the wound to the rear of Alice Cooper's cranium. Also a close range wound, but not a contact wound, the .22 bullet had traveled downward twenty degrees and was found lodged in Alice's brain just above her left eye socket.

Pulling the daily out of the typewriter, LaStanza spotted Jodie coming into the squad room. In a high-collared off-white blouse and a full dark green skirt, she looked every bit as fresh as she had at the autopsies hours earlier. It was pushing a hundred outside and there wasn't a hint of perspiration on Jodie's face. Her eyebrows, however, were furrowed.

She plopped into her desk across the aisle from LaStanza's desk.

"So," LaStanza said in his Calliope Project street voice, "What it is?"

Jodie leaned back in her chair and said, "Joan Cooper bought the gun yesterday around one p.m. She was alone. She only bought six rounds of ammunition."

"And ..." LaStanza prodded. Snowood looked over the top of the sports section at Jodie.

"And Alice Cooper left work an hour early last night. She gets off at midnight. Her mother came and got her. The manager saw them drive off in the T-Bird. They were alone."

"Good," Snowood injected.

Jodie was anything but pleased. She gave him a sour look.

"What'd I say?" Snowood opened his arms to LaStanza, letting the paper fall in his lap.

"Go ahead and tell him!" Jodie said.

LaStanza shook his head no. He ran his hand down the front of his light gray tie, which was a shade darker than his extra light gray shirt and a shade lighter than his dark gray suit pants. Instead, he passed Jodie the daily report.

"Well, is anybody gonna let me in on what I said wrong?"

Jodie turned to Snowood and said, "I was thinking this morning that the husband may be involved. This is all too ... convenient. He's a cop. He coulda staged all of this."

Snowood shook his head no and went back to his paper. "Glad I'm heading across the river this evening. I got my own mysteries to solve."

Jodie shot LaStanza a hard, inquiring look. He looked back at her with eyes void of any expression.

"I hate it when you do that!"

It was a Sicilian trait, the ability to look someone coldly in the eye without revealing anything in your eyes, like Al Pacino at the end of *The Godfather*, when his wife asked if he had his brother-in-law killed.

Go with the facts, he told himself automatically. He'd told Jodie that a hundred times. Murder aren't solved by taking shots in the dark. *Stick with the facts and you can't go wrong.*

The phone rang. LaStanza snapped up the receiver and said, "Homicide. LaStanza."

"Dino. It's your friendly neighborhood crime lab with your test results." It was Fat Frank Hammond from the lab.

"Good." LaStanza grabbed a pen and pad.

"We got a negative on Alice Cooper. But we got a hit on Joan Cooper. Positive for antimony and barium. She definitely fired a gun."

LaStanza hurriedly jotted the results of the neutron activation test of the both women's hands he and Jodie had ordered at the autopsy.

"Also," Hammond said, "one print from the gun was clear enough to ID. It belonged to Joan Cooper."

Good. That was fast work, already comparing the latent prints from the scene to the prints taken at the autopsies.

"This was a policeman's wife and daughter?" Hammond asked. Uncharacteristically, he didn't sound as if he had a mouthful of fried pie.

"Yeah," LaStanza said. "Thanks for rushing it through."

"Damn," Hammond said, "Anybody I know?"

"Frank Cooper at the Third District."

"Don't know him. How's he taking it?"

LaStanza let out a sigh. "We can't find him."

The Cooper house was at the corner of Cleveland and South Bernadotte, a white wood frame house in dire need of painting. Its front yard was dominated by a huge magnolia tree, so large and thick no grass grew between its exposed roots. Small puddles of water were dammed-up between the knotted roots.

Jodie knocked on the wooden front door. LaStanza stood to the side, wiping sweat from his brow. At least it was shady under the magnolia. They received the same answer they had the previous night and that morning on their way to the autopsy. Nothing. Jodie's business card was still stuck between the door frame and the door.

LaStanza led the way next door, to another wood frame white house. This one sported a fresh coat of yellow paint. A middle-aged woman with a blotchy white face and curlers in her salt-and-pepper hair leaned out the front door.

LaStanza opened his jacket to show his badge and said, "I'm Detective LaStanza and this is my partner, Detective Kintyre. We're trying to locate Frank Cooper next door. Have you seen him?"

The woman crinkled her abundant nose and opened the door wider, revealing the iridescent orange muu-muu she wore and fuzzy green slippers. LaStanza smelled red beans cooking behind the woman.

"Isn't Frank a policeman?" the woman said.

Why can't it ever be easy?

Forty-five minutes later, LaStanza and Jodie pulled away from Cleveland Street fortified with several more facts. Frank Cooper was 'a drunk.' Frank Cooper 'came and went at all hours of the day and night.' Frank Cooper 'hadn't been home for three days.' Joan Cooper was a 'closet drinker.' Alice Cooper was a 'quiet girl with no boyfriends.'

The most important fact given by the next door neighbor was the fact that Joan Cooper was in therapy, treated by a psychologist on Canal Street by the name of Dr. Billy Bob Benson.

"Sounds like a born-again preacher," Jodie said.

LaStanza pulled out the computer print out of Frank Cooper's motor vehicle record. Beside the T-Bird, Frank Cooper owned a 1978 brown Oldsmobile Cutlass. There were no Cutlasses parked anywhere on Cleveland Street or around the corner.

"You remember to call the Third?" Jodie asked as she turned off So. Bernadotte on Canal Street and headed down toward the river.

"Yep. Cooper's AWOL. He was due

back this morning from his two days off."

Dr. Billy Bob Benson's office was on the second floor of a blond brick building near the corner of Canal and Jefferson Davis Parkway. A red headed receptionist in a low cut red blouse and a tight black skirt said the doctor was busy with a patient.

"Y'all can wait," she said, waving to several cushioned chairs in the small waiting room. LaStanza plopped in one of the chairs and leaned his head back against the wall. The air-conditioning felt good. He opened his jacket and closed his eyes.

About a half hour later voices came from the doctor's office. LaStanza watched a well dressed woman in her forties wave good-bye to the receptionist.

Jodie was already standing. Dr. Billy Bob was in the doorway. A tall, balding man with huge bags under his eyes, the good doctor said he only had a few minutes, but they could come in.

He didn't even blink when Jodie told him about Joan Cooper and Alice. His head nodded slowly, up and down, up and down as Jodie continued.

"We'd like to know," Jodie said, "exactly what was Joan Cooper's problem."

Dr. Billy Bob's wrinkled face tried to smile. He cleared his throat and said, "I can't tell you. That's confidential information."

LaStanza saw Jodie's chest rise. Through gritted teeth she said, "Doctor, the confidentiality of privileged communications between physician and patient does not extend beyond the patient's death." Jodie's eyes were narrowed and dark.

Dr. Billy Bob shook his head and shrugged his shoulders.

"She's dead," LaStanza said. "You can't violate her rights."

"Well," Dr. Billy Bob said as he rose. "Nonetheless. You cannot see her file." The detective's bluff didn't work.

LaStanza turned to Jodie and said, "I'll stay while you get the warrant."

Jodie rose and walked out, closing the door loudly behind her.

LaStanza put his hands behind his head and smiled at Dr. Billy Bob. "I guess we'll just have to wait 'till my partner comes back with the search warrant. Judges love to sign warrants for doctor's offices. Especially psychologists." That was no bluff.

"But," Dr. Billy Bob was angry now. His hands were on his hips. "You can't wait in here. I have a patient due any minute."

LaStanza leaned back and said, "I'm not going anywhere."

"But …!"

"What are you going to do, doc? Call the police?"

There wasn't much in Joan Cooper's file. She'd only seen Dr. Billy Bob twice. Joan Cooper was depressed, had been depressed for a long time. LaStanza didn't need to read beyond that. He'd seen the effects of depression before.

"Depression can be so ugly," he told Jodie on their way back to the Bureau with the original file, "so powerful, sometimes people take the ones they love the most with them." Although Dr. Billy Bob vehemently objected to them taking the original file and even offered to make a copy once Jodie returned with the search warrant, Jodie was too angry.

She even poked him in his sunken chest with her index finger when he wouldn't get out of her way fast enough.

"Next time a police officer asks you for help," she said, jabbing her finger against his chest as the good doc retreated across his office, "maybe you'll think twice before being so uppity."

Turning to LaStanza, Dr. Billy Bob blinked his bat-like eyes and said, "But. But."

Following Jodie out, LaStanza leaned over and told the doc, "Don't you hate it when they poke you in the chest like that?"

Before they got back to the office, their lieutenant called them on the radio. Sergeant Frank Cooper just walked into the Bureau.

His elbows on the desk in the tiny interview room, Frank Cooper buried his face in his hands and cried. His large shoulders shook. The man was a wreck, unshaven, red-eyed, wearing a sweaty Hawaiian shirt and baggy khaki shorts and dirty sandals.

"Why?" Frank bellowed like a wounded bear. "Why did she have to take Alice with her?"

The first question Jodie had asked, when they settled in the interview room was how he found out about it. Joan had left Frank a note on their kitchen table. He brought it with him. On a piece of yellow ruled paper Joan had written one word, "Good-bye." Frank went next door. The neighbor with the blotchy face and the iridescent orange muu-muu and fuzzy green slippers told him.

Jodie sat across from Frank, her arms folded, another sour look on her face. Jodie had said it on the way back to the

office. "Frank did it." Frank killed them. He might not have put the bullet in the back of his daughter's head or press the revolver against his wife's head and squeezed the trigger. But he did it with a bottle. No, with plenty of bottles.

LaStanza touched his partner's shoulder as Frank Cooper wept.

"I'll go check this out," he said, holding up the pink sheet of legal size paper Frank Cooper had presented to them when Jodie asked where he'd been the last three days.

The squad room was surprisingly empty. LaStanza moved straight to his desk, sat and took out the Louisiana law enforcement officer's telephone directory and called the Natchitoches City Police Department. He asked for the detectives.

"Detectives Bureau. Dugas." The voice had a slight Cajun accent.

"This is Detective LaStanza. New Orleans Homicide. I need a little help, partner."

"You got it. What can I do for you?"

Dugas called back ten minutes later with the information.

"Yeah," Dugas said. "That jail sheet's genuine. We arrested a Frank Cooper at 6:05 p.m. the night before last. We released him this morning at 10:00 a.m. And no, he didn't tell us he was the police down your way."

"Can you fax me his fingerprint card?" LaStanza said.

"Sure. We got fax machines, indoor plumbing, microwave ovens. We even got cable TV up here in the country." Dugas was laughing now.

LaStanza gave him the fax number.

"I owe you one," he told Dugas.

"Anytime, padna."

"One more thing. How far is Natchitoches from here?"

"I just looked it up. It's 240 miles."

LaStanza took the fax down to Fat Frank Hammond in the crime lab. Hammond had already pulled Frank Cooper's from Internal Affairs. It took him less than a minute to say, "That's him, all right."

Peeking back into the interview room, LaStanza waved Jodie out and told her the news.

"I don't like it," she said. "It's all too neat."

"You gotta go with the facts."

"I know," she stammered. "I'm just so *angry*!"

"Can I talk to him a minute?"

She nodded and opened the door. Frank Cooper was sitting back in the uncomfortable wooden folding chair, his arms limp at his sides, his face streaked with dried tears. He looked at LaStanza with bleary eyes.

LaStanza sat across from him and said, "Why Natchitoches?"

"I woke up there. I woke up in Oklahoma City once."

"They didn't know you were a police officer," LaStanza said, knowing what the man's response would be.

"Would you advertise?"

Frank leaned his elbows back on the desk and said, "Aren't you Anthony LaStanza's boy?"

LaStanza nodded slowly. He felt a tug in his gut, but caught himself before his eyes expressed anything.

"I worked for your Dad back when I was a rookie." Frank began to rub his eyes. "He was the best captain I ever worked for."

LaStanza put his elbows on the desk and stared back into the man's eyes when he finished rubbing them. He looked right through the man's eyes, all the way to the back of the Cooper's head. It was called the Sicilian stare. When he was a little boy and his father pulled it on him, it used to scare the hell out of LaStanza.

Frank blinked and slowly, very slowly leaned back in the chair.

Sure, my father drinks, LaStanza told himself. *I've seen the depression creep in and turn my mother into an aloof old woman. I know what the bottle can do to a cop's family. But don't look for sympathy here.*

"You know," LaStanza said. "In Homicide we don't care about why. We don't even have to prove motive to get a murder conviction." He narrowed his eyes slightly and said, "A good detective works on how it happened to learn who did it. Once we know who, it's all over."

Frank Cooper was free to leave. He walked out without looking back.

Jodie, leaning against LaStanza's desk, was still angry. Her jaw was set, her eyes thin and cat-like. Across the front of the file folder, beneath the names Alice Cooper and Joan Cooper, she wrote in black mark-a-lot, "30—29S." Murder—Suicide.

"Damn," she said through gritted teeth. "It's all such a waste."

"No it's not," LaStanza said, dropping his note pad on his desk.

"What's that supposed to mean?"

"We got the truth."

O'Neill De Noux is the author of five books featuring New Orleans cop Dino Lastanza, of which the latest, The Big Show, *is available in the UK,*

TRUE ORIGINALS

King of the Streets
'Baker has added something new to the crime scene'
Literary Review

New York Graphic
A jolting ride through the night-time streets of
Manhattan, a first novel of sheer brilliance:
compulsively readable, funny as hell

Like a Hole in the Head
'Brilliantly fast and funny debut novel ...a guaranteed
flat-out good-time read' *GQ*

Rumble Tumble
'It's a bit like life - except with all the flabby boring bits
left out and all the weirdly wonderful bits jacked up to
the max' *Loaded*

Kneeling at the Altar
'A labyrinthine case of deceit, persecution and abuse
involving the Christian Brothers' *Oxford Times*

Losing the Plot
Screenwriter Alan Tate has lost the plot - or has it lost
him? - and once the corpses start piling up the game
doesn't seem so funny any more

Death and the Language of Happiness
'Straley flawlessly expresses both his and our own
underlying anxiety about the world around us in this
superb series' *San Francisco Chronicle*

Phreak
Georgina Powers finds herself in the midst of a gang
war in cyberspace and a turf war in real life while
investigating a phone phreaking scam...

GOLLANCZ
Paperback Originals

Available from all good bookshops at £9.99 each.

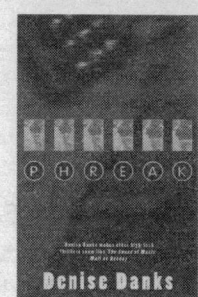

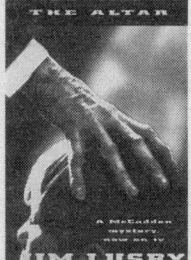

Frankie Bosser Comes Home
by Jerry Raine

'I loved it … shows that *Smalltime*
was no one-off'—Ian Rankin

*Phil Gator has been bumming his way
through France and Spain for three months,
lying low after pulling a petrol station
robbery, and the first thing that happens
when he gets back to England is that a white
Transit van drives through a puddle and
soaks him to the skin. Everybody laughs.
Some welcome.*

*So when he spots the Transit van in the
car park of the Railway pub, it's only
natural to give the driver some payback,
rough him up a bit. Trouble is, the old guy,
name of Stanley Bosser, turns out to be
connected.*

*To Frankie Bosser, a real bigtime hard
man. When he comes home from his Italian
hideaway and discovers Dad didn't die of
natural causes, not surprisingly he's keen
to discover who did him over …*

THE VW CAMPER VAN pulled off the motorway at the Woodvale turn-
off and Phil Gator climbed out. He hoisted his rucksack on to his shoulder
and was ready to shut the door when the driver reached over with a joint
in his hand.

'Here, one for the road,' he said, laughing and pushing his long dark
hair away from his eyes.

Gator smiled and took the offering. He was already fairly stoned but
one more wouldn't hurt.

'Thanks a lot,' he said. 'Mind how you drive.'

'I'm used to it,' the driver said. 'I'm on auto-pilot.'

Gator shut the door and watched the VW pull away, then reached in his jacket for a box of matches. He lit the joint and inhaled as he walked up the exit ramp.

It was a wet June afternoon but the rain had momentarily ceased after a violent thunderstorm about thirty minutes earlier. Luckily Gator had been inside the VW then and had been able to watch the rain through a haze of dope rather than being outside getting wet. It had taken him three lifts to hitch his way up from Dover, and now he was finally on the outskirts of his home town.

Walking with a spring in his step and enjoying the dope, Gator thought about his three months away from England. He had been bumming his way through Spain and France, lying low after committing a robbery at a petrol station in a town a few miles away. With a stretch in prison three years before for an attempted robbery on a building society in Croydon, he had decided to clear out until things cooled down a little. He had walked out of his mechanic's job at a small garage in Horley, kissed his mother goodbye, then caught a train to the coast and the first available ferry. Now he was returning with a good tan, but with the dread of having to find a job and get back in the swing of things. His nine hundred pounds from the petrol station robbery was all gone.

When he reached the top of the exit ramp he turned left towards the hill that led down to Woodvale. Cars were circling the roundabout, either heading back down to the motorway or joining the slow queue into town. Woodvale had become a traffic bottleneck since the M25 had reached it some ten years before, but rather than add to the general well-being of the town it had only created new problems; Woodvale was now a town that people passed through rather than lingered in, and many of the shops in the centre had closed down. It was still a desirable place to live though, and there were many opulent homes in the surrounding areas owned by business types who commuted into London. As for Gator, his mother lived in a council house in one of the less fashionable streets.

At the top of Woodvale Gator let his momentum take him down the slope. He was feeling tired from his hitching and also from the joints he'd been smoking. He was on a cigarette now, and he watched the rainwater in the gutter running down the hill. He passed a couple of pubs and hotels on his right, while on his left was countryside, the distant woods still showing gaps from the hurricane of 1987.

At the bottom of the hill the road flattened out as Gator approached the level crossing at Woodvale station. He noticed the rainwater had gathered in the drains, leaving large puddles by the side of the road, and moved over to the left so that passing cars wouldn't splash him.

He was coming to a sizeable puddle now and watched it closely as he approached. When he was right next to it a white van sped by as close to the kerb as it could get, and crashed through the water. Gator jumped sideways at the noise but it was too late. The water hit him like a tidal wave and soaked the whole of his right side: his jacket, his jeans, his rucksack and his trainers. The cigarette he'd been smoking was extinguished and he threw it in the gutter. He looked at the van as it drove on.

'You bastard!' he shouted, waving his fist.

He tried to brush the water from his clothes. Other cars were passing and he sensed the passengers smirking at him. He swore again and carried on walking. So that was the kind of welcome he got. Back in the country just a few hours and already the English population was showing him its pathetic sense of humour. He wished he were back in Spain lying on a beach.

His earlier drowsiness had now gone. As he carried on walking, he could feel his anger, and also a sense of despair, growing. Passers-by were looking at his wet trousers. Did they think he'd pissed himself?

There was no way it had been an accident because the puddle hadn't stretched into the middle of the road. The driver had had to drive right next to the kerb to make contact with it. So what was his problem? Gator had seen only one man in the van, so it wasn't as if he'd done it to get a laugh from a passenger. It was just a mean-bastard thing to do. He felt himself getting even angrier.

When he came to the Halfway House pub he turned left and started walking down a road parallel to the railway line. On his left were some warehouses and another pub, imaginatively called the Railway. Gator walked past the smell of beer and glanced into the car park. He felt his pulse quicken when he saw the white van that had just splashed him parked there. And sitting inside, having a smoke, was the driver.

Gator marched into the car park and approached the van. As he got nearer he could see the man looking at him, a puzzled look coming on to his face. Gator took the rucksack off his right shoulder and dumped it by the front wheel. Then he walked to the driver's door and opened it.

'Thought that was pretty funny did you?' He snarled, pointing at his wet clothes. The driver looked at him blankly.

'What do you mean?' He said, cigarette smoke coming from his mouth and the cab. He was in his sixties, in dusty working trousers and a white T-shirt. He had a craggy red face, receding hair and the rough hands of a manual worker. Gator grabbed him by the T-shirt and pulled him on to the Tarmac. The van-driver resisted but Gator had him standing in front of him in less than ten seconds. Although the man was slightly taller than him, Gator grabbed him by the throat and slammed him against the van.

He liked the look of fear on the man's face.

'You should watch the way you drive, you know,' Gator said in a voice so quiet the man hardly heard.

The man was just saying, 'What ...?' when Gator punched him hard in the face. The man's head snapped back and hit the van with a bang. Gator then hit him in the stomach, and as the man doubled over he kneed him on the chin. The man slid unconscious to the ground.

Gator picked up his rucksack and walked away. He could feel the strength surging through his arms. A small group of passers-by gathered on the pavement and was watching him. They gave him disapproving looks as he walked away.

'What did you do that for?' a pensioner asked him.

Gator sneered and said, 'That's just the kind of bloke I am—if it's any of your business.'

He carried on walking and could hear their admonishing remarks behind him. He felt like turning round and swearing at them but decided it was best to leave it alone, and put some distance behind him before the cops turned up.

Read on... *Frankie Bosser Comes Home* **by Jerry Raine is published in paperback by Victor Gollancz, price £9.99. Available from all good bookshops.**

Jerry Raine is from Yorkshire and currently lives in Sevenoaks. He is also a singer/songwriter who has supported the likes of Christy Moore and Iris DeMent on their UK tours. His first novel, Smalltime, *made a real stir.* Frankie Bosser Comes Home *is his follow-up.*

Phreak
by Denise Danks

Computer journalist Georgina Powers is investigating a phone phreaking scam in the East End of London. Her contact and toy boy, Abdul Malik, a top-rank phone phreaker, is found dead at the bottom of a skip. His neck's broken and there's lipstick smeared on his University of Santa Cruz Banana Slug T-shirt. Her hacker friend, Chronic, a local drugs dealer, does a runner and when the police arrive, she's in the frame.

Not only do the police want to nail her, but a Bengali protection gang want to know what happened to the Abdul aka Little Stevie Wonder, the boy who played with phones. Georgina calls on an old friend, East End villain and ex-boxer Tony Levi, to help her out and finds herself in the middle of a gang war in cyberspace and a turf war in real life.

I HAD A FEW PROBLEMS WITH THE BODY. One, I knew who it was. Two, I didn't know if he was breathing. Three, he had my lipstick on the front of his University of Santa Cruz Banana Slug T-shirt.

Abdul Malik lay among rubbish bags at the bottom of a large metal drum, his head twisted this way and his body that. Ten foot off the ground, I held on to the rim of the bin and looked down at him. Chronic Delaney was next to me holding tight too, staring down, like me, into the shadows. The sweet and sickly smell rising up on the night air reeked of interminable decay, of wet plastic, damp paper and the rotting remnants of quick lunches. My fingers ached and gave way and I slid down the cold steel to the ground. Chronic hung on for a moment longer before he followed.

'What do you think?' he said.

'I think he's dead,' I replied.

'You do?'

'Yup.'

'Oh, shit.'

It was not something he was given to, but Chronic began to stammer.

'N-n-no point in calling an ambulance then.'

'We should call the police and an ambulance. He looks dead, but we can hardly see him. I only think he's dead.'

We both stood motionless in the narrow road behind the square telco building. I looked up at the dull flat stonework and blank windows that served as the exterior panelling of stacks of interconnected rooms and corridors leading into and out of a central core of semiconductors and software that could switch the stuff of a billion telephone conversations and datastreams every second of every day. Chronic looked up too, pushing his lank fringe out of his eyes.

'Think they've got a phone?' I volunteered.

'You got to get your stomach on the rim, hook on with your hips and lean down to get to the bags. The bin's almost empty so it's a long way to reach. He could've fallen,' Chronic said.

'Gimme the torch.'

With trembling hands he unzipped one of six outside pockets on his black parka and gave me the rubberised flashlight. I switched it on and the shadows leaped up our faces.

'Right. You ready?' I said, and he cupped his nicotined fingers in a cradle for my booted foot and heaved me up high enough to rest my elbows on the bin's edge. I pointed the beam downwards and the circle of light shuddered as Chronic hoisted himself up beside me.

As we watched intently for signs of life, we learned that death is very different. It was Abdul Malik all right. There he was lying on a bed of yellow plastic bags and old McDonald's cartons. We could make out the T-shirt he liked to wear in honour of his favourite movie. His legs were twisted to the right in his low-waisted baggy jeans, as if he were running to hell in his Nike trainers. His brown arms were outstretched. One hand clutched the neck of a large bag and held it to his side like a favourite toy. He was looking over his left shoulder, his stunned mouth gaping out of the marble mask of his face, his dull eyes staring blindly beyond the light into the darkness, his hair a fixed halo of black rays. On his shirt, there was a smudge of deepest red and tucked into the waistband of his jeans, a mobile phone.

The still detail held us in silence and disappointment until the binary stutter of a fluorescent striplight flickered in one of the offices above.

Chronic moved fast, sliding down and leaning against the cold metal of the dump bin for cover. As I followed, he caught my swinging legs and helped me down, nervously lighting us both a cigarette. I took at least two deep drags before I could speak.

'You know what the problem is here?' I said, puffing and blowing.

'He ain't dead?'

'I wouldn't say that not being dead was a problem, Chronic.'

'I fucking know that. So what is the fucking problem?'

'He's got my lipstick on his shirt.'

Chronic took a couple of swift inhales and moved from one foot to the other.

'He was a boy, weren't he?' he said.

I pulled my cigarette from my mouth and inspected the telltale red wax on the filter. The image of my lips was stuck to it like a fingerprint.

'God damn it,' I said, and a whooping sound of sirens spliced into the even hum of city traffic.

Chronic moved away from me. He threw his head back, closed his eyes and began to whirl, turning silently before me like a shadow in the deepening twilight. He seemed to be holding something, a stick that I couldn't see. To the left, to the right, his shoulders jolted with the imaginary force of a recoiling machine-gun. Long red flares of burning tobacco streamed out behind him like the tails of a night kite while his body jerked back and forth and his hair fell over his face. He raised his no-show Kalashnikov aloft, pumping his arms in triumph and then he stopped, just like that, and turned to me, his eyes all craziness and confusion. He waited one speechless moment before he legged it, leaving me alone with the dead body of Abdul Malik, formerly known to his friends as Little Stevie Wonder, the boy who played with phones.

Jesus, I wanted to run too.

Read on … *Phreak* by Denise Danks is published in paperback by Victor Gollancz, price £9.99. Available from all good bookshops.

Denise Danks is a journalist, screenwriter and author. She has run a technology news agency and been a director of a publishing company and the editorial director of a daily online IT news service. She is married with two children and lives in London.

Rumble Tumble
by Joe R. Lansdale

'Quotably funny, filthy, page-turning, deep-dish Texas stuff'
—Time Out

Hap Collins is beginning to feel old. Working nights as a bouncer, living his days by the grace of his best buddy Leonard Pine and his good woman Brett Sawyer, he's greying at the temples and thickening at the middle. And he feels that bad things are coming.

They are. Brett's teenage daughter Tillie has taken to drugs and prostitution, and needs a quick and merciful rescue. It will be no easy chore, starting with a treck from LaBorde, Texas, to Hootie Hoot, Oklahoma, a place even more god-forsaken than it sounds.

On the road, their motley band expands to include a six-foot-four ex-Pentecostal Preacher and hitman, plus his brother, a red-headed midget with an attitude. Not to mention Leonard's adopted son, Bob the armadillo. Ranged against them stands a biker army turned vice barons and stone-mad killers …

WHEN I GOT OVER to Brett's she was sitting in an aluminium chair on the front lawn fighting lovebugs and mosquitoes. I could see her from the curb where I'd parked. I got out and went over there, smiling. Brett wasn't smiling, however, and I got a nasty feeling in my gut, like maybe I'd waited too long to make up my mind one way or another.

'You like bugs?' I asked.

'Not really, 'she said, and this time she smiled. It was a little strained, but it was a smile.

'You look like maybe you're smiling around something sour.'

'I'm glad to see you, 'she said. 'Especially now.'

'Something wrong?'

'Yeah. Let's go inside.'

Inside, we picked lovebugs out of each other's hair and opened the screen and threw them out. There was a pot of coffee on, and Brett poured us cups. We sat at the table, then she looked at me and tears began to squeeze out of her eyes and run down her cheeks.

'Brett, what's wrong, honey?'

'It's Tillie, Hap.'

Tillie was Brett's wayward daughter. A young woman who had gotten mixed up in drugs and prostitution and whose last letter home was hopeful because her pimp had stopped beating her as much and her limp was better. Brett had tried to talk her out of the life, had offered to have us come get her, but she didn't want out, or didn't know how to get out, or it was some kind of stubborn pride thing. It was hard to say. Frankly, I tried not to involve myself unless Brett involved me.

'What's the score?' I asked.

'There's a man in a motel wants to talk to me about her. He called this morning. Says she's in trouble and I should talk to him.'

'He didn't tell you what about over the phone?'

Brett shook her head. 'He wants money.'

'To tell you what kind of trouble she's in?'

'I'm supposed to go over there around one o'clock and bring five hundred dollars. I told him I had to have someone drive me. I didn't want to go there by myself.'

'That's a smart idea.'

'He said that was okay.'

'I don't like the sound of it,' I said.

'Neither do I, but he said Tillie was in deep shit and I ought to know about it. He said Tillie paid him some to tell me she was and that I'm supposed to pay him some before he tells me what the problem is, and he said if cops come he won't tell me anything and everything is off. But I come with one person and five hundred dollars, he'll tell me what I need to know.'

'A real Good Samaritan.'

'I got a gun,' Brett said. 'I can use it, and it's legal. But I still don't like going over there by myself, gun or not. Me with all that money. I don't know he's got someone with him or not. But him talking about Tillie like he knows her, I got to go see.'

'No problem. We'll both go.'

MY WRECK WAS IFFY just driving into town, so we went in Brett's blue Plymouth Fury. Like me, she had recently traded cars, and though this one was many years old and not exactly a road racer, it had been regularly serviced, and could get up to seventy miles an hour without the assistance of a tow truck. It's also nice to be driven around town by a good-looking redhead, even if you're on a bicycle built for two.

On the way over to the motel the lovebugs pelleted the windshield and collected beneath the motionless wipers like dead soldiers in trenches, left greasy yellow and green spots all over the glass.

We got to the LaBorde Motor Inn about ten minutes before one and parked in front of a row of doors. I had brought the pistol from my glove box, and I stuck it under my shirt against my spine.

Brett has a thigh holster, and she wore a skirt so she could wear the holster and the snub-nose .38 she owns. It's not that she goes around wearing a thigh holster and a .38, but recent events had led to this, and she has a license. In Texas, with right training and certification you're allowed to carry a concealed handgun. It's a law Leonard loves and I hate, but I'm a hypocrite because, unlike Brett, I never bothered to get a license.

We walked to the metal stairs, went up and found the number the caller had given Brett, and knocked. Thirty seconds didn't pass before the door opened and a face showed over the chain inside the door, and it was some face. It looked like first base after a hot season in the Astrodome: pocked and beaten and not too clean. He stuck the face out enough so I could see his nose had been broken and some teeth with it, and recently. Behind the face I could see a body that looked as if it ought to be used to hold up something heavy. He took the chain off for a better look at us, and we got a better look at him. He wore a dirty white dress shirt and black pants with grey pinstripes and shiny black dress shoes, except for the toe tips, which looked to have been dipped in shit.

'You Brett?' he said.

Brett nodded.

'We told you not to bring nobody,' he said.

'You, or whoever I spoke to, said I could have someone drive me,' Brett said.

'We thought you meant some other woman,' the face said.

'I didn't say that,' Brett said. 'What's it matter?'

'I don't know it matters,' said the man, 'but we didn't think you'd bring no man.'

'Well,' Brett said. 'I don't know why you shouldn't have thought it.'

'Hey,' I said, 'do I look dangerous to you?'

'Naw, you don't look dangerous,' he said, and he walked away from the door and we followed inside.

The first thing I noticed was a midget sitting on the bed. I think that's normal, noticing a midget first. He had on a tailored blue Western suit and shiny blue cowboy boots and a gold cowboy shirt with silver snaps and a string tie with a silver cow head clasp holding it together. The suit looked as if it had once been expensive and nice, but now it was covered in filth and so was the shirt. The steer horns leaned a little too far left and somehow gave the midget an unbalanced look, as if he had been laid out without the use of a plumb line. I figured originally a hat had gone with the outfit, but now his blazing red hair was scattered over his head in such a way if you took a photo of it, it might look like a man with his head on fire, like Brett's ex-husband. He had a big thick cigar in his mouth, but it wasn't lit, and his feet dangled off the side of the bed almost two feet from the ground. He had a face I couldn't judge for age. He might have been thirty or forty or fifty. For all I knew, he was twenty-one and constipated or had just previously passed a kidney stone.

Second thing I noticed was the big guy had drawn a little silver automatic out from behind his back. The rest of the room sort of lost interest for me after that.

Read on … *Rumble, Tumble* by Joe R Lansdale is published in paperback by Victor Gollancz , price £9.99. Available from all good bookshops.

Also by Joe R. Lansdale and available from Victor Gollancz: *Mucho Mojo, The Two Bear Mambo, Cold In July, Savage Season, Bad Chili*

Joe R Lansdale is the author of over two hundred short stories and a dozen novels, and has edited several anthologies of dark suspense and western fiction. He has won the British Fantasy Award, the American Mystery Award and three Bram Stoker Awards. He lives in East Texas with his wife and three children.

Walking With Ghosts
by John Baker

'John Baker brings heart, invention and wit to the business of adapting the tough-guy novel to the realities of contemporary Britain'—Ian Ousby, *Independent on Sunday*

Edward Blake was a political lobbyist, one of those Thatcherite 80s success stories. When his wife India was kidnapped, he didn't trouble the police, just paid the twenty grand. When she didn't show up, and the kidnapper went to ground, he did call in the law, and they came to the conclusion that the whole thing was a set-up between India and some secret lover.

But then, three months later, she turned up in a box in an allotment shed near York racecourse, where she had been left to starve to death. Then the police got really interested, especially when they found out about the two and a half million pounds' worth of life insurance he'd taken out on her the year before. But with no proof, they had to let Blake go in the end.

The insurance company are less than keen on paying out, however. Jill Sheridan, insurance assessor, needs someone to do some legwork, poking around in odd corners of Blake's life, and her thoughts turn to an old flame: Sam Turner ...

SAM HAD PROBLEMS with insurance. You could only insure the things that didn't matter. Houses and cars, the material trivia of life: things that could be replaced. New for old. You couldn't insure people. Not really. The insurance companies said you could, but it wasn't true. When you lost someone you loved they'd make a cash settlement. A bunch of fifties to replace flesh and blood. Courage, spirit, laughter. New fifties, though. Crisp, new ones, to replace an old love.

Jill Sheridan opened the door of her office and came across the reception area towards him. Sam got to his feet and took her hand. She was thirty-seven, lean machine, dressed in a navy Hermes suit, classic cut, with a white silk blouse showing at throat and cuffs.

'Jill. Looking good, as usual.'

She stood back to frame him from a different angle. 'You look like shit, Sam. Had a bad night?'

He grinned and shrugged his shoulders. Followed her into her office. The brass plate on the door: JILL SHERIDAN—CLAIMS ASSESSOR. Behind her desk was a picture window that looked out over York. The skyline dominated by the Minster. In the distance the blue smudge of the North Yorkshire Moors.

She stood close to him and they took in the view together.

'Different to the last place, 'Sam said.

'Yes. It felt strange at first, but I'm getting used to it. At least it's not haunted.'

Sam laughed. 'There must be a ghost in every other building in this town. Romans, Vikings, Normans. They all had their day, and they've all left the odd strangler behind.'

'There's one in your office, isn't there?'

He laughed again. 'Celia and Geordie keep bumping into a shady Victorian lady on the stairs. But I haven't seen her since I gave up drinking.'

She waved him into a chair and went behind a desk that housed only a telephone/fax/intercom gismo. No pen or pencil, no notepad. Polished wood and the box of technological tricks. 'Thanks for coming. Can I get you something? Coffee, isn't it?'

'Yeah. Unless you've gone over to the powdered stuff.'

She punched a key on the intercom. 'Will you let us have a couple of filter coffees, please? Mr Turner'll have his black and strong, no sugar.'

'Your memory's holding up, 'Sam told her. 'But how do you work in here? No PC or terminal. What happens if I ring in with info? You can't even take notes.'

Jill smiled. 'Always the practical Sam. Whatever happens on the telephone is recorded. Holly intercepts the tapes and does the necessary. If there's something that needs my action, she prepares it and puts it in front of me.'

Sam shook his head. The year before he married Dora, he'd been keen on Jill, and they'd had a brief affair. He could date the beginning of the end of that affair from the time he'd heard her say that she'd 'actioned' something. That, and the fact that his clothes never seemed to suit hers. Wherever they went he'd felt like a poor relation. Nice woman, though. When everything came to an end he'd missed her for days.

'Why did you call?' he asked.

'I've got a job for you.' A hint of a smile passed over her face, as if a secondary thought had come to mind, unrelated to whatever it was she wanted to communicate to Sam. A memory of some kind? 'It's rather complicated,' she hesitated, avoided eye contact for a moment. 'But I've heard you're having a bad time. If you don't want to take this one on, I'll understand.'

'We need business, Jill. I'm not the only one in the office.'

'What I've heard, Sam, you're not in the office at all.'

He shook his head. 'Exaggeration. I can't get in as much as I'd like. But everything's covered. There's Geordie and Marie, Celia, all raring to go.'

Jill Sheridan looked over the desk at him. She looked into his eyes, and Sam looked back. 'I mean at home. How is she, Sam?'

He blinked a couple of times. Sighed. 'She's in pain some of the time. Other times she's coherent. We talk a lot. Talk through the night.'

'I'm sorry,' said Jill.

'There's nothing anyone can do. Sometimes it feels like we're the only two people in the world. It's a special time.'

There was a knock on the office door, and Jill's PA entered with a tray, jug of coffee, cups and saucers. Sam watched her legs and behind as she served the coffee, wondered briefly how many legs and behinds he'd checked out in a long career. And then his thoughts returned to Dora, and he wondered what it would feel like to be a widower all over again.

When Holly left the office, Jill said, 'I want you to handle this job yourself.'

'I'll give it all the time I can. I'm not gonna promise anything, Jill, except you'll get the same attention you did in the past. This time it might be Geordie who handles it, or Marie. Maybe both of them, instead of me. But at the end of the day you'll get better service from us than you'll get from anyone else.'

She smiled. 'I wouldn't dream of giving it to anyone else.'

'So what've you got?'

'Edward Blake.'

'I thought that was all over. You mean you haven't paid him yet?'

Jill shook her head. 'You remember the story?'

Sam showed her the palms of his hands. 'Only what was in the papers. You'd better fill me in. I never thought I'd be working on it.'

Jill spoke with a clear voice, as if she was making a presentation. 'Edward Blake is a political lobbyist. He came to prominence in the eighties, and made money under Thatcher and Major. In the spring his wife , India, was kidnapped. But he didn't got to the police. According to Blake he received a call from the kidnapper, and paid a ransom of twenty-five thousand pounds. But India was not released, and nothing more was heard from the kidnapper.

'When Blake did call in the police, a search was launched, but nothing was found. There was no real evidence to confirm that she'd been kidnapped, apart from Blake's story, and the police thought she'd run off with a lover. They reasoned that India and her lover had stung Blake for the twenty-five. Anyway, the whole thing died down, the newspapers found another cause to stick on the front page. We had several weeks of minor royals in and out of each other's playpens. But then, three months later, India Blake's body was found in a box in a garden allotment shed near the racecourse. She had been left to starve to death alone.

The police took Edward Blake into custody, held him for a time, and seemed fairly convinced that he had been behind it. Especially when they discovered that he'd insured her for two and a half million pounds the previous year.'

'You still think he did it?' asked Sam.

Jill shrugged her shoulders. 'We want you to look into it. Two and a half million pounds is a lot of money. But if you say the man's kosher we'll pay out.'

'The police have written him out of it?'

Jill nodded. 'He has finished helping them with their inquiries. There was a time when they were convinced he did it. But since the DNA tests they've left him alone.'

Sam finished his coffee and looked at the jug. Jill moved it closer to him. 'She was pregnant, wasn't she?' he asked.

'Yes. Only just. The presumption is that she was raped by the kidnapper. What is certain is that whoever the father was, it wasn't her husband.'

'Is that all you've got? Sam said. 'Why haven't you paid the guy?'

Jill shrugged. 'It smells,' she said.

'These things always smell a little,' Sam said. He sniffed. 'Yeah, there's a real whiff, but it's not like it makes your nose fall off. I bet if it wasn't two and a half mill you'd have paid him by now.'

'Oh, sure, Sam. Of course we would. But I'm hoping that if we pay your daily rate for a couple of weeks, we might save ourselves a lot of money.'

She walked to the lift with him. 'I hope Dora'll be all right,' she said.

Sam didn't say anything.

'She's lucky to have someone to take care of her.'

Sam smiled. 'You don't need taking care of, Jill.'

'I know,' she said. 'It's a bitch.'

She touched his arm as he stepped into the lift, dug out the soft smile, the one with the hint of concern in it, and flashed it at him as the doors closed between them.

Sam looked at his reflection in the full-length mirror that made up one side of the lift, and shook his head. Why didn't they just pay the guy? Jill acted like it would be coming out of her personal bank account instead of corporate funds expressly put aside for the purpose.

Still, why should Sam Turner worry? It meant work for the business, paid work. And the thing was about work from Jill, she paid well, and she paid quickly.

The job would consist of straightforward leg work, interviews with the dead woman's associates, maybe a little surveillance on Edward Blake. Sam wouldn't need to get too involved himself, Geordie and Marie could handle it easily enough.

Two weeks, maybe two and a half. He'd be able to spend more time with Dora.

It would have been too complicated to go into with Jill Sheridan, But Dora, Sam's wife, had known the murdered woman. They hadn't been close, but Dora had been upset when India Blake had disappeared, and shocked when the dead body was discovered. Dora had followed the case closely, sometimes reading extracts from the newspapers to Sam when he got home in the evenings.

He stopped in at Betty's for coffee instead of going straight to the office. Sam was still surprised that he was married at all. He'd watched himself getting closer to Dora, talked himself out of it a dozen times, then watched himself making up his mind to go through with it. He and she had recognised the lawlessness in each other. That's what they called it. Whatever it was, they shared a bond.

And now she was falling apart.

Read on... *Walking With Ghosts* by John Baker is published in paperback by Victor Gollancz in February 1999, price £9.99. Available from all good book shops

Also by John Baker and available from Victor Gollancz: *Death Minus Zero* and *Poet in the Gutter.*

Born in Hull in 1942 and educated at the university there, John Baker has worked as a social worker, shipbroker, truck driver and milkman, and most recently in the computer industry. He has twice received a Yorkshire Arts Association Writers' Bursary. He is married with five children and lives in York.

fiction

two dead detectives
simon clark

*The corpse is a staple of crime
fiction—but rarely so vividly as in
The Dead Detectives...*

THE DEAD got in the way of finding
the body. They streamed across the
meadow whistling, jeering, shrieking as
only the Mad Dead do.

Detective Chief Inspector Victor
North shook his head. This was a sorry
spectacle. There was nothing for it but to
wait for this flood of lost spirits to pass
by.

"Why do they do that, sir?" asked the
young detective. "What makes them cry
out like — like they're in agony?"

North glanced at the young man who
stood beside him. Detective Constable
Chadwick had only crossed over six
months ago. He still had much to learn.

"They've refused to adapt," North
told him. "Only when they accept who
they are ... or rather what they have
become ... will they be as rational as you
or I."

Chadwick rubbed his jaw. There was
as much a look of fear in his eyes as curiosity. "Some people don't take to being
dead, do they sir?"

"They do not, Chadwick."

"But how on Earth do we find our
man in that lot?"

"We don't." North was a gruff old
soul, but his voice could be surprisingly

gentle at times. "We just sit it out, Chadwick. Don't worry they'll pass soon enough."

"But what are they looking for?"

"A way back to their own bodies of course."

"But that would be against — against … "

"Nature, Chadwick?"

"Yes sir. I suppose so, sir … once you're dead, that's it."

"You're not wrong, Chadwick."

"But what I don't understand is why part of us — our spirit or soul whatever they call it — is here on Earth yet other parts have gone on to … well, wherever it is they've gone to."

North felt for the young man. Clearly, this existence was still very much new to him. New, strange and downright perplexing. Painfully so, in fact. But then he, North, had more than seventy-five years to become accustomed to this way of being. Something which he now regarded as a reward after forty years service to the force. The last fifteen of those being at Scotland Yard. Then of course, there'd been twenty years of a healthy, happy retirement with his wild flowers. Shame about not seeing the book in print, though; well, beggars can't be choosers and all that.

Chadwick, here, was a different kettle of fish. Died young, poor chap, at the wheel of his high-speed pursuit car. Left a pretty young wife and children … sad, so much to live for .. the transition would be hard for the poor devil.

North watched the young man struggling to express the little he'd learnt about his new existence here in the meadows outside the small town of Tudor-Le-Street.

"I mean sir … you said a little while ago that the ancient Egyptians had got it just about right; that humans have more than one soul … or … or was it one soul that's actually a number of different components? And that when we pass on—"

"Die, Chadwick, die: plain and simple. Don't give death euphemisms."

"I know, sir, but, where do the other parts go? Didn't you say that part of our soul might be reincarnated? But why am I standing here in this field. And I feel like me … well the me that I've always known. I can see my hands, my feet, sometimes I feel hungry, and sometimes I could murder a pint of Guiness, yet I know my body was cremated more than six months ago. And right now I'm scattered all over the crematorium's bloody flower beds—"

"Chadwick—"

"Excuse my French, sir."

"Chadwick, listen to me, you're questioning too much."

"Ours is not to reason why and that kind of thing." Chadwick sounded a tad bitter.

"Yes, I'm afraid so, Chadwick. Accept what you've become. If you don't you'll become one of those damned lost souls across there. Moping all over the country, yelling, shouting. Pulling those dashed stupid faces. You wouldn't want that, would you?"

"No, sir. I suppose not."

"Good man! Brace up then."

"But it's the little things that bother me, sir. I know being dead is bad enough. But I bought our Jason a computer for Christmas. I hid it in the loft where he'd never find it. The little tyke looks high and low for his presents. Of course before I had time to tell Jackie where I'd put it — booofff — wet mud on the A64 and here I am. Poor kid'll probably be as old as I am — was — before he stumbles on it all covered in cobwebs and crap …"

"Chadwick." North held up a finger. "That's enough. Listen, old fellow, life will go on for your family."

"But sir—"

"No. You must let go. Your first responsibility is to your self. You have to shape a new life here."

"Life?"

"Well, after-life then. But it seems as real as the life you left behind, doesn't it?"

"Yes, but, damnit all, sir."

"And if you don't hold onto yourself; if you don't occupy this." North tapped his temple. "You'll loose mental definition. Once that happens you've lost yourself and you'll become one of those."

He stabbed a square ended finger at the Mad Dead streaming across the meadow. They were nothing less than a tidal wave of psychosis; a purpling mass of bruised ego, id and memory; the spirits of men and women fusing, separating, fragmenting; a wash of demented spirits that had yearned so hard for something they could never have they'd lost every shred of sanity they'd once possessed.

North watched a chain of maybe a hundred men holding hands and running along a track. The saying 'the blind leading the blind' was familiar enough to North. But this was the mad leading the mad. Every second or so one in the chain would call, "This is the way! This is the way!" Then the line would break and reform with the one who'd shouted the words in the lead. Then another would

shout: "It's this way! I know it's this way!"

The line would break, reform, break, reform, and so on; each demented spirit believing it knew the way back to life. And each man in the line holding onto his neighbour's hand with a fierce, grip, terrified lest he should be left behind.

And so the Mad Dead formed into these herds that roamed the country. Dead, mad … lost.

North cast a knowing eye over Chadwick. The man's Adams' apple bobbed in his throat; his eyes had turned glassy as he watched the Mad Dead sweep by. North knew that the raw excitement of the mob was exerting its grip now. In a moment Chadwick would feel that same mad fire in his heart, that desire — that impossible desire — to make the homeward journey to life. The emotion would blaze within him and carry him away, shrieking, laughing, wailing, crying.

Leaning forward, North gripped Chadwick's arm just above the elbow.

"Why are we here this morning?" North asked, his Yorkshire tones firm. "What has brought us to this rather pleasant meadow?"

Chadwick blinked, as if bringing himself out of a day dream.

He blinked again, took a deep breath and looked round.

"Chadwick? Why are we here?"

"The body, sir. We've had a report that a body's been found?"

"Good man, Chadwick. Now. Whereabouts exactly?"

"Down by the river."

"Are our informants reliable?"

"I believe so, sir."

"Who are they?"

"The shepherd boys. They were looking for a lost lamb and — sir, why do the ghosts of dead shepherds pretend to still mind sheep?"

"Now, now, Chadwick. I didn't want to go into this again."

"But there are no lambs; no sheep come to that."

"If you'd pay a little more attention to what I have to say, Chadwick, you'd find your life here easier and a lot more rewarding."

"I know, sir, but it doesn't make sense, does it?"

"What doesn't?"

"Dead shepherds pretend to look after sheep; dead doctors treat the sick; dead teachers teach make believe children … "

"Then it must be obvious to you, isn't it? In life our professions define who we are. So why not in death?"

"Sir … " Chadwick looked shaken. "I'm sorry, but I think it's all those people and their screaming that's unnerved me this morning."

"Don't worry, Chadwick. You'll get use to it. And you'll see queerer sights than that mark my words. Now, to business. Our informants?"

"Yes, the shepherd boys. They called me at around eight this morning to say they'd seen the body of a young man lying face down in long grass down by the river. They think he'd been murdered, sir."

North nodded. Now he let Chadwick speak. The young man's mind was safely rooted in sanity once more. They had a murder to investigate. That would deflect the young man's attention from the Mad Dead. Making a church and steeple from his fingers, a characteristic 'contemplation' device of North's he gazed over the meadow. The stream of revenants

had almost passed. Occasionally one would break away from the rest, race across the grass to himself and stare fiercely into his eyes. There was an expectancy there. That silent agonised stare. North knew were asking the same question.

Which way back to life?

The trick was to ignore them. After a moment they'd break that nightmarish eye contact and run on. Eventually they'd rejoin their own kind. Then resume their quest which would undoubtedly continue until the end of time itself.

North was an old hand now. The Mad Dead didn't bother him. If anything now it was the songs of the prehistoric dead that moved him. As they sat on their mounds up on Jackdaw Ridge and hallelujahed the rising sun, or wove beautiful melodies around the moon. Now that did have the power to send a silent shiver thrilling through his old bones.

But great heaven, what a pleasant day it was (once you'd discounted the Mad Dead and their shenanigans, of course). There was a blue sky lined with the purest white jet trails. The church spires and rooftops of the town shimmered in the heat haze. Wild flowers added dashes of yellow and blue to the expanse of grassland rolling out before them. Butterflies flitted to and fro. And meanwhile a bumble bee got busy with a wild rose.

Along the road behind him boys on bicycles raced by laughing. No doubt they were headed for the dam. There they'd swim and shout their heads off all day long.

Presently the Mad Dead passed by.

Then there was only one figure racing madly to and fro across the grass.

He was shouting out in a high voice, "What's happening? What's happening, what's happening/ Woss' 'appening?"

Chadwick gave North a quizzical look.

North nodded. "That's our man." He set off across the meadow. "Come on, Chadwick. We've a homicide to investigate."

Two

North wasn't going to get any sense out of the dead man. He saw that straight away. The dead man's ghost rushed backwards and forwards across the grass. His eyes were wide. His face was the image of sheer fright. He babbled over and over: "What's happening, what's happening?"

Chadwick said, "He's not going to be much use to us for a while, is he, sir?"

"A long while at that.

"What's happening, what's happening?"

"Quoth the dead man," North added weightily.

Now the recently dead man rushed up to his own lifeless body sprawled there in the grass and stared down at it. The man clapped a hand over his mouth as if he'd vomit. Not that there was any chance of that again. The man had traded the physical for the elemental.

"What's happening?" Again the useless question. A moment later he turned and ran away from his own corpse as if it would bite him.

When he was half way across the field he stopped and looked back.

A faint cry came to the two dead detectives: "What's happening? What's happening?"

North rubbed his jaw. "No, I think it'll be a long time before we can get any sense out of him, Chadwick. A common enough symptom with the violently killed. Right, Chadwick, down to business. What do you make of it?" North nodded down at the corpse.

"Well, sir. Mid-twenties. Recently killed. Casually dressed in jeans and a T-shirt."

"Expensive clothing?"

"Not at all, sir. The jeans are pretty old, not a quality make. And the T-shirt looks as if it's being through the washing machines a good few times."

"But look at the shoes. Expensive footwear is easy to spot in any day and age."

"Yes, that's odd, sir … I'd have expected him to be wearing trainers, but these are brogues. Probably hand-made. Look, leather soles."

"So how does a young man in cheap clothes wind up dead in rich man's shoes."

"Nicked them, sir?"

"Possibly, Chadwick. Now to cause of death?"

"Well … without being able to turn the body over, I'd say these two … " he indicated two bloody holes in the man's back. " … are exit wounds from a small calibre weapon."

"That's a fair deduction. Instantaneous death?"

"Impossible to say, sir."

"But there's a trail of blood across the grass as far as the body here."

"The corpse might have been dragged."

"Unlikely. The blood isn't smeared, it's fallen as drops." North pressed his fingertips together into a church roof and steeple. "Also, you'll note there's a copious amount of blood immediately around the corpse."

"So his heart was still pumping the blood out through the wounds a while before he died?"

"That would be my guess, too, Chadwick. In short we can imagine this man was shot twice, escaped his attacker —"

"In expensive shoes."

"In expensive shoes, Chadwick, then mortally wounded he ran down this meadow where he fell into the long grass and eventually expired."

"At night, sir?"

"Again I'd hazard a guess in the affirmative. Perhaps he was shot somewhere up on the road — at night — ran down here. Fell into the long grass. His attacker either fled straight away or followed him but was unable to find him in the dark. The question now, Chadwick, is did any of our lot see him?"

"Our lot? Oh, I see, sir. Any of the dead?"

"Absolutely, Chadwick."

"No, not that I'm aware of, sir. The shepherd boys found him this morning as they—"

"Looked for a lost lamb. Yes, yes, I recall, Chadwick."

"What now, sir?"

"Does the corpse yield any more clues?"

"Clean shaven."

"Then he may have shaved before going to meet someone in the evening."

"I can see a wallet in his pocket."

"Was the motive robbery? Perhaps we'll find out when our mortal colleagues begin their investigations."

"So we have to wait for someone — someone mortal — to find the body?"

"Yes, Chadwick. Alas, yes."

Three

Someone found the body less than twenty minutes later.

"Now that is surprising," Chadwick murmured as a middle-aged man with an abundant crop of silver hair came upon the body. "You would have expected to see the man express shock. Not relief." They watched as the silver haired man studied the body for a moment. Then he quickly pulled off the corpse's shoes and lobbed them into the river. All the while he shot glances back over his shoulder to make sure no-one was watching him.

"I reckon we've found our murderer, sir."

"Indeed we have, Chadwick, indeed we have."

"But what's he doing?"

"Come, come, Chadwick your eyes are a damn sight younger than mine."

"I mean I can see what he's doing. He's thrown the shoes into the river. Now he's going through the corpse's pockets. See … he's found a piece of paper, he's reading something on it … now he's putting it in his own pocket."

"So there is nothing wrong with your eyesight, Chadwick. I'm relieved." North gave a grim smile. "Filthy business though, isn't it? Murder?"

They watched as the middle-aged man grinned down at the corpse; then he gave it a playful slap on the face; much in the way an old friend might greet another.

Then the man's face darkened. He gripped the corpse by the hand and dragged it through the grass toward the river.

"So the crime isn't over yet, Chadwick."

At that moment the two detectives were distracted by the ghost of the murdered man who rushed through the long grass toward the man dragging the corpse. "What's happening? What's happening? What's happening?"

At that moment he saw the middle-aged man's face. The ghost shrieked and slapped the palms of both hands to the sides of his head. "Morton!" He cried, then circled the man pulling the corpse, shrieking all the while: "Morton! Morton! What's happening? What's happening?"

Of course Morton, if that was the murderer's name, being mortal heard and saw nothing at all. Saw nothing, that is, but a river, a meadow, and perhaps butterflies rising up, disturbed by the corpse's passing. And heard nothing but a skylark singing high in the sky.

The ghost departed shrieking.

"Oh, sir … "

"What is it, Chadwick?"

"We've caught him red handed, sir. Are you sure we can't do anything?"

North sighed regretfully. "Nothing, Chadwick. Absolutely nothing."

They watched the man drag the corpse down to the river where he rolled it into the water. There he weighted it with stones.

A moment later it was invisible beneath the surface.

"Damn, I hadn't expected that," Chadwick hissed. "Now there's a good chance no-one will ever find the body."

"And we will be the only ones to know that the perpetrator was an individual by the name of Morton, who will probably return to his everyday life, and grow old and contented with his pipe and slippers afore a roaring fire, hmm?"

"Something like that, sir. Just think, though, the injustice of it."

"I think there's been some rough justice meted out already. Look at Morton's shoes. The man has taste, hmm?"

"They're the same kind of shoes as the corpse was wearing. But sir … " Chadwick was near speechless. "You don't kill a man for stealing your shoes."

"No, you don't Chadwick. You're a civilised man. But I've seen a man murdered for taking nothing more than a smear of another man's hair-cream."

They watched as the middle-aged man dried his hands on the grassy bank and then smoothed back his handsome head of silver hair.

North reflected. "But I think there was more to it than that. We have to give our imaginations their head, Chadwick: might we not suppose that Morton there is a criminal himself? Perhaps the unfortunate young man chose the wrong man's house to burgle. Perhaps the young man discovered a secret or two he shouldn't have known. Morton there, found the young man. Lured him here somehow, perhaps with an offer to buy that piece of paper we saw drawn from his pocket. Of course, Morton had no intention of honouring such a deal. He shoots the young man. Bang bang! Mortally wounded, the young man escapes to this very meadow only to be found the following morning. Now we see the concluding events."

"Morton hiding the body, you mean?"

"Yes. And it's a pity. A great pity."

"Where's a policeman when you want one, eh, sir?"

North frowned for a moment then gave a slight, some might say a ghost of a smile. "Quite, Chadwick. If only the police could be alerted right now."

"Wait a minute, sir."

"What is it, Chadwick?"

"Over there, by the bushes." Chadwick's voice brightened. "I think our prayers might have been answered."

North looked in the direction of Chadwick's pointing finger. There behind the bushes stood a man. He was around seventy with wispy hair and held a small dog in his arms. He'd clearly seen everything.

"I think justice might be done after-all, sir." Chadwick sounded pleased with himself now.

North wasn't so sure. "I hope you're right. But I'm very much afraid ..." He paused and looked back at Morton. "Yes ... I'm very much afraid events have just taken a turn for the worse."

Morton had seen the old man as well. As soon as their eyes met the old man began limping away as quickly as he could along the river bank to where the bushes grew more thickly.

He couldn't outrun the younger man. That much was clear. Was he now planning on hiding?

Chadwick let out a breath. "Oh, good grief ... Morton's got a gun."

They watched Morton stride energetically toward where the old man had taken refuge in the bushes. The revolver he held in his hand was a hefty thing in glittering chrome; its barrel had all the prodigious girth of a cucumber.

"Oh, no ... " Chadwick was dis-mayed. "You know what's going to happen now, don't you, sir?"

"Yes, I do, Chadwick ... tragically, our numbers are going to be increased by one."

"Are you sure there isn't anything we can do?" Chadwick watched Morton march through the grass to where the old man tried hard to conceal himself under a bush. The dog whimpered in the old man's arms.

"Chadwick — I've told you: we observe, we consider, we discuss, sometimes we draw conclusions ... but we cannot interfere."

"But the old man's going to be shot. This is monstrous. Surely we can do something?"

"Yes, there is one thing we can do, Chadwick, old man."

Chadwick looked at North suddenly expectant.

"And that, regrettably, is to turn our back on what will happen next." North's expression was grim. "Poor ineffectual creatures, aren't we, Chadwick?" He sighed and looked away to the church spires rising above the town. "Now, that is a crime isn't it, old man? When a policeman has to look the other way."

With that he turned and walked to where the ancient dead sang about the great mysteries. He tried not to hear the gunshots when they at last violated this pleasant summer's day.

And all the birds fell silent. But the ancient dead sang on ...

Simon Clark is the author of many excellent horror novels, the latest in paperback being Vamphirric. *His latest book in hardcover is* The Fall, *from Hodder & Stoughton.*

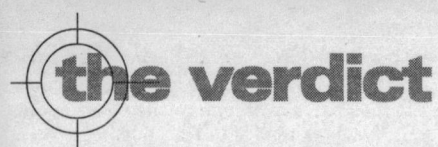

the verdict

The latest in books, film, and sound reviewed by people with time for crime

'a surrealistic noir epic' – GQ

BOX NINE BY JACK O'CONNELL, NO EXIT, £6.99

THIS IS THE FIRST of O'Connell's novels set in Quinsigamond, a futuristic version of Worcester Massachusetts crossed with the LA of cyberpunk novels. There's a new drug around town, called Lingo, which gets you speaking in tongues and also drives you to fiercer rage than the worst crank you ever saw. The high is great, but the price is high.

Connections to Vonnegut's Ice-Nine are obvious, but we're dealing with something deeper here. O'Connell's more relevant in-

fluences appear to be early Thomas Pynchon, Don DeLillo, Julio Cortazar's *Hopscotch* and the movie version of *Blade Runner*. It may seem a strange mix to apply to a small city in central Massachusetts, but it does work, particularly because of O'Connell's alternately manic and dreamy prose.

Leonore Thomas is the drug cop investigating Lingo. Problem is, she's a speed freak, gun fetish, thrill-seeker, who might be more at home on the other side of the fence. In a city torn apart by ethnic gangs, the big drug lord is Cortez (Cortex? Cortez the Killer?) and the microcosm is more like a slide full of bacteria wiggling under a microscope.

O'Connell is one of those writers who can bend his prose to what he's doing, form as an extension of content. There aren't many of them around. If you haven't hooked into Quinsigamond yet, this is the place for your first hit. It's almost free. And kudos to No Exit for a cover which captures perfectly the layers of atmosphere in this book. *[That's a first then – Ed]*

Michael Carlson

A GOOD HANGING AND OTHER STORIES BY IAN RANKIN, ORION, £5.99

A WELCOME REPRINT OF a collection of twelve short stories, originally published in 1992, featuring Lothian and Borders' DI John Rebus, which go far to support Rankin's position amongst the elite of modern British crime writers. The short story format allows Rankin to demonstrate that his talent doesn't just extend to complex, atmospheric novels like Black and Blue that explore the complicated, flawed character of John Rebus, but that he also has a great talent for devious, complex puzzles. *A Good Hanging* contains several excellent short stories in the classic mould, like *Playback*, a classic exposition of the supposedly unbreakable alibi, and *Monstrous Trumpet*, where Rebus's deductive skills in solving the mysterious theft of a slightly dodgy sculpture receive assistance from an unfortunately named French policeman.

There are also several more conventional stories of detection in Rebus's bleak Edinburgh—particularly good are the title story, set during Rebus's least favourite time of year, the Festival, and *Being Frank*, where a tramp's conspiracy theories lead Rebus along a rather different tangent. The character of John Rebus is explored in pieces like *Sunday*, a reflective piece on the off-duty policeman, and *Auld Lang Syne*, where a face from the past at Hogmanay confronts Rebus with a dilemma. Overall, what can I say? If you've read Rankin's other novels, you'll certainly devour these with relish, and if not, you'll probably enjoy them just as much. It's also nice to note that Rebus can get on with a days work without worrying about Big Ger Cafferty for once...

William Penn

GO BY SIMON LEWIS, PULP BOOKS, £8.99, 1901072053

A BIT OF A diversion from the norm for me, this one, but I surprised myself by liking it far more than I thought I would. *Go* is a loosely connected series of pieces about Lee, Sol and Vix, jet trash wandering around Goa, Hong Kong and China, and how their lives intersect. Lewis captures the grubby, desperate atmosphere of his locations superbly, from a Deptford nightclub through the dazed, unfocussed Goan rave scene to Hong Kong on the cusp of change. Lee, Sol and Vix, who meet each other in Goa, Hong Kong and China, are all fleeing past troubles in Britain, and the story turns from one to the next, exploring how they have come to be where they are.

The prose is suitably gritty and the dialogue believable, but unfortunately, its hard to care about the main characters, who drift rather aimlessly through the novel, supposedly fleeing their pasts but never really getting anywhere. The plot is loose, concentrating more on the influence of the past on the present, although the ending of the novel attempts to inject a little more tension into the proceedings, but with little success. Too frequently, Simon Lewis seems to be intent on writing 'What I Did On My Holidays', although he has a great talent for capturing the alien culture experienced by Westerners in Asia. *Go* is an engrossing, if ultimately unsatisfying, read, and frequently smacks too highly of style over content, but none-the-less worth reading for the reader bored with novels based in the more usual run of society.

William Penn

DEAD WRONG BY CATH STAINCLIFFE, HEADLINE, £17.99, ISBN: 0747219842

FORGET MERCHANT BANKER NICOLA Horlick as the modern superwoman, there's a new contender in town. Sal Kilkenny, single mother of two and gutsy part-time Private Investigator. This is Sal Kilkenny's third outing and is easily the pick of the trio. Her first crime novel was *Looking For Trouble* which was picked up by Manchester publisher, Crocus, and ended up on the John Creasey shortlist.

Many single mothers might list sleeping as their spare time hobby but that's not Sal's style. Empowered by motherhood, she takes every opportunity to tread the grey streets and leafy suburbs of Manchester, cleaning up the city for her growing generation.

As a force for good, Sal is a realistic and endearing creation. Her tenacity marbled with a motherly compassion are proof that a single person—in both senses, can make a difference. Staincliffe is good on contrasting the innocence of her toddlers—nicely revealed in moments of uncosy domesticity, with the drugged-out feckless youths who form the thrust of Staincliffe's story.

It's a story that begins with a murdered Asian youth and ends with a well handled chase scene which left me quite breathless. In between, Sal is hired to prove the innocence of the white teenager accused of the murder, and to discover the identity of a man stalking a young mother.

Manchester is Staincliffe's home town, and she's continually comparing the beauty of the old with the ugliness of the new. She also sets her story either side of the day the IRA decided to remodel the town centre, and the repercussions of that bombing are laced throughout the novel, Plenty of realism then, but also some echoes of hope,

This is first person narrative country inhabited by the likes of Sue Grafton's Kinsey Millhone (Kinsey jogs along the beach, Sal goes swimming in the municipal bath), and Evanovitch's Stephanie Plum. Staincliffe lacks the humour of both these writers but then again you'd never find Kinsey or Stephanie in Mothercare.

David Howard

DEAD FISH BY RUTH CARRINGTON, 4TH ESTATE PUBLICATIONS, £5.99, ISBN: 1857028775

WHEN DR GEOFFREY QUINN arrives home in the middle of the night, after three days of absence, he finds his house on fire. To add to his misery and confusion, he is arrested on the spot for the murder of his wife, Nikki, and his two children are missing... presumed dead.

When Allison Hope is called upon to defend Dr Quinn, she is faced with an apparently insurmountable task. The defendant is a man who, seven years earlier, became a local hero for his part in the jailing of a vicious psychopath, Simon Bonniface,

and who has no recollection of at least 24 hours out of the 72 hours he was missing over the weekend of his wife's death.

Chief Superintendent Manning, the arresting officer, is convinced of Quinn's guilt as are, albeit reluctantly, some of Quinn's friends and neighbours.

Allison's life partner, George Kristianssen, a private detective, is drafted in to help uncover the real happenings on that fateful weekend. Together they uncover more than even they bargain for... a high power illicit sex and drugs ring, with invitation only parties open to the select few, an arms deal funded by the drugs ring and, as they lurch closer to the truth about that weekend, a rising body count,

Allison seems to be a normal woman, despite the fact that she is conjured up by a man, with skeletons in her own closet that rattle alarmingly throughout the course of the case.

This is the first in a series of Allison Hope novels, written by established crime writer, Michael Hartland, under the pen name Ruth Carrington.

Dead Fish is a fine read... With a plot that keeps you guessing right to the end, and a keen insight into the various threads of law and order within the UK, this was a book I couldn't keep my hand off.

There are three questions... did Dr Quinn murder his wife, where are his children... and when's the next Allison Hope novel being published?

Helen Bryant

BLIND DATE BY FRANCES FYFIELD, BANTAM PRESS, £15.99

"HOW DO YOU make people love you?" Caroline Smythe asks herself, a question that seems to haunt all the characters in *Blind Date*, and a theme that ties together a convoluted, multi-layered and ingenious story.

Pretty, compliant Emma Kennedy is brutally murdered in her own house, by some-

Murder One for all the Pulp Fiction your heart desires.
Murder One where you can find all the Usual Suspects. If it's in Print, in English, we have it. If it's not in Print, we might well have it too. The **ultimate** mystery superstore.
Mail Order all over the world.
Catalogue on request.

Visit our spanking new, criminal website at www.murderone.co.uk **and** e-mail:106562.2021 @compuserve.com

one she invited in, probably one of the troupe of inadequates whom she is known to befriend. Her eight year old son is in the house but does not witness the murder. Emma's older sister, Elizabeth, a policewoman is sent undercover to extract a confession from the prime suspect, Jack, a lonely man with a history of violence. The case against Jack collapses in court, the judge ruling that the evidence Elizabeth gathers is inadmissible, due to having been extracted under emotional duress. Jack commits suicide, Elizabeth retires from the force under a cloud and the case remains unsolved. Elizabeth goes to her childhood home in a seaside town to recuperate and is then injured in a seemingly motiveless attack, when she is doused in caustic soda when leaving a pub in the town.

The answers to Emma's murder and the assault of Elizabeth are hidden in the complicated relationships of the sisters' family and friends. The novel begins with a sense of finality and failure. Emma's murder remains unsolved, the files on the case remain open, but the impetus to solve it seems to have been lost. Has the key to the case died with Jack, or is a murderer still at large?

The theme of the search for love is expressed in the shiftlessness of lonely, urban life, the devise of the dating agency, the complexity of mother and child relationships, people not feeling loveable, people trying too hard to be loved. Fyfield has created an extremely plausible plot, with parallels to the Rachel Nickell/Colin Stagg case. The novel is tense and full of menace. There is a recurrent theme of people being scarred physically and mentally, damaged by their inability to face up to who they really are. Fyfield observes the small details of people's dress, their behaviour and mental ticks brilliantly. It is this observation and the strong sense of place in the novel that gives it its depth and its pace, which manages to be both hectic and tense and quiet and reflective at the same time. Diana Kennedy's

love for her house by the sea, Elizabeth's for her London tower are symbolic of their need for a place where they can be themselves and feel safe.

Blind Date keeps you guessing right to the end. Questions still linger. *Blind Date* reveals Fyfield getting better and better.

Sara Grant-Thorald

MOTHER, SON AND HOLY GHOST BY REG GADNEY, FABER AND FABER, £9.99

THE MILLENNIUM APPROACHES. The zealots of the Trinity Chapter religious cult are preparing for the Resurrection of their leader in the first minute of the first hour of the first day of the Millennium. Near King's Cross, the corpse of a young American researcher, Jane Moorfield, is found on some derelict wasteland. Did she die of a massive heroine overdose? Her sister, Caroline, doesn't think so, and enlists Alan Rosslyn of the business intelligence consultancy ASG to investigate. The sinister causes of Jane's death involve both the wealthy recruits of the cult and the British security services. Gadney here pulls off an interesting trick: there are echoes of John Buchan in this headlong dash to a tense New Year's Eve finale in Trafalgar Square, but the bloody violence is very much of the 1990s and gives this well-honed thriller a truly compelling edge.

Barry Forshaw

LOS ALAMOS BY JOSEPH KANON, ABACUS, £5.99

THE BUILDING OF THE US atomic bomb in the New Mexico desert has served as the backdrop for a lot of fiction, and some very dramatic non-fiction as well. But by moving it into the world of the crime novel, Joseph Kanon has done one of the things which genre fiction often accomplishes more effectively than the so-called mainstream, and that is to move the issues of the present, and other pasts, into the story of one very specific past.

Thus, in much the same way that a presumed homosexual murder in Albuquerque winds up having pronounced effects on the entire atomic project in *Los Alamos*, so too the story of Michael Connolly, a War Department PR man sent to investigate and keep a lid on the murder, eventually leads to revelations which cause the reader to reconsider the genesis of the Cold War, of the McCarthy era, of the Red Scare, and of the strangely "un-American" group of scientists who created the atomic age out there in the middle of the American nowhere.

The science isn't the big thing, atomic or otherwise, (though I don't know if the term quantum mechanics had been thought up then) and really its only the romantic subplot, with its too easy Red shadows in the background that creaks in the slightest. *Los Alamos* delivers its genre promise, while at the same time covering the birth of a new age, one which ushers in a bleakness of the sort the world had never seen. Robert Oppenheimer, later driven to suicide in the witch hunts, confesses to his joy at watching the bomb explode successfully, even as he knows its power will soon be beyond his control. Connolly and his love achieve the American essential, as her husband terms it, of a happy end. But we know there is no happy ending to this story. And it's all the more powerful for that. It is a shame that *Los Alamos* was not published and reviewed as a major mainstream novel in Britain. Perhaps Kanon's next, *The Prodigal Spy*, which promises to take us through the McCarthy era, will be.

Michael Carlson

THE NAME OF THE BULLFIGHTER BY LUIS SEPULVEDA, TRANSLATED FROM SPANISH BY SUZANNE RUTA, ALISON & BUSBY, £7.99

JUAN BELMONTE IS NAMED after a famous bullfighter, and the name is apt. A former guerrilla fighter now exiled from Chile, he is working in Hamburg when he approached by an old man in a wheelchair who wants him to return to Chile, to track down and recover a horde of medieval coins looted from the Nazi vaults by two German policemen.

From a start in Hamburg to a finish in Tierra del Fuego, Belmonte is forced to relive his radical past, and forced to deal with people who might once have been his allies, former operatives of the East German secret police, now out of work after reunification, who are also after the coins. Like a bullfighter, he is caught in a ritual sort of battle, with a hugely dangerous but often stupid foe. And, of course, bullfighting is a sport trapped in the past.

This is a post-Berlin Wall novel, rich in the ironies of the way our political compasses appear to have been realigned in the wake of the Reagan/Thatcher revolution. Luckily for Belmonte, he has a personal motive, his lover and former comrade, who is now on life-support in Santiago. Personal motives are more pure, and Veronica is both motivation and symbolism. The thriller elements are strong enough to keep the airport reader involved, but the writing is good enough so this book will probably slip through the cracks, to be found, like the stolen coins of the story, in the serious literature in translation section of your bookstore.

Michael Carlson

NEVER HIT THE GROUND BY KIRK LAKE, PULP BOOKS, £9.99, ISBN 190107207X

OH DEAR. WRITING about books that are terrific is usually fun. Writing about books that are abysmal is usually even more fun. Why, then, is it so frustratingly difficult to write about a book that's just *blah*? Not too exciting, yet not exactly boring either? Not terribly original, yet quirky and odd enough to be straying from the beaten path every once in a while? What can one do except perhaps try to emulate the unsatisfying qualities of the book by writing a rather bland and unexciting review?

Which isn't too hard actually, considering that this is another one of those stories about a loser dabbling in big-time crime and not being too successful with it. Will the two transvestites in the subplot get a job in porn movies or not? Will Ray Gardner finally close the big deal that will make it possible for him to leave a life of petty crime behind? Will his employer (the one with the slightly sick interest in Siamese fighting fish) get him first? Do I care? No, I don't. Some people you just shouldn't hang out with, and if Ray Gardner had read the right books, he'd know that. Stay away from stock characters, otherwise you'll become one yourself. Unfortunately, this book is full of stock characters: the girlfriend with the golden heart, the big boss, his gently psychotic henchmen, the best friend/sacrificial lamb character etc. The plot is maybe not predictable at every turn, but also not entirely unfamiliar.

The saving grace of Lake's book (that is, the reason why I kept reading) is the language; very contemporary, believable, and real. Gritty, sometimes coarse, yet musical in a way. There's not a single wrong note in it; it never seems contrived or attempting very hard to sound authentic or 'urban.' It's such a pity, then, that all the rest is marred by a bad case of 'Been there, read that.'

Frank Thielmann

NIGHT DOGS BY KENT ANDERSON, ARROW, £6.99

IT'S PORTLAND, OREGON, mid 1970s and Hanson, a decorated Vietnam veteran, is a patrolman covering the North Precinct, where the streets are a battle and the cops assigned there are those the department would rather forget. And it's summer, when the cops open the season on killing the wild dogs roaming the streets at night, with a prize to the partners racking up the most confirmed kills.

This is a cross between Wambaugh's 70s tragi-comedies of LA cops on duty (they even refer back to Wambaugh's TV series *Police Story*) and Tim O'Brien's mainstream novels, where the ghost of Vietnam haunts every action. For the most of the book Anderson carries this double burden well: and if certain elements are predictable (the partner about to retire gets killed, the beautiful ethereal hippie chick turns out to be into handcuffs and violence) there is a good deal of humour which works, and a wonderful set-up with Hanson being stalked by a DEA task force and his best buddy from Vietnam re-entering his life as a drug dealer targeted by said agents.

Problem is, after building up the pressure almost to exploding point, Anderson lets it blow away, as the feud with the DEA agents dissipates, and his buddy's situation is resolved without outside interefernce. Which is a shame, because you've really gone along for the ride up to that point. In his introduction, James Crumley says no one's ever written like this before. Well, yeah they have, and we've seen this ending in Robert Stone, we've seen the set up, most recently, in Stephen Hunter. This is not meant to put you off this book, which is a good one. But good as Anderson is as a writer, with a new twist on its finish, it could have been great.

Michael Carlson

ONE LAST TOWN BY MATT BRAUN, ST. MARTIN'S PRESS, £5.99

MATT BRAUN WRITES WESTERNS. His best ones are based on historical fact, which seems to provide him with the depth of character and event which he otherwise doesn't really generate. *One Last Town* deals with Bill Tilghman, Oklahoma's most legendary lawman, and the last epic showdown between the Wild West and the Roaring Twenties.

As one of the 'Three Guardsmen,' Tilghman was responsible for cleaning up the former Indian Territory, and played a huge part in its becoming a state. Now the time is

1924, and Tilghman is 70 years old, but still working on special assignments for the governor of the state. Oklahoma is awash in oil, and the boom towns are overflowing with crime, especially because prohibition is the law of the land. As if that weren't enough, the Klan is also riding rampant.

When the town marshal of Cromwell disappears, Tilghman is sent in to clean up the town. Now we're dealing with automobiles, airplanes, and tommy guns; and organised crime as big business, not just gangs of train robbers on horseback. Braun does well with the modern action, and with the anachronistic nature of Tilghman and his job. And, as befits a crime novel, he also sets up an interesting little mystery: just who is the Mr Big controlling the crime in Cromwell: but he reveals the answer far too soon, robbing it of its suspense. Of course Tilghman never figures out he could just go to the telephone operator and find out who the town baddy calls: it is 1924 after all.

This mix of Wyatt Earp and the Untouchables works well. It's surprising it hasn't been done more often, but then, there weren't many Bill Tilghmans around, were there?

Michael Carlson

THE BLOOD BROTHERS BY GENO WASHINGTON, THE DO-NOT PRESS, £6.50
ISBN 1899344446

OVER SIXTY YEARS AGO, black anthropologists were caught on the horns of a dilemma. Did they print folk tales as spoken by African-Americans, thereby subjecting their interviewees to ridicule for not speaking standard English? Or did they re-write the tall tales told to them, distorting the truth to make their findings acceptable to a polite society readership?

Geno Washington's debut novel reminds me of this concern. (Yes, *that* Geno Washington: the sixties soul legend immortalised by Dexy's Midnight Runners. If nothing else, *The Blood Brothers* is a celebrity

novel to end up bracketed with what Julian Symons called the 'curiosities and singletons' of crime fiction.) Ploughing through the adventures of Robbie Jones—Vietnam vet, secret agent, surgeon and ladies man— it's clear that he can tell a story as energetic as his on-stage performances. It's clearer still that he can tell a mean folk tale and write a tall, short story with explosive pace. Thus Robbie wakes up in hospital and lets us in on his dark secrets: a plot to give Idi Amin syphilis; friends and lovers slain and betrayed, covert operations in Southeast Asia. Readers of 1970s pulp will have heard it all before, but Washington rehearses such scenes with considerable charm and an episodic rock-hard, side-splitting punchline.

The problem with this is that it won't stretch to over 300 pages. The issue of vernacular speech raised above matters here because, pretty soon, the author takes his eye off the ball. As a result, each colourful character starts to sound the same, often fluctuating between Huggy Bear's jive talking and RAF-style 'old chaps' in the same sentence. The kind of banter that would be impressive around Chester Himes' campfire doesn't make the transition into print at all well. Readers will be won over by the knockabout humour of the first chapter, but as Jones soldiers on, they'll get a sense of *deja vu*.

Raymond Chandler once advised crime writers to have a man come in the door with a gun every time they ran out of ideas. It seems that Washington has modified this maxim, lobbing explosives through the window when either the protagonist seems to be winning or the plot is floundering around. This makes for tedious reading: what starts off as breakneck pace ends up as a novel stuck in a single gear. What's more, the good gags based on similes and metaphors—'in a dress so tight you could see what she for dinner' and so on—failed to get a laugh when they pop up in every other chapter. It's like reading Garry Bushell on acid. When each new character is introduced as being 'so big his dick must have hung in the water when he went to the toilet', how can you tell them apart? Do Arabs really eat sandwiches made from fried camel balls all the time? I think not. Without wanting to sound PC, Washington shows that ethnic banter and stereotypical homosexuals can be the refuge of the lazy writer. By the time Robbie is on his umpteenth escape bid from Mauritania's military prisons, you wish a warder would just put a bullet in him.

Some of these problems seem down the editing. The repetition of phrases from one chapter to the next stands out a mile. Likewise, readers who can spot the typos a mile off will wonder why no-one at the publisher did. Overall, a disappointing debut that could have been invigorating if tightly edited and kept to under thirty pages.

Graham Barnfield

HELL ON WHEELS BY DANIEL EVAN WEISS, HIGH RISK, £7.99, ISBN: 1852424397

BOOKS ABOUT PEOPLE WITH any sort of disability fall into two categories; those that ring true and those that seek to glamorise their subject; you know the sort of thing, these people are so brave in spite of it all, they are wonderful in the face of adversity, in other words they are stereotypes to make the rest of us better. In *Hell on Wheels* David Evan Weiss avoids such clichés and gives us Marty, a former tennis pro who has lost his legs and copes in his own way—by being bitter at times, sulky at others and just getting on with it at still others. He is never less than believable.

So you have the basis for a good mainstream novel—but he can't remember the details of his accident or who is responsible, and this is where the mystery element creeps in. The book charts his efforts to find out as well as his dual romance, with Lucy on the one hand, who has looked after him since he lost his limbs, and with Esther

on the other, an old girlfriend now married to someone else.

So far, so intensely serious, you could think, but it isn't. Marty is sassy, witty and in on a whole load of disability jokes that would be closed off to the rest of us. He tells his story so that it keeps you hooked and entertained even if you do end up wincing a couple of times. There are flaws, mind you; at one point Marty goes to the police precinct and they get his file out—before he has told them his name. Clever, that. And the dialogue slips occasionally, particularly when he's talking to his women, you can lose track of which words belong to whom.

But these are minor points. It's a satisfying read with a nice pointy sense of humour attached, and that's becoming something of a rarity in a world where the hardboiled school of crime writing is so fashionable. More of this, please—and fast.

Guy Clapperton

BAD DEBTS BY PETER TEMPLE, HARPER COLLINS AUSTRALIA, $12.95, ISBN 0-7322-5748

YOU WILL NEVER READ a bad blurb—the question is will the book live up to the claim? *Bad Debts* is hailed as *"wonderful, quintessentially Australian stuff, an absolute pearler of a read"* and I can verify that—I have not read such a good and entertaining crime book in a long time. You had to know there was more going on in Melbourne than *Neighbours*.

Jack Irish, barrister and solicitor, also debt collector, trainee cabinetmaker, punter and football fan, rethinks an old case when one of his clients is shot after he is released from jail. The trail seems to lead to a framing and cover up involving corrupt policeman, a charity foundation, a multi-million dollar property deal and much else besides. But a midway interview with Police Minister, Garth Bruce, reverses Irish's understanding of the case creating an impossible and hopeless situation and even his new found girlfriend leaves. Meanwhile important witnesses are dying off and the prospects are not looking good, generally. Irish often considers giving up the case as a bad loss but persists.

Interleaved in all this is some shrewd insight into the horse racing business,(Dick Francis eat your heart out) led by former jockey Harry Strang and his oppo, Cam Delray. They are two of the well drawn characters in this book, some of which you want to meet and maybe drain a Tooheys, or two, with.

The tension and enjoyment keeps going right down to the wire and even after the satisfying ending there is still the matter of the 'plunge horse,' Dakota Dreaming, and the thousands of dollars riding on it to come.

The bad news is that *Bad Debts* is only published in Australia so you'll need a mate there or try the Harper Collins Australia web page:

www.harpercollins.com.au/order.htm
Martin Spellman

HACK BY JOHN BURNS, PAN BOOKS, PBK, £5.99, 0330354884

BARRY HARDNOSE TAKES THE Case might by an alternative title, of this first Max Chard mystery, after the powered by booze, fortified by fags, Steve Bell cartoon journo. John Burns is a former crime reporter for the *Express* and Max Chard, as Chief Crime Correspondent of *"a red-top tabloid,"* is a thinly disguised version of himself. The discovery of a *"green cuisine queen"* with a bullet in the brain in St. Catherine's Dock involves Chard in a fast moving celebrity scandal. The heart of this is a topical and effective theme that is spoiled by the cynicism and arrogance that pervades the rest of the book. The neat twist at the end is . the best part and reveals a real killer. Chard is the narrator of this story but it is difficult to identify with someone who seems to hate everybody and everything. This accompanied by populist, right-wing politics that is always assumed and too often stated. Apart from himself and his girlfriend, Rosie Bannister, all the other characters are thinly drawn when they are not clichés or mere cardboard cut-outs. Some professional journalists take a jaundiced view that there is nothing new under the sun (geddit?); it has all happened before and there is no need for constant attention for unforeseen developments. Things centre on themselves and the world of hacks in general. The information flow is outwards only and best accomplished after a lot of boozing and lunching. The result is well known and perhaps a reason why more people seem to read books on their way into work these days. The story has to be fast moving, in case you notice the flaws. I think it was George V Higgins who said if you use coincidence in a story it should always work against the main character. In this one there are several bluffs, one crucial to disclosing the main scandal, and they all pay off. The police seem to do nothing except fish corpses out of the dock and then go round the pub to collect their bung in return for some useless information. Even a basic police investigation would have linked the first victim to the killer and the gun in a short time and ruined even the ending twist. *Hack* in paperback is published with the hardback of *Snap* the second Max Chard mystery. Right that's my piece done—time for a livener?

Martin Spellman

INDIGO SLAM BY ROBERT CRAIS, ORION, £16.99, ISBN: 0752813439

FEATURING PRIVATE EYE ELVIS Cole, this one is a slow starter dealing with the children of currency forger Clark Hewitt. When a Seattle chapter of the Russian Mafia became involved I thought it showed some promise but then it fell back into formula stuff and the flaws became irritating. The initial tug of protecting the children is referred to so often it becomes a pain. Instead of developing the plot seems to centre on this aspect and other motives seem forced and contrived. Cole refuses to inform or involve the authorities, even when it is in his own interest, particularly with the Russian thug, Markov, who almost kills him. His efforts to protect the children get so out of hand that they reach irresponsible levels. Why does the youngest child, Charles, *return home* when, the text has already explained, he does not really have one and his own room is devoid of comforts?

Real, live, ugly, Russians have replaced the communist bogey. One of the Mafia is a Spetsnaz who fought in Afghanistan. It is all there—Cole allies himself with some anticommunist, Vietnamese—"Old wars were merging with new wars. The Russians had supported the North against Nguyen Dak, and the Russians still supported the North's Communist regime today. It would all be the same to these guys. A war they needed to win to go home." Thus two groups of counterfeiters, from former enemy states are given ideological motives when both are as criminal and anticommunist as each other.

Too many of these kind of books are creeping in and are likely to lead to a serious deterioration of the US hard boiled crime novel, in my view, as its essential realism is undermined. It is probably unstoppable because it is too easy—recycling anticommunist themes as anti-Russian Mafia, etc. They could be described as 'Third Cold War' novels. The first began in 1945, the second in the 1980s with Ronald Reagan's offensive, now this for the post Soviet era. The US could not beat the Soviet Union while it was around but now Russkies can be sorely thrashed from California to the New York island. But a new situation requires fresh treatment not the old one resprayed or dressed in new clothes.

So it all ends up as you might expect. Why it is called *Indigo Slam* is not explained and is a mystery to me.

Martin Spellman

NOWHERE TO HIDE BY JAMES ELLIOT, PIATKUS, £5.99, ISBN 074993042X

THIS IS TOP LINE crime and no mistake. An engaging and absorbing story of a high class call girl who not only witnesses the hit of a Mafia *accountant* but gets away with some cash and something else they want back very much. A deadly chase is on. The writing is crisp and tight—no hanging out or about here and at the end of each chapter you are dying to know what happens next and who is next to die. It is also clearly based on good research in the Intelligence Division and Organised Crime Unit of the New York Police Department.

Excitement and interest is maintained—just as Don Genero is arrested, which should solve her problems, all the stakes are increased. There are some real evil characters—it is almost a pity some were not saved for a sequel or two. The chapters on the hit at the *Golden Cockatoo* in New York's SoHo are a set piece in tension building.

There is also a great feel for both the

geography and atmosphere New York. You almost want to take the book and retrace the steps of some of the incidents. So many crime books are set or filmed in New York City it is worth reading a guide book, if you have not been there, as it will increase your enjoyment and appreciation of the setting. Where exactly is Central Park, the Upper West Side and Fifth Avenue?

If I had to find fault with it I would say it is about 40 pages too long. The pitcher of narrow escape probably goes to the well once too often. This is James Elliot's second book after *Cold, Cold Heart*.

Martin Spellman

ELEVEN DAYS BY DONALD HARSTAD, FOURTH ESTATE, £9.99

FOUR PEOPLE ARE FOUND murdered in a farming area in Iowa, and the killings bear the hallmarks of satanic ritual. Enter Deputy Sheriff Carl Houseman who drinks a lot of coffee and hardly ever sees his wife. He's one of the good guys who is suddenly catapulted into finding guys and gals who are very bad indeed.

The opening chapters intrigue as the Deputy examines the gruesome torture-murders. We're shown life in a countryside Sheriff's department, from the lack of modern technology to the almost endless junk food that the overworked police consume. There are a few humorous sideswipes at inadequate bosses plus glimpses into the lifes of people who aren't as dull or as undriven as they originally seem. But for this reader *Eleven Days* just didn't grip. It must be me because the endorsement on the front describes it as 'gripping and unsettling.' I was only unsettled by the number of doughnuts the police were eating. I guess I'm just not a police procedural fan. Not that this is a bad book. It's written with clarity and would be useful for s writer who wanted to replicate police work in an American farming community. And it's supposedly inspired by actual events, which might make it of inter-

est to some true crime fans. Harstad writes about what he knows with obvious sincerity and his style doesn't appear to be derivative. With its rising body count and unexpected shoot-outs *Eleven Days* would work better on celluloid than it does on paper, a rustic big brother to the movie *Seven*.

Carol Anne Davis

LIGHT ERRANT BY CHAZ BRENCHLEY. HODDER & STOUGHTON, £16.99

BEN, WHO FIRST appeared in Chaz Brenchley's novel *Dead Of Light*, is back. He goes home to do a favour for a friend and finds himself once more amongst his amoral relatives. Relatives who have the power to maim people at a distance, as Ben can himself. But Ben tries to use this supernatural gift to good effect whereas his kin uses it to terrorise the locals. Let battle commence...

Brenchley is superb at making the reader relive sensations, from the morning craving for strong coffee to the emotional and physical trauma of being beaten up. There are also nice touches of humour, such as a chapter called Ben Behaving Madly and a wry look at sanitary towel advertisements depicting blue menstrual blood.

This is quiet horror and—perhaps because I'm more used to reading fast-paced thrillers or edge of seat true crime—I found the first half of *Light Errant* dragged somewhat plot-wise. Later the images became more grotesquely rousing and helped compensate for the somewhat subdued storyline. There are some truly chilling scenes involving dead hostages, including one in which a man unwraps a severed head, fearing that it belongs to the girl he loves.

Brenchley has a nicely immediate style that is never derivative and encouragingly dialogue-intensive. Check out his outstanding short story collection *Blood Waters* (Flambard Press, 1996) for an example of the man at his best.

Carol Anne Davis

SLAUGHTERMATIC BY STEVE AYLETT, PHOENIX HOUSE, £9.99

WHEN A BANK ROBBERY begins with *"it's a money-or-your-life paradigm,"* you know you're headed for an alternate type reality where language is the most powerful weapon and Steve Aylett has more fun wielding that weapon than the Entropy Kid does with a Kafka gun. There are echoes of cyberpunk novels and of the word play of William Burroughs in this novel, but it flows relatively smoothly, or about as smoothly as it can flow when it's jumping from reality to well, maybe, not reality, who knows?

Mark Steyn wrote in the *Spectator* that the reason American kids are shooting up their schools, apart from the fact that they all have guns lying around their rooms the way I used to have, say, baseball cards, or slingshots, was that the constant playing with videogames had robbed violence of its context. Thus those of us who read dime novels, or listened to radio serials, or went to the movies, or watched TV, learned that violent behaviour had its human cost, even if that cost seemed minor and shooting baddies (or goodies) was a lot of fun.

But video games remove the context, and all that's left is that shooting anything that moves is a lot of fun. Of something like that. Well, if that's the country we're at, then this here is the national anthem. It's wonderfully inventive, throwing off conceits (which also means you never have to develop them!) and even giving these two dimensional vehicles for verbal fore-and-aft play a hint of another dimension. As Corey the Teller says *"there are two ways of bringing someone around to your way of thinking—softly, or hardly."* Aylett does neither, but it seems to work.

Michael Carlson

SOHO BLACK BY CHRISTOPHER FOWLER, WARNER, £8.99 ISBN 07515 25596

CHRISTOPHER FOWLER IS THE director of a film production company based in Soho,

'Distressingly brilliant'
THE GUARDIAN

SLAUGHTERMATIC

STEVE AYLETT

so it is reasonable to assume that he is writing what he knows in his latest novel, set in the film world of Soho. The author clearly loves films even though the production process appears to be even more harrowing than the contemporary horror with which he made his name. (One of his splatterpunk stories is so gruesome that years later it is still throbbing away malignantly somewhere inside my head.)

We are used to reading novels in which screenwriters complain about their lowly status in the business. This time we see the action through a good-hearted producer, someone perhaps too nice to succeed in a cut throat business. Until he drops down dead and then it's no more Mr Nice Guy. The convoluted plot would be ruined by summarising it, suffice to say that Bryant and May, the two cops with the contrasting working methods, have their work cut out. Fowler cuts between short scenes which evoke vivid mental pictures, skilfully interweaving a narrative that will keep you guessing. I liked the narrator so much that it was a wrench knowing that you won't see him for a few chapters or so.

There are echoes of many films here, often signposted although, as usual, one is never sure when homage becomes theft until the reason for all this finally becomes clear. Throughout he keeps you guessing if there will be a rational explanation for the occult and horror trimmings and the denouement will not let you down whether you are into horror, crime or just sharp, modern fun.

Elmore Leonard sometimes whets producers' appetites by suggesting in a novel that a character resembles a certain film star. Fowler has gone one further here by including a prospective review of the film that could be made from this book. There is also an amusing review of a film made by one of the bad guys. I don't know what he has against the angelic (and highly talented) Jane Horrocks though. Unless I am confusing the reviewer inside the novel with the author. As for Jeffrey Bernard having been an *"an intelligent, contented alcoholic;"* shome mistake surely. Pointless pedantry aside, film fanatics will enjoy this book as will Soho obsessive and anyone who likes a humorous, well-written tale with a proper beginning, middle and end, plenty of surface gloss and much entertaining bitchiness. A splendid entertainment with depth beneath the surface sparkle.

Mark Ramsden

SNAP BY JOHN BURNS, MACMILLAN, £16.99

MAX CHARD IS a hack, crime writing for the Daily Gazette, in fierce competition with the rest of the bottom feeders of Fleet Street. The quality of Chard's tabloid journalism is reflected in the book: Burns takes you through the progress from event to story through Chard's eyes, and you watch as lies, speculation, fantasy, and cruelty are melded to fit a template designed to render every story emotionally familiar and soothing: junk food for the eyes. Who needs Jerry Springer when you have the *Mail* and the *Sun*?

Burns is so good in his portrait of Fleet Street that it steals his novel's show. In fact, in the same way that the office politics of the Richmond morgue are usually the most interesting part of a Patricia Cornwell novel, here the newsroom politics of the Gazette provide a subplot more interesting than the murder itself.

Oh yes, there is a murder, of a Dutch au pair, and it might be drug related. This leads Chard in strange directions, and people keep bunging him money, just like people keep falling in love with Kay Scarpetta, and those who do are usually the killers. So too in *Snap*, though clues drop like lead balloons in the middle of the circles Chard runs around in. Not that he notices. Like a good tabloid story, *Snap* is fast paced, formulaic and clichéd. And like a tabloid, it provides a product that's recognisable, momentarily satisfying but ultimately not very rewarding.

Michael Carlson

SURVIVAL OF THE FITTEST BY JONATHAN KELLERMAN LITTLE, BROWN, £15.99

THIS IS THE TWELFTH of Jonathan Kellerman's books featuring psychologist Dr Alex Delaware. In Survival of the Fittest, Alex is forced to go undercover to infiltrate META, a sinister MENSA-type organisation which seems to have connections with theories of eugenics.

Alex and maverick LAPD detective Milo Sturgis suspect that the organisation may not be only concerned with rather unpleasant theories, but could have some connection with a series of murders which have been committed across a wide area of Los Angeles and over a considerable length of time. Initially all the murders seem unconnected and remain unsolved. However, all the victims are disabled in some way. There is also the matter of the inexplicable suicides of a brilliant young scientist and of a young cop known as a bit of a loner.

The case begins with the seemingly motiveless murder of the retarded fifteen year old daughter of an Israeli diplomat. The victim's father seems to be obstructing the LAPD investigation and has brought in his own police detective, Inspector Daniel Sharavi who brings with him an awful lot of undercover hardware and expertise in guerrilla warfare. After initial suspicion, Milo and Alex agree to work with the Israeli.

LA has so many murders. Kellerman creates a fine atmosphere of cynicism, burnout, and too many crimes to solve in a big, chaotic city. There are some very nasty and very mad people around and poor old world weary Milo Sturgis gives the impression of have met rather a lot of them. Milo is an appealing and attractive character, an overweight, gay cop, seen as a bit of a pariah in the LAPD. His relationship with Alex Delaware is a nice touch of humanity in a novel which is rather bleak about human nature.

Linking the apparently unconnected crimes which have been committed in a wide area of LA occupies most of the action. The search is for a very subtle serial killer and the target seems to slip through one's fingers at every turn. The eugenics connection is extremely sinister, as are some of the characters unearthed in META. The sense of tension towards the end is almost unbearable, as Alex goes undercover to try to find information from a particularly repulsive and well-drawn character, META siren and pert babe Zena Lambert.

The writing style is compelling. Kellerman excels at short dialogue and the minimum of description setting a scene. Though some of the technical stuff is a bit mindboggling, it has an authentic feel. Speaking as someone with a low boredom threshold for too buch overblown, boysy technical stuff I can say that I was never bored. Kellerman manages to keep the killer as a grey and mysterious presence right up to the end of the story. Is it a killer or group of killers? One sick individual or a whole organisation? How well will Alex's undercover persona stand up to the infiltration of META? One is given a subtle sense of unease about the undercover operation which proves to be well founded.

The best laid plans do go disastrously wrong at the end and one is left with the feeling that it is going to take Alex rather a long time to recover from this case. It all leaves a rather nasty taste in the mouth, and unfortunately seems all too plausible. If Alex and Milo can cope with another case after this, I will look forward to reading it.

Sara Grant-Thorald

TOO CLOSE BY HILARY NORMAN, PIATKUS, £16.99

NICK MILLER IS IN the wrong place at the wrong time.

As a child he moves next door to seven year old Holly Bourne and an obsession that will profoundly effect both their lives begins to grow. Holly's elder brother Eric has recently been drowned in an accident in a local pond. Eric was Holly's hero and fall guy, taking the blame for all her misdemeanours, protecting her and giving her unconditional love. Holly blames herself for the accident and begins to close down emotionally. She also feels that her mother blames her for the accident.

As soon as Holly sees Nick she knows that everything has changed. She emerges from the emotional darkness. She knows that a higher power has sent him to replace Eric. *"Nick Miller had come to change Holly's live. He belonged to her."*

In the first few pages Hilary Norman sets the scene for Holly's sinister and dangerous obsession with Nick, which builds from a childhood friendship to an intense adolescent sexual relationship and on into college days. When Holly becomes increasingly possessive and unbalanced in her behaviour Nick finally chucks her for good.

He rebuilds his life, meets another woman, gets married, has a baby and Holly

Bourne is a distant and unpleasant memory.

Holly has always flirted with petty crime, as a way of controlling and testing first Eric and then Nick. She thrives on power, planning a way Nick will beg for her forgiveness, will need and want her forever. Brilliant and very attractive, Holly has no difficulty in using her attributes and knowledge as a top lawyer to make trouble for Nick and things get very nasty indeed, particularly when Holly goes missing and ends up once again living next door to Nick without his knowledge.

Hilary Norman creates the slow build up of tension in the story very cleverly. There is an economy in the writing which allows her to set the scene very quickly before heightening the tension. Obsession, particularly sexual obsession, could seem a little hackneyed a theme, but the way the plot twists and turns does not make for a dull read. I was also a little suspicious of the harpy woman versus the delightful cosy family unit plot, a la Fatal Attraction. However, the characters are too well drawn for this to become irritating; as Holly becomes more deranged, she becomes at once more pathetic and sympathetic. Nick's wife is a barely reformed alcoholic and hardly perfect, the stress she is under constantly threatening to drive her back to the booze.

At the end one feels sadness more than anything else. Early tragedy blights an already disturbed character and the scene is set for disaster. Norman creates a fine sense of claustrophobia for Nick. His very existence is the reason for Holly's madness, and he constantly feels the guilt that he could have acted differently, perhaps in some way he is responsible for his own problems.

This is a 'this could happen to you' sort of book, demonstrating that one can find oneself in a very nasty situation just by living in the wrong house, particularly when the dispute is about more that the height of your hedge.

Sara Grant-Thorald

THE MAMMOTH BOOK OF TRUE CRIME (NEW EDITION) BY COLIN WILSON, ROBINSON, £6.99, ISBN 1854875191

"THE MOST COMPREHENSIVE and fascinating collection in the history of crime" reads the by-line on the back of the book. Does the book it live up to this claim? Er, yes, and no.

I first heard of Colin Wilson several years ago, when I read a book that he had written about Jack the Ripper. Being, to my mother's mind, slightly sick (and more than a little fascinated as to why that mystery had never been solved), I read the book cover to cover because it promised to shed new light onto the perpetrator of those crimes.

Anyway, although I enjoyed the book immensely, I was in no better position after reading the book than before. The usual suspects, some hint of a clue – and some interesting psychological reasoning, but no real light shed anywhere.

When I started to read this book, and it IS a mammoth, I tried to shut out any misgivings that I had about it. If you are interested in a catalogue of crimes, ranging from blackmail to railway murders and beyond, then THIS is the book for you.

The book is separated into 70 or so chapters, each dealing with a particular echelon of crime, with a neat summing up at the end from Mr Wilson.

There are a few criticisms (sorry Mr Wilson). As each chapter deals with a different aspect of crime, the author makes no distinction between cases and, if you are unfamiliar with those cases, it is easy to get confused. I would have preferred each case to be dealt with separately – or at least introduced separately.

The other criticism is that Mr Wilson occasionally refers to cases that do not appear in the book, most noticeably that of Jack the Ripper and The Moors Murderers. While these cases are infamous, not everyone is conversant with the kind of detail that Mr Wilson alludes to.

To its credit, this book is probably the most up to date true crime book in print at present, as it mentions the Gloucester Street murders in its pages alongside those committed at Rillington Place. But, because it is so packed, there is little opportunity to delve deeper, which is probably a good thing if the truth be known.

The Mammoth Book Of True Crime is an excellent reference book, and well worth reading for Mr Wilson's analysis of each genre. This is not a bed time book (I tried it and spent the night awake), but it IS a fascinating catalogue of the most horrendous crimes that can be committed against another human being.

Helen Bryant

TRUE TO FORM BY YVONNE ANTROBUS. VISTA, £5.99, ISBN: 0575603690

THIS IS YVONNE ANTROBUS' first novel, staged against the elite world of horse racing.

The heroine, Sukie Buckley, is a widow who tries to continue the lifestyle she built up whilst married. An ex-boarding school girl, Sukie resorts to catering and cleaning jobs to make sure that she can keep up with her old set of friends. These friendships are, at best, one sided, with Sukie being there for them in their hour of need while they continue to play at their lives, convinced that she can handle anything that they, or life, throw at her.

Her friendship with Amanda, which has existed since boarding school, is stretched to the limit when Sukie discovers Amanda's husband, Jerry Wearing, dead at their London flat. Jerry is discovered in rather a compromising position, wearing nothing but his old school tie and Georgio perfume (not his normal tastes by any means).

Using her old cleaning job to case his offices at Amanda's request, Sukie discovers a card advertising an Escort Agency – and the game is a foot (or perhaps in this case, a hoof).

Her suspicions roused, Sukie decides to play amateur sleuth and begins to make enquiries. Jerry's partnership with two others within their exclusive circle of friends over the ownership of a racehorse, Triumvirate, is thrust into the limelight time and again when the other two owners are attacked. The first, Rosamund Officer, is attacked, the second, George Graham-Jones, is left hanging in his own barn, dressed to the nines, having apparently committed suicide believing his wife to be having an adulterous affair.

As the death toll, and apparent accidents, continue to rise within Sukie's small group of friends and associates, Sukie is forced to play a dangerous game of cat and mouse to find Jerry's killer. Someone is systematically destroying the Triumvirate partnership – but who? Can the deaths and accidents be attributed to one person, or even to one group of persons?

As the net draws closer Sukie finds herself wondering whom she can turn to, or truly trust. Can she confide her fears to her newest acquaintance Bob Tiechgraeber, recently arrived from the USA with a strange passion for the sport of Kings? Or can she trust Henry Whippet, the playboy jockey who often rides for the partnership and does strange things to her pulse rate?

Her investigations take her from London to Newmarket, Royal Ascot and into the face of danger at every turn. Sukie must unravel this Chinese puzzle and discover who, or what, is picking its way through the horse racing elite one by one.

True To Form started off slowly. The way that the characters were introduced was often confusing, so I had to keep thumbing through the pages to redefine relationships, but the story line was good, and it ended with a nice little twist.

Definitely one for Saturday night bath time, with a good wine and some chocolate!

Helen Bryant

FIVE PUBS, TWO BARS AND A NIGHTCLUB BY JOHN WILLIAMS BLOOMSBURY £9.99, ISBN 0747540578

I THOUGHT I HAD cornered the market in titles twice as long as the average person's attention span but, no, here is John Williams with *Five Pubs, Two Bars And A Nightclub*. I'm usually prejudiced against short stories but, as these are all set in Cardiff, and some of the same characters weave in and out of this collection, the whole thing is as satisfying an experience as reading a novel. Already I can sense vague mutterings. Did he just say Cardiff? Isn't that in Wales? Yes, but this is the way Elmore Leonard would write about it—spare, funny, non-judgmental and with the right music in the background.

There is no doubt John has researched this city, as the Cardiff-based *Bloody Valentine* proved. This courageous attempt to investigate a miscarriage of justice led to death threats and the pulping of an early edition due to a possible libel action from the Police. Not surprisingly, John now writes fiction. His protagonists are mixed race villains, mostly portrayed as loveable rogues but we are also reminded that 99 per cent of all known villains are crap, which can't be said often enough. This is not a book for the armchair hardman. It doesn't glamorise these ham-fisted goons but it doesn't condemn either. It's just the way things are.

This collection is certainly up to date, what with the Nation of Islam and faked documentary films about drug-smuggling. The pirate radio story is a little gem and the Welsh Angry Brigade story stirred uncomfortable memories of the underground scene in Liverpool, where I grew up.

How much you like this book probably ultimately depends on how much you like days and evenings spent watching smoke circulate in pubs while your vision gradually goes out of focus. It's a slow burn book, saturated in alcohol, dope and music. It does not aspire to glitz and glamour. It is not contrived or fake. Real people do the things they actually would do at the pace they would do it. There are occasional surprises but no tricks. No one gratuitously uses words like iatrogenic, no-one turns into a monkey—in other words it's not Will Self. And thank fuck for that.

The humour is gentle, the pace reflective—life as it is actually lived rather than on the telly or in the movies. People say what they actually would say rather than what a scriptwriter straining for effect would have them say.

Although John recorded the world's first Welsh hip-hop record in 1986 and has wide musical tastes, he is not afraid to confess to liking folk music. Perhaps the reason John and partner Charlotte Greig (who performs folk-based music) have moved back to Cardiff is to be able to practise this most secret of perversions in the relative peace of a smaller city. Although he may have just returned to Cardiff to run for Mayor. After all, which writer could possibly have the necessary gravitas to compete with Jeffrey Archer in London? I mention folk music because these tales are like modern folk songs—honest and memorable. Cue collapse of Bloomsbury marketing department terrified of any association with terminally unfashionable folk music. Start again—this is a celebration of real life rather than trick endings, pointless puzzles or macho posturing. A warm, good-hearted book.

Mark Ramsden

ACID CASUALS BY NICHOLAS BLINCOE, SERPENT'S TAIL, £5.99, ISBN 1852427086

SERPENT'S TAIL ORIGINALLY published Nicholas Blincoe's debut novel in 1995. It was reprinted in 1997, and has now been re-issued with a new 'club mix' style cover in place of the inspired original cover, depicting a scene-of-the-crime type body-outline, in white powder rather than chalk.

Acid Casuals is a terrifically fun novel, excitingly plotted—despite, or in spite, of what might appear to be a most unlikely hit-job involving a transexual with a penchant for giving blow jobs—and well-paced throughout. It is also genuinely funny in places, and as such, should be read with caution, because laughing out loud on the train can cause people to look at you as if you are the carriage looney. Usually, novels that try to be funny—especially those written by 'comedians'—are tedious, requiring the reader to wade through so many over-long scenes which are intended to be humorous but feel like limp padding. Blincoe, however, manages to introduce scenes or lines that are genuinely funny, and places them in such a way that the plot never loses its impetus.

Although it's four years old, it's still fresh and well worth a read. For those who don't know, the plot involves the aforementioned transexual, now called Estela, the Manchester club scene, a money laundering operation, a manic VJ (that's video-jockey) called John Quay (aka Junk) with only one eye (the other one lost to shooting speed), car chases, shoot-outs, some sex and lots of drugs.

The moral, for those of you who like books with a moral, is simple: 'drugs can make you into the kind of person you need to be.'

Acid Casuals would make a terrific *Budda of Suburbia*-type four-parter on Channel Four, but that is not to be. Instead there is a film planned. As long ago as *Crime Time* 9, the film adaptaion of *Acid Casuals* was 'at the script stage', written not by Blincoe, but by Mike Hodges *[Who he? Ed.]*—apparently Hodges had got the script as far as a second draft, which Blincoe described as 'really good.' However, there's been no further news on how the film's shaping up since then, but let's hope it's in production. Until then, powder your nose, charge into Waterstones with your piece blazing, and grab a copy of *Acid Casuals*.

Eddie Duggan

KNEELING AT THE ALTAR BY JIM LUSBY, VICTOR GOLLANCZ, £9.99, ISBN: 0575066067

I GROANED WHEN I saw the cover blurb for Jim Lusby's latest McCadden mystery. After all, it seems as if these days it's compulsory to have child abuse in fiction, whether Booker Prize winner or crime potboiler. On balance, this book mountain adds little to our understanding of the subject—fortunately Lusby avoids the cursory and fashionable treatment of the subject to develop instead a complex picture of rumour, gossip and suspicion. The prevalence of hidden agendas in the Waterford-based cast of characters all make for a world in which investigation is impeded by self-defence mechanisms which unwittingly block the search for a missing boy.

One of the great strengths of the narrative is the way it hinges on a contrast between a tight-knit community and the outsiders it despises. Rather then rip the events straight from the headlines, it shows instead how irrational fears can make ordinary people into the raw material of a lynch mob. Lusby writes as one who can get his characters' dirty laundry out in public without turning it into the Jerry Springer show.

Presenting us with a provincial detective inspector who avoids stoicism and forced eccentricity makes for an engaging tale. Doubts as to whether 'kneeling at the altar' refers to the local Christian Brothers school or fellatio in US prison slang are skilfully sown in our mind. What lets it down is the dialogue where, with the exception of the council estate characters who eff and blind a bit, all the characters sound the same. Not everyone has to be Philip Marlowe, but it's nice when the creations on the page have distinctive voices of their own.

Graham Barnfield

THE BLESSING FILE BY CAROLYN MORWOOD, WOMEN'S PRESS, £6.99, ISBN: 0704345862

Lyn Blessing is an Antique Bookseller and aficionado with a problem... well, actually several problems, but one in particular.

Her City Centre bookstore is being haunted by her dead sister's doppelganger. To make matters worse, her boyfriend (sorry, her ex-boyfriend, if *only* he'd get the message) won't leave her alone and keeps cluttering up her shop front with flowers—and her 'phone with messages.

After several coincidental meetings with 'Adele' in and around the shop environment, Lyn is convinced that the girl is in trouble. The meetings in her shop have a particular pattern, and Lyn becomes increasingly convinced that there is something fishy going on.

Her own curiosity, combined with the striking resemblance between her sister and the mystery girl, forces her to investigate further...with near disastrous consequences. On one occasion, she is chased down a dark alley by a stranger intent on capturing the evidence she is carrying regarding the meetings in her shop. On another she is hospitalised following a brutal attack at her childhood home, and is forced to rely on some of her oldest friends.

There does, however, seem to be a common between the various incidents, the young girl, and a young man with pale hazel eyes, whom Lyn dubs 'the watcher'. But there is someone else, in the shadows, pulling the strings...and Lyn needs to find out who that is, and what is happening around her home and shop.

Her investigations throw her from pillar to post, forcing her to re-evaluate old friendships, and her own guilt at not being there for her sister before she died. Not knowing who to trust, she turns to the police, but the upper echelons are unable, or unwilling, to pursue the investigation to the depth that she knows it requires.

Finally she makes the connection between the strange visitations by the mystery girl each Friday lunchtime and the watcher... but it is too late for Lyn to help the girl—who is obviously in over her head

"A great book. The hardest, purest American prose since Faulkner's *Sanctuary*."
Terry Southern

BEAM ME UP, SCOTTY

Michael Guinzburg

and desperate to escape.

An excellent book, with enough twists and turns to make you dizzy. I was completely engrossed—and must admit I accused just about every character of being the puppet master. I was surprised (yet again) when that person was revealed (although I had my suspicions, you understand).

This is Carolyn Morwood's first crime novel—and I for one am eagerly awaiting publication of the next.

Helen Bryant

BEAM ME UP, SCOTTY BY MICHAEL GUINZ-BURG, REBEL INC., £6.99, ISBN 086241-845-3

SEX, DRUGS, violence, gore by the bucket. Charles Bukowski this ain't, though, not by a long shot. Imagine a Beavis and Butthead version of Pulp Fiction, with a lot more drugs and just one gun, and you're halfway there. I strongly suspect that this is one of those books where, if you don't like them, people accuse you of "not getting it." Well, folks, there's nothing to get in this one, trust me...

Crack addict Ed has finally made it through rehab and is now in the process of getting his life back together. His main focal point in a world full of temptation is HDA, *Hard Drugs Anonymous*, a mildly amusing support group (Lesbians! Transvestites! Sex-hungry hookers!) founded on the teachings of two rehabilitated Midwestern farmers and filled with outcasts from all corners of society, thrown together by the need for speed/crack/coke/paint-thinner/sausage rolls/name your poison. In between group therapy, though, Ed discovers that there is a high to be experienced that beats even crack: namely, killing off drug dealers.

What starts out as a very peculiar way of dealing with his addiction soon becomes a new addiction in itself for Ed. And that's about it, really – we follow him through the book as he goes to support group meetings and kills people. One wonders whether the book will pick up anything as it rambles on – a plot, tempo, characterisation, anything. But no such luck.

See, this book's idea of fun is to feature a lethal bull terrier by the name of Natasha. Oh, how we laughed. From the moment the dog was introduced, I wondered how many pages it would take until it ran off with somebody's penis in its muzzle. True, longer than I thought (page 213), but this still serves as an example of the predictability we're dealing with here. Even worse than that are the book's pathetic attempts at satire. Poking fun at support groups and support group jargon is easy enough. Unfortunately, the author fails to succeed in even that, instead falling back on repeating over and over again the graphic confessionals of the group's members. Your point, please, sir? To be fair, though, I should mention that there is one truly hilarious scene where Ed tries to find out if there's a support group for people who kill people:

"Are you an overeater? A gambler? A debtor?"

"Keep going."

"Are you a gay fundamentalist?"

"Please, lady, it's bad, really bad."

Apart from this bit, though, the book falls flat on its face most of the time. The language is quite fruity and used to such an extent that the shock value soon wears off. Besides, 'motherfucker' looks slightly silly when it's spelled 'mafocka' – sorry, but that's how it is. The characters are two-dimensional and sometimes behave in thoroughly inexplicable ways; why, for instance, does Ed's wholesome, apple-cheeked Midwestern wife turn into a drug-addicted hooker halfway through the novel? Is this supposed to tell us that 'it could happen to anyone?'

It's all rather annoying, really, because one keeps thinking that with a bit more effort (well a lot really), this could have been the *Catch-22* of drug literature. Oh well. All in all, the best thing to say about this book is that its tremendously misleading title (referring to the crack addict's mantra, spoken before drug intake) will probably make sure the book ends up under the Christmas trees of Trekkies all over the world. Blimey, are they in for a surprise...

Frank Thielmann

CALL THE DEAD AGAIN BY ANN GRAINGER, HEADLINE, £5.99, ISBN: 074725642X

CALL THE DEAD AGAIN is set in Bamford, a small country village which has, if you are to believe the majority of the inhabitants, been left untouched by the crime wave that has engulfed the rest of the UK.

Our heroine, Meredith Mitchell, works for the Foreign Office and, on her way home from a course, picks up a lone hitchhiker near the outskirts to the village. Her companion for the last stage of her journey, is an extremely confident, but secretive, young woman who asks to be dropped off at Tudor Lodge, the family home of the Penhallows.

Despite her misgivings, Meredith drops

her off and continues her journey home, fuelled by the promise of a quiet weekend with her partner, Superintendent Alan Markby. By the next morning, however, all hope of her quiet weekend is dashed when he is called to attend an incident at Tudor Lodge. The owner, Andrew Penhallow, a Brussels based Lawyer, has been found dead in his back garden dressed in his pyjamas and holding a water bottle.

The murder investigation plunges the couple into a web of intrigue and soon Mitchell and Markby have more than their strange love life to ponder.

Members of the press quickly swamp the village, and pretty soon tongues are wagging about old arguments between Andrew and various members of the community, not to mention the odd whisper about him leading a double life.

The Police seem to have enough on their hands attempting to investigate the circumstances leading up to, and including, Alan Penhallows murder, when a series of small time theft's around the village come to light—and an attempted murder of another member of the community add to their workload. But the question remains—who actually killed Alan Penhallow?

With the murder happening so quickly after the arrival of the mysterious young lady, Markby has a few questions of his own to ask. Who is the mystery girl and what was her relationship with the late Alan Penhallow? *Is* she responsible for this seemingly senseless murder?

As Markby, ably aided by Mitchell, moves closer to the truth the intrigue deepens and the final twist to the plot is completely unexpected—as they should be in all good mystery books!

A really good read—this novel comes highly recommended for a long train journey—it kept me entertained during a particularly 'interesting' trek from Kidderminster to Birmingham Snow Hill.

This is the eleventh book in the Mitchell and Markby series of murder mysteries, and, if this book is anything to go by, I shall be off down to the bookstore to get the other ten.

Helen Bryant

POINT OF ORIGIN BY PATRICIA CORNWELL, LITTLE, BROWN, £16.99

THERE HAVE BEEN DISSENTING voices recently when Cornwell's amazing success has been discussed. Did her disappointing last book, *Hornet's Nest,* signal that the splendid run of Kay Scarpetta thrillers was played out? Thankfully, this latest thriller is Cornwell back on form, all cylinders firing. When the psychopathic Carrie Grethen breaks free from custody, Scarpetta and her group of intimates and associates are soon in deep water again. Blaming them for the death of her equally homicidal partner, Grethen inaugurates a campaign of terror while Kay tries to solve the problem of an incinerated body in a farmhouse. The usual riveting medical detail is matched by the kind of grisly narrative that the author is mistress of, and enthusiasts can relax in the knowledge that Cornwell's star looks set to glitter for quite some time yet.

Barry Forshaw

ANGELS FLIGHT BY MICHAEL CONNELLY, ORION, £9.99

HOWARD ELIAS, A high-profile black lawyer, is murdered and his body is dumped in a funicular in downtown LA. As Elias specialised in lawsuits alleging police brutality and racism, most LAPD cops are reluctant to touch the case. When detective Harry Bosch is put in charge, his investigations in his own backyard are, unsurprisingly, explosive in their results. Connelly's *Blood Work* was a book that leapt out from the dizzying mass of thrillers published recently, and here again he succeeds in ringing the changes with a novel that has both the bite of authenticity and a grasp of plotting that makes Bosch's descent into a world of corruption and betrayal a truly splendid read. The beleaguered detective protagonist is characterised with assurance and wry understanding.

Barry Forshaw

CRUEL TO BE KIND BY TIM WILSON, HEADLINE, £5.99, ISBN: 0747256543

WHAT A BOOK! *What* a book! Oops, sorry, have I already said that? Well, blow me, what a book! (And, no I do not know Tim Wilson, nor am I set to gain financially from this recommendation—it is just a good book).

I had, until recently, never heard of Tim Wilson (sorry Tim, but truth must out)… nor had I any inkling, when picked up this paperback, that I would spend the entire day avoiding people so that I could finish the book in peace. I am reliably informed that Mr Wilson has written other novels—which I shall have to acquire at a later date just to make sure that this wasn't a fluke.

Anyway, I waffle (no surprise there then)—down to the story…Laura Ritchie is a recently bereaved widow with a seven year old son. Her husband, David, is involved in a road traffic accident and is killed by a local builder whilst on his way to the train station one morning. Up until that moment Laura had been considering leaving him and putting her unhappy marriage behind her, until, of course, fate plays her ace card.

She is left in a vulnerable state, as she discovers that David was heavily in debt—and leading a double life. Just when she thinks that things can't get any worse—they do. The van driver, full of remorse, turns up at the family home… and offers his condolences and assistance. He is convinced that he is totally responsible for taking a loving father and husband away from his family.

Despite Laura's best efforts to steer him away from what he considers his duty to the family, she finds herself fending off a man who is hell bent on becoming their guardian angel—and won't take no for an answer, or any other answer either!

Laura tries to break free from his unwanted attention, realising that his offer of assistance is rapidly turning into the need to totally control both her and her sons' life.

Tim Wilson does not just write about the situation, he allows you to begin to identify with the characters… and you find yourself completely wrapped up in the situation with the same feelings of hopelessness as Laura herself.

This book is compulsive reading, from the very first time that you are introduced to Mike, the earnest and completely insane van driver, you start to feel uneasy about his overtures… and rightly so. But, hey, not all angels are good.

Helen Bryant

CRIME SANS FRONTIÉRES, BY CHRISTOPHER BELTON, MINERVA PRESS, PBK, £6.99

MY DOUBTS ABOUT THIS book were first raised when I read the title. I'm no French scholar, but shouldn't it be 'frontières', with an e-grave, rather than an e-acute? Also, on further examination, Minerva Press seems to be something other than the Minerva we all know and love. Whoever they are, they should have employed proof readers or copy editors to remove structures like 'He must of been hit,' and 'to walk to towards the elevator,' as well as the wrong kind of 'it's', although the latter misuse is becoming widespread in recent times, as our own editor knows full well.

But what of the story, I hear you ask. It's a tale of computer crime, launched by an underground Japanese criminal organisation, with far-reaching effects around the world. Accordingly, the first chapter deals with the activities of a number of different software bandits in such detailed computer-speak that reading it was like attempting to plough through a user-hostile software manual. Anyone with little or no experience of computing would, I'm sure, give the book up at that point.

If you can survive this initial baptism by fire, the going gets better. We travel to Geneva, where an international organisation to combat computer crime is alerted to the activities of the criminal group by the deaths of key persons in various other countries. Everything points to Japan, and so two experts are sent there from Switzerland to investigate further. As they begin their probes they place themselves and their Japanese hosts in considerable danger from the rogue elements, resulting in a bloody climax which is described in graphic detail.

The author seems to know Japan well, and also the customs of its people, and this aspect of the book works well. Despite a rather slow start it eventually builds into a fast-paced read, which, apart from the caveats already made, should be of interest to those with a penchant for the subject of computer crime.

Dave Moore

DANGEROUS DAVIES AND THE LONELY HEART BY LESLIE THOMAS, HEINEMANN; £15.99 ISBN: 0434004413

CONFESSION TIME. IN my early teens I picked up one of Leslie Thomas' Virgin Soldiers books which was lying around our house and eagerly searched it looking for the 'dirty bits'. I didn't find any, and haven't picked up one of his books since. Prejudice at such an early age! Ho-hum.

So when *Dangerous Davies and the Lonely Heart* dropped through my letter-box, up popped that old familiar voice declaring "*Hmm, I won't bother reading that*." But then I turned a few pages and something curious happened ... I was hooked,

Those of you who've read my reviews before may have noticed that I'm not averse to having my crime fiction leavened with a little humour. Leslie Thomas has it by the tanker load. Why wasn't I told?

Dangerous Davies and the Lonely Heart is Thomas' fourth novel in an occasional series featuring the eponymous Davies. In the three previous outings Davies was employed by the Met, where he acquired his epithet—he was given cases too frightening for others.

At the beginning of the latest novel he is attending a Police dinner which turns out to be his retirement *do*—only owing to an administrative error nobody has told him. Now out on the streets of North London, Davies sets up as a Private Eye (wisely deciding not to call his agency *Dangerous Investigations*), and immediately finds life as an independent investigator far harsher than the Police force he is used to—"*lots of other blokes are with you, all plodding on together, like an army*." Instead he bumbles along pursuing several initially unsuccessful investigations which involve, amongst other things, finding a missing scientist and tracking down a murderer who is preying on women registered at a lonely hearts agency.

But with Thomas the plot, thoroughly entertaining as it is, is not everything. Characters are obviously his trademark, and in this novel there's a whole parade of marvellously quirky creations, from Davies' sidekick Mod, the amateur philosopher struggling with the Information Highway, to Davies' estranged wife Dora, with whom he lives (separate rooms) in a Willesden boarding house. His characters exist almost on dialogue alone with minimal amplification from Thomas.

This is a funny, touching, warm, candy floss of a book.

David Howard

THE BREAKER BY MINETTE WALTERS, MACMILLAN, £16.99 ISBN: 0333747127

FIRSTLY, I SHOULD point out that I'm such a fan of Minette Walters that I'd probably find dramatic tension in one of her shopping lists. That said, I should also say that I found her last novel *The Echo* a disappointment.

Now she's back with her sixth novel, *The Breaker*, which is by some way the best crime story I have read this year.

Minette Walters is almost unique among modem crime writers in eschewing a series character. Instead, she uses either Police officers or journalists—Walters is a former magazine editor, as her investigators, and in *The Breaker* the task falls to the Hampshire constabulary.

More particularly it falls to PC Nick Ingram, who is not only the upholder of all that is good but is also an old fashioned romantic lead, compared to the more blatant sexual charms of porn movie actor and principal suspect, Steven Harding.

Suspect in what ? Well, murder of course, but Minette Walters is far from being a formulaic crime writer. She's always pushing against the barriers of crime fiction, searching out the new, and in this case the topical date-rape drug, Rohypnol, is central to her story.

The plot revolves around the discovery of young pregnant mother Kate Hill-Sumner, who is found raped and murdered on a Hampshire beach near the yachting town of Lyminton—the setting for Walters' investigation.

As ever, she is brilliant at drawing her readers into the story. After two chapters of *The Breaker* I was so hooked that I refused to answer my phone.

Complications to the plot arrive swiftly. Kate's three year old daughter is found walking the streets of a town twenty miles away, apparently abandoned. Her husband is away at a conference in Liverpool but nobody saw him for twelve hours either side of the time of his wife's death. As the story unfolds we learn that Kate was disliked by many and that her marriage was more one of convenience than a love match. Walters squeezes the plot, pointing the arrow of suspicion to all points of the compass before unravelling the complex strands in an exhilarating final few pages.

What is it that makes Minette Walters work so engrossing? She plots well, but so do many other writers. Her characters leap off the page, but again the same is true of many of her colleagues. Ditto, her dialogue, which has greatly improved since her debut novel *The Ice House*(I 992). The secret

perhaps is in her rare and intuitive understanding of human nature. She gets beneath the skin of her characters, understands their pain, and then switches on the pressure until they crack.

The Breaker confirms Minette Walters position not only at the top of the British crime writers tree, but flying some way above it.

David Howard

FADE TO GREY BY JANE ADAMS, MACMILLAN, £16.99, ISBN: 0333721543

JANE ADAMS leapt to prominence with *The Greenway*, stumbled slightly with *Cast the First Stone*, and regained her footing with last year's *Bird*. Now she's back with her fourth novel and the third to feature DI Mike Croft.

Is it any good? Well, yes of course it is. Adams couldn't write a bad book if she tried but *Fade to Grey* just falls short of the truly outstanding. That said, this is her most ambitious work yet, told with that familiar lack of sensationalism that has always been her trademark.

Fade to Grey begins with two crimes investigated by police forces two hundred miles apart. One is the latest attack in East Anglia by a serial rapist; the other a murdered woman found in a burnt out car in Devizes. A hundred pages into the story the investigations converge when the name of one murdered woman is found in the address book of another.

Jane Adams employs cinematic techniques to rapidly cut from scene to scene, often with time lapses as brief as ten minutes. It's a staccato effect that begins confusingly but ends up working exceptionally well. It's also the ideal device for contrasting the chalk and cheese personalities of the two investigating officers. Adams has always been good at portraying the teamwork that's the backbone of modern police procedure, and DI Mike Croft is teamwork personified. On the other hand, Charlie

Morrow, heading the Devizes investigation, seems at times to have escaped from an episode of *The Sweeney*.

Pornography and snuff movies form the basis of an all too believable plot littered with broken lives and the quick fixes that lead them deeper into obsession. Adams keeps the suspense right to the final pages. Her depiction of violence is admirably brief, serving only to propel the story to its chilling conclusion.

One day Jane Adams will write the seminal psychological thriller. *Fade to Grey* isn't quite it, but by any yardstick it's a top notch book by a rapidly maturing talent,

David Howard

SURVEILLANCE AND THE CITY BY DOLAN CUMMINGS, URBAN RESEARCH GROUP, £7.00

WHO'S WATCHING YOU? No-one's entirely sure, but it's common knowledge that a mixture of local authorities, city centre managers and police officers can conjure up your mugshot at the flick of a switch. As this incisive pamphlets points out, gone are the days when would-be private eyes were chewed out over hopelessly grainy images that produced too few convictions. Today CCTV allows all-comers to get results while staying indoors for a stakeout.

It doesn't stop there. As Cummings shows, CCTV is simply the most high-profile part of a broader culture of organised distrust. He looks at how a wide range of quasi-legal categories and institutions—from 'anti-social behaviour' to 'case conferences'—are blurring the distinct between civil and criminal law, public and private life. Pulling together the strands of a wider trend, he analyses the way that new assumptions effectively underpin the control and monitoring of estates and city streets: guilty until proven innocent. In the process, many everyday activities—fixing your car, playing your stereo—can be reclassified as crimes. Particularly striking is the case of David and John Finnie in Coventry, served with an exclusion order from Stoke Heath estate and, in John's case, sentenced to a term of imprisonment for breaching it. Both had already served custodial sentences—presumably paying their debt to society—for the very offences which brought about these new, retrospective penalties. The underlying logic is that they were clearly 'criminal types'.

In the age of Jack Straw, some might find Cummings's conclusions controversial: 'more freedom, rather than less, is more likely to generate a sense of common purpose in the city'. Nevertheless, if you want a spot-on portrait of contemporary behind-the-scenes policing, *Surveillance and the City* makes disturbing reading.

Graham Barnfield

DYING FOR POWER BY JUDITH CUTLER, PIATKUS, £5.99, ISBN: 0749930810

DYING FOR POWER IS the fifth in a series of books by Judith Cutler about a female college lecturer, Sophie Rivers, who is outspoken, and confident—most of the time.

The book starts in Berlin, where Sophie is enjoying (for want of a better word) a holiday with her gay male friend Courtney. Here she meets Greg, an Australian engineer currently working on the re-design of Berlin in readiness for the Millennium. Despite walking out on him half way through the holiday due to cultural differences, Greg becomes a central character to the book (and, despite holding the same reservations as Sophie, I couldn't help myself admiring the man by the end of the book).

Returning to Birmingham, and to her job as an English lecturer at William Murdock College of Further Education, she is surprised when one of her ex-students presents himself as her new boss.

To make matters worse, since Dan Godfrey's arrival, together with that of Ms Fairborn as Principal, strange things have been occurring at the college. More than their fare share of arson attempts, including one that results in a fatality, a near fatal attack on a fellow lecturer, and, ultimately, her own suspension after reported inappropriate sexual behaviour towards members of the Asian community who attend her class.

However, these strange occurrences are not limited to Sophie's professional environment, the cross-cultural community project she was involved in is raised to the ground following (suprisingly) an arson attack, her car windshield is broken, her house is targeted for an interesting, and particularly vile, deposit.

Slowly Sophie, ably assisted by Greg (the Australian almost boyfriend), Chris (her ex-lover who is a DCI) and Afzal (more than a friend and a fine lawyer), starts to piece together the evidence... and their discoveries put Sophie in mortal danger.

Could all of these events be linked in some way? Is there a hidden agenda at William Murdocks', and would that agenda be more important than the livelihood, and indeed the very lives, of those unwittingly involved? And who, if anyone, is the lynch pin?

Set in and around Central Birmingham, *Dying For Power* is a strange mixture of places I know, have walked past, and have heard of—and a compelling mystery/thriller.

I could do no more than read the book... and stumble around trying to tie all of the loose ends, in both of Sophie's lives, whilst doing so.

I was unprepared for such a realistic view of cross-cultural friendships—and for the twists and turns in the plot.

Greg wasn't so bad after all—why? Read the book and you'll find out.

Helen Bryant

BABY TALK BY JUDITH JONES, CONSTABLE, £16.99

CHILDREN SEEM TO BE a fashionable subject for crime writers at present and here's another variation—not child abuse or child abduction, but child 'grasses.'

Bill James (for it is he by another plume) has always excelled on exploring and exposing that grey area of the law where police and villainy begin to sing from the same song-book. With children informants James could scarcely have chosen a better subject to display his 'dirty realism' skills.

The police controller of the child grass is Kerry Lake, making her first appearance and convincingly portrayed by James as a detective trying to live up to her fast-track reputation.

Perceived morality is so often at the heart of good crime fiction and Kerry Lake, so at home within the rigid confines of the law, is less assured when, in the early stages of *Baby Talk*, she is confronted with a moral dilemma. Whether to dance at a charity dinner arranged by her boyfriend's company with a wealthy businessman benefactor she is investigating for child murder.

A small decision perhaps, but her acceptance of his offer has repercussions throughout the novel and serves as a coda for the whole book. It also sets the story up for an engrossing start.

The businessman in question is Tom Ingle-Blake, whose smiling public persona and shady underbelly are reflected in Kerry Lake's own domestic circumstances—her live-in boyfriend is convinced of his innocence whilst she knows that Coventry Tom, as he is known, is guilty. Proof is of course everything and that's where the child ,grass' plays his sordid part.

As ever, it all goes horribly wrong, and Kerry Lake is more than a little to blame for the events that lead up to James' neatly honed ending.

A morality tale for the nineties then. So if you like your crime fiction with grit in its teeth and tears in its eyes this could be for you.

David Howard

FOUNTAIN OF SORROW BY PAUL CHARLES, THE DO-NOT PRESS, £6.50, ISBN: 189934439X

THIS IS THE THIRD book in a series about Detective Inspector Christy Kennedy.

Set in and around Camden Town, where (oddly enough) the author (himself) lives. The book spans an unspecified number of decades—from a rather too well documented rape scene in the prologue (carried out by four young men), to the eventual demise of three seemingly unrelated middle-aged men in unusual circumstances by an unknown assailant.

The first's mutilated corpse is found near a bridge in Camden Town with his throat ripped out after an attack by a savage animal.

The second is found within days of the first, bludgeoned to death near a fountain.

The third has been dead for some time—but again under suspicious circumstances which are surprisingly similar to the savage animal attack.

Christy Kennedy, a Beatles fan, is set the task to find the killer, or killers—and investigate the lives of the men who have met such a sorry end.

While all this is going on in his work life, his girl friend, ann rea (whom I thought was a grammatical error) leaves him to fend for himself and takes herself off to the sea side to visit a frail old gentleman with whom she used to lodge. After a few days, she starts to drop *very large* hints about the identity of the killer (like we needed any).

The problem was that, having read such a graphic scene in the prologue, I was left in very little doubt as to *who* was killing off these men...and I had to wade through the rest of the book to discover that my suspicion was correct.

There were *so* many suspects that it really could only be one... but I won't spoil the suspense by smirking and telling all. I reserve judgement and suggest that you read the book yourself to fully appreciate it. *Enjoy*.

Helen Bryant

NOM DE GUERRE BY JEFF GULVIN, GOLLANCZ, £15.99

WHEN INTERNATIONAL TERRORIST Storm Crow—real name Ismael Boese—bloodily escapes while awaiting trial (after threatening to explode a chemical bomb in London), Detective Jack Swann follows him from the UK to the US and teams up with an FBI agent to piece together Boese's movements. While this may initially seem like a serviceably gripping adventure thriller with Carlos the Jackal as its inspiration, Gulvin has other fish to fry: the labyrinths of betrayal and personal responsibility are as important as the mechanics of the thriller plot. Gulvin's main aim is to keep the pages turning (and here he scores a palpable hit), but he is fastidious in his characterisation, and his villain in particular is something of a unique creation.

Barry Forshaw

PERMISSIBLE LIMITS BY GRAHAM HURLEY, ORION, HBK, PBK £16.99/£9.99, ISBN 0752813110/3129

HURLEY'S TRACK RECORD AS a thriller writer is solid (even though one or two books seemed to be written on auto-pilot), and if this new one takes a little time to settle down, it quickly asserts itself as probably his most compelling book yet. Ellie Bruce is struggling to pick up the pieces of her life after the death of her husband in a flying accident. She finds that her husband's life and secrets were largely closed to her and, to survive, she is forced to learn to fly the WWII fighter that her husband's company was built around. Hurley constructs a dramatic and satisfying narrative focusing on a woman's search for the truth about herself and her husband, while finding time to deal with the legacy of World War Two.

Barry Forshaw

NICK'S TRIP BY GEORGE P. PELECANOS, SERPENT'S TAIL, £7.99, ISBN 1852425628

ALTHOUGH THIS IS THE third of George P. Pelecanos's Nick Stefanos novels to be published by Serpent's Tail, chronologically speaking, it is the second in the series.

Here, in Stefanos's first 'real' case, set a year after the events related in the first novel, *A Firing Offence*, an old friend, Billy Goodrich, turns up to ask for Nick's help in finding his missing wife, April. While the case of the missing wife is the pretext for *Nick's Trip*, Stefanos undertakes a number of other journeys during the course of this investigation.

First there's the literal journey, which develops chronologically forwards through the investigation, and proceeds geographically south from Washington DC, as Stefanos and Goodrich travel south, deep into the woods of Maryland, to Tommy Crane's pig-farm...

Then there are Stefanos's other journeys: he journeys back in time to reserchez the temps perdu of his own youth, recollecting the set lists of bands he went to see with now lost friends, and recalling various youthful escapades, usually enjoyed under the influence of more recreational drugs than a member of the serious crime squad could swear under oath to have found in your pocket.

While every Pelecanos novel is something of a journey around Washington DC, in *Nick's Trip* it's fascinating to watch Stefanos revisit the sites of his youth. Travelling to Brooklands, now a poor black district, but once a 'nice' area where his grandfather, 'Big Nick' had property, allows Stefanos to reminisce about the pleasant Sunday strolls of his childhood and to compare the new 'poorer, harder' DC with the old.

Needless to say, there is a fair bit of drinking, lots of driving around, and plenty of relationship stuff. Nick Stefanos carries a lot of pschyo-baggage and rarely wastes an opportunity to air his emotional laundry. Apart from the 'Greek' aspects which allow him to explore his relationship with his ethnicity, and his grandfather, Big Nick (now *there's* something for the Freudians), Stefanos has a habit of re-running his childhood in his head. This tends to make him something of a Peter Pan figure—in a sense he resists 'growing up' by continually seeking to return to the past—and this fatherless private dick recalls some 'male bonding' moments from his adolescence with an attention to detail that is surely a cry for therapy. As he remarks to Billy Goodrich, 'I expected things to be like they were ... when we were kids.' Here too, as ever, the women who are close to Stefanos fare reasonably well. Although Stefanos's old friend Jackie tests Stefanos's capacity for male-female friendship to the limit, she does provide the possibility of a sojourn to San Fran at some later date. Meanwhile, his new friend Lyla McCubbin, managing editor of *DC This Week*, can serve as both a source of information for later investigations as well as provide the love interest.

Pelecanos's writing is highly self-conscious, and this is apparent in the way in which the first-person narrative suffers from the all-too-present 'I'. For example, in one passage of eleven consecutive sentences (pp. 42-43) narrator Stefanos uses 'I' nine times. This serves to draw attention to what can only be described as self-obsessed narration; it is as if Stefanos/Pelecanos is trying just a bit too hard, with the effect is that, in places, the story has something of an 'overwritten' feel to it. (There's also a highly improbable telephone conversation with April Goodrich's doctor, if this is the place to air such niggles). That said, the novel is well plotted, thoroughly enjoyable and highly entertaining. And Pelecanos's style does improve, as his later work—especially the recently published *King Suckerman*—attests.

If you've already read Pelecanos, you'll know exactly what to expect: slickly written rites of retro-passage stuff, in which we *always* know what every character in the scene is wearing; and precisely what track is playing on the juke-box or what cassette is currently in the tape machine.

If you haven't tried Pelecanos before, he's certainly well worth reading, if only to see for yourself what all the fuss is about (the truly brilliant Barry Gifford, for example, declares in a blurb on the jacket, *"to miss out on Pelecanos would be criminal"*). And of course, to see how Stefanos resolves the case of the missing wife, and to see how he manages his various 'return journeys', both those that take place in the past, and those in the present. Stefanos is alright: anyone who kisses 'hello' as a wind-up deserves to be given a chance.

Eddie Duggan

AUDACIOUS PERVERSION BY MARK SANDERSON, DO-NOT-PRESS, £6.50, ISBN: 1899344322

AFTER READING ABOUT THE antics of Martin Rudrum, the man who sits on the train quietly doing the Times crossword will never look quite the same again.

If you like a good murder mystery, don't bother with this one. The author more or less tells you the plot on the first page and by the fifth page you will have met most of the victims and probably decided you could cheerfully kill them yourself.

There are one or two little twists in the plot but not enough to really startle. This may be because, with the exception of the killer, the characters lack any depth, the murders lack any discernible motive and the perversions mentioned in the title seem a bit too contrived. The police are too stereotyped and I'm sure they are never quite as thick as the author makes out.

On the plus side the murders, when they occur, are grisly and the descriptions of them graphic to the point of inducing the desire to vomit. In between killings the author fills in with episodes from Martin's unhappy childhood, and his not much happier adult life.

A thoroughly depressing book which left me wishing I hadn't read it.

Leon Whittick

THE MAMMOTH BOOK OF NEW SHERLOCK HOLMES ADVENTURES EDITED BY MIKE ASHLEY, ROBINSON, £6.99. ISBN 1854875280

THE TITLE PRETTY WELL says it all; the book contains twenty-six new Holmes short stories. I liked the book when I first saw it, although some reviewers were of a different opinion. Many of the writers have an SF or fantasy background, and I suspect that put some readers off.

It is true that many of the plots are a touch flimsy. But then Richard Lancelyn Green says in his introduction that the apocryphal Holmes tale *"need not be a great detective story, but it has to be a convincing story of the great detective,"* and this is quite true. Many of the original sixty tales are lightweight, to put it politely, and it is the mere presence of Holmes and Watson, rather than any complex problem solving, which attracts the aficionado.

There are some names here which are familiar in the Holmesian world, though perhaps less so outside it—David Stuart Davies, Barbara Roden, Denis O Smith, Barrie Roberts, Roger Johnson—and some who are better known for other genres, such as Peter Tremayne, Edward D Hoch, Michael Moorcock, HRF Keating. Whatever their backgrounds, most of the authors do manage to capture at least some of the magic, that chemistry between Holmes and Watson which makes even a slender plot readable.

There are variations, naturally; and once again it is unfortunately our American friends who show up worst. I like the Americans—they keep giving me awards, honorary memberships, and doctorates; although even if they didn't I like their optimism and no-BS approach—but it has to said that the average American attempt at writing about Victorian London is less than impressive, if not downright crap. The currency seems to be a particular handicap; but you know all about that anyway.

I particularly liked Peter Tremayne's *The Affray at the Kildare Street Club,* an episode from Holmes's early days; F Gwynplaine MacIntyre's *The Enigma of the Worcestershire Vortex,* a mix of SF, real-life characters and classic detection; Zakaria

Erzin‡lioglu's *The Adventure of the Bulgarian Diplomat,* and Basil Copper's *The Adventure of the Persecuted Painter.* And Roger Johnson's *Adventure of the Grace Chalice* captures the Holmes/Watson magic particularly well, though the answer to the problem should be obvious. I have to declare something of a personal interest; Roger is a pal of mine, and so are some of the other writers in this collection; but one can try to be objective, and, objectively, none of the stories in this book come into the 'absolutely dire,' category, while many are quite impressive.

However, I have to differ with Richard over his introductory mention of the book's gimmick—*"it has a scholarly status as it is arranged in chronological order with a connecting narrative."* Sherlockian 'scholarship' (always a contentious field anyway!) in connection with pastiche is necessarily spurious; the stories either work on their own or they don't. I found the connecting narrative an irritation and a distraction; and the complete chronology at the back is a waste of paper, meaningless to those not into Sherlockian scholarship, and far too superficial to interest those who are. And the bibliography is highly selective.

However, the bottom line is impressive; disregarding the editorial input and the occasional dud, seven pounds for five hundred pages has to be a bargain, even if your interest in Holmes is only marginal. Recommended.

John Hall

WHILE OTHER PEOPLE SLEEP BY MARCIA MULLER, THE WOMEN'S PRESS, £6.99, ISBN: 0704346411

TWENTY SO YEARS AGO, when the world and I were young(er), Marcia Muller introduced Sharon McCone, a woman detective, to the world. With such accolades as the Private Eye Writers of America Life Achievement Award under her belt, I found the thought of reviewing one of her books a bit daunting. Did I say a bit? I hid it under a pile of other books for ages – and even then, I could hear it crying out 'read me, read me.'

So, I bit the bullet, and lived to tell the tale!

Someone in San Francisco is impersonating Sharon McCone… and is doing a very good job of it.

More used to investigating and solving other people's problems Sharon is forced to use her own methods to track down the identity thief before he or she takes away her own sense of identity completely and leaves her with nothing to call her own.

An incredibly capable detective, Sharon is completely thrown when she discovers that the OTHER Sharon has been handing out her own business card to potential clients. To make matters worse, her home has been violated – and she is shocked to discover that her doppelganger has a similar taste in wine, and clothing, but not, unfortunately, her taste in men.

It becomes increasingly apparent that the identity thief knows too much about Sharon for her to put it all down to experience and the hunt is on. Despite her pride in her ability to detach herself from her cases, Sharon finds her anger building as she chases after the thief, and becomes more isolated from her friends and family as she tries to discover just who is trying to become her.

Whilst all this is going on in her own personal life, she is asked by a very close friend to tail his male partner who has been acting very strangely over the last few months. So, she has to tread a very fine line between her professional and private life indeed.

There is only one way to catch a thief…does Sharon catch her 'man'? Well, read on and find out.

An extremely well written thriller, and, no I didn't just say that because Ms Muller is an established novelist, I HAD to finish it. And, just when you think that it is all over… well, you'll just have to read the book and find out for yourselves.

Helen Bryant

THE NAKED CITY: URBAN CRIME FICTION IN THE USA BY RALPH WILLETT, MANCHESTER UNIVERSITY PRESS, £10.99

'SPATIAL THEORY'—largely based on the study of buildings, towns and, most importantly, cities—appears to offer a stimulating and practical alternative to some of the more self-indulgent academic concerns, especially in the discipline of cultural studies. Thus, in his classic *City Of Quartz*, Mike Davis took a magnifying glass to Los Angeles and in the process exposed some of the most destructive trends unfolding in contemporary America. Significantly, for readers of crime fiction, Davis claimed that a key tension in LA's public image was whether to present itself as the home of sunshine, or of *noir*. This suggests a ongoing battle between town planners, Hollywood and the lingering image of the hard-boiled detective.

Hull University's Ralph Willett further develops such themes in *The Naked City*. Central to his investigation is 'urban discourse'—the recurrent feature of a narrative that not only tells us which city we're in, but also infuses—and perhaps enthuses—the reader with particular geographical pressures and sensibilities. The book's circular sweep takes in all the key locales: from San Francisco to the East Coast, down to Miami and back west to New Orleans—taking in Chicago on the way.

By piecing together various strands of textual evidence, Willett attempts to identify the common features around which different writers organise their respective settings. Thus, the City of Angels becomes the 'Big Nowhere': shapeless, sprawling and dominated by desires that 'nourish crime and violence' (p.34). San Francisco remains a playground *and* commercial centre of the rich and powerful, while New Orleans—especially as depicted by James Lee Burke—invokes a primeval wildness that counts *Angel Heart*'s Mickey Rourke among its victims.

Throughout the text we find a constantly shifting dialogue between crime writers and cultural theorists, sort of Walter Mosley meets Walter Benjamin. It's here that the problems start, however; the book's ambitious scope undermines its central thesis. Each city gets a flying visit, with little rationale offered as to why specific authors were selected as personifying their particular city. Also notable are some of the absences—LA with only a passing reference to James Ellroy; next to nothing on the nation-wide, best-selling bigotry of Mickey Spillane. Whereas Willett's little-known 1992 pamphlet on hard-boiled fiction presented a concise summary of the genre, the sprawling theme of 'urban discourse' generates new mysteries and confusions faster than it can solve them. However, perhaps this is highly appropriate, given today's widespread perception that American cities are in a dilapidated and chaotic state.

Graham Barnfield

TOMATO RED BY DANIEL WOODRELL, NO EXIT PRESS

IT'S CUSTOMARY to remark on the literary skill employed in any half-well written crime novel. In fact, most of the time, this is a kind of knee jerk relief at not encountering the kind of stupifyingly bad writing so endemic to the genre. There's the other problem, too: the strikingly well written crime novel can all too often end up being adopted as literary fiction, and (in some people's eyes) lost, therefore, to the fold. Which is why Dan Woodrell affords such pleasure. His books may not be to everyone's taste, but writing of a signally individual kind often isn't. However, Woodrell numbers E. Annie Proulx and Roddy Doyle among his admirers—which is an indication of the strength of his dialogue (clearly appealing to two writers who specialise in that area). And Woodrell's blackly comic novels are unashamedly in the crime genre. Literary, yes, but still satisfyingly gutsy enough to keep them from the more rarefied sections of the Sunday arts papers.

Give us a Kiss was an intoxicating mix of raunchy sex, vigorous family feuding, and the American vernacular. His characters behaved in an outrageous fashion, but never due to any synthetic promptings of the plot: as with all the best writers, Woodrell allows plot to develop out of the behaviour of his characters, rather than having the exigencies of the narrative propel things along.

The St Bruno trilogy (*Under the Bright Lights*, *Muscle for the Wing* and *The Ones You Do*) were perhaps a touch too idiomatically American for the more insular British reader, but *Woe to Live On,* despite being a civil war novel, was mordant and blistering in its exploration of violence.

Tomato Red will probably be Woodrell's breakthrough book. From the first arresting passages of its first person narrative and the deliberately quotidian, down-to-earth references (trailer courts, dog food factories), the reader is gripped inexorably in a highly spiced goulash of caustic humour and clumsy violence. The protagonist is threatened when caught housebreaking, and shortly finds himself on a whirlwind ride of sex and double-dealing with Woodrell's in-your-face women and colourfully drawn lowlifes.

In fact *Tomato Red* is almost *Give us a Kiss* through a lens, darkly. The earlier novel with it's 'educated hillbilly' first person narration and it's comedy of violence and errors was a cheery affair by comparision. The narrator of Tomato Red is as intelligent as the narrator of *Kiss*, but is lacking in that characters breadth of vision. && and his confederates are always trapped in the smallness of their own vision - the most visionary of them wants only to ... Inevitably, lacking the (mostly mental) tools to forge any kind of break with the life they are trapped in (and, the book makes plain, trapped with the complicity of the surrounding society) they are crushed. Woodrell delineates clearly a society of have not's, often sentimentalised in American fiction, who exist cheek

by jowl with the have-a-great-deals.

Woodrell's admirers (Proulx, Doyle, Val McDermid, and the reviewers of the *Times Literary Supplement*) will probably be falling over themselves to persuade us to buy *Tomato Red*.

And this time they're right.

Brian Ritterspak

STRAIGHT, BENT & BARBARA VINE BY GARRY DISHER, ALLEN & UNWIN, £7.99

Here's something really unusual: the Australian writer Disher is also a teacher of creative writing, and incorporates into these fast-moving narratives a virtual manual on the art of writing thrillers. Juggling classic ingredients from all genres (the insurance investigator involved in a murder, the wrongly implicated suspect, etc.), Disher has cunningly mixed the familiar with surprising twists. This mix-and-match approach could have ended disastrously, but Disher has come up with a concoction that should delight every crime and thriller aficionado.

Barry Forshaw

garry disher talks

MY NEW BOOK, *Straight, Bent And Barbara Vine* (Allen & Unwin), is a collection of crime short stories, in three parts: the straight stories are traditional (e.g., a murder mystery), the bent stories poke gentle fun at some of the conventions of the genre, and the Barbara Vine stories are psychological mysteries. The crime story is very difficult to write. They must be convincing and yet satisfy without recourse to cheap tricks. I hope mine work. I've also included a short, personal study of the craft of writing crime fiction at the start of the book.

My six Wyatt novels, and the Wyatt stories in the latest book, were inspired by Richard Stark's Parker novels of the 1960s. I admired the cold, relentless tone of them (a tone in keeping with the character of Parker) and wanted to write about a similar character. I'd like to believe, however, that Wyatt is distinctive and not a clone of Parker. I also felt that private eyes and police officers were rather thick on the ground—there was room for a crime—from—the—inside series. That's the only direct influence I'll own up to. There are many crime writers I admire without necessarily being influenced by them—Elmore Leonard, James Lee Burke, Tony Hillerman, Sjowall and Wahloo, Laurence Gough, Ruth Rendell, Bill James, John Harvey.

All of the unpublished work has been thrown out long ago. In recent years, as I've become a better writer, there have been times when I've spent a few months on novels that didn't work, and rather than throw them out I've taken the key incident and turned it into a short story. There are two in the latest book: *Trusthouse* and *Scrapings*.

I never miss the authors I've listed above, and try to keep up with a handful of others. Sometimes I'm disappointed, but rarely abandon a writer completely. One writer I no longer read is Andrew Vachss. I simply can't believe in his hero. I can't suspend disbelief.

Regarding any bloodshed in my books: gratuitous violence is an insult, and offensive, but modern life is violent and deserves serious treatment by writers. And there's violence and Violence—crime writers haven't tackled domestic violence, or the effects of violence on individuals, with much thought.

I find sex scenes difficult to write, and would rather gloss over the details. Sex scenes in crime fiction are often badly handled, as though writers are including them to titillate or to give the hero a love interest (I've sometimes been told by editors to include more sex), when everything in a book should be there to advance the story rather than fill in time.

I don't think it is possible to be apolitical as a writer, especially as the gap between rich and poor grows more extreme. The best crime fiction has always taken a stance on aspects of modern life—the justice system, racial inequality, pollution, official corruption, the influence of new technologies, revealing social tensions. Crime fiction, more than any other type, tells us about the world we live in, often acting as a barometer of social tensions or articulating the viewpoint of society's victims. Often, under the wisecracks and sardonic tone of many crime novels, is a sense of real anger and outrage.

I've been a full—time writer for many years, and treat it as a daily job, going to my desk each day at about 8 am and writing until about 1 pm I devote the afternoons to research, typing, editing, correspondence, etc. I write the first draft with a blue pen on the backs of scrap A4 paper, then transfer it to the computer and write the subsequent drafts on that (copyediting each draft as I go along with a red pen). I can't think through the keyboard very well; I need to feel the scratch of the nib on the page.

I wear three writing hats—I write crime fiction, children's fiction and 'literary' fiction. They have separate audiences, but one thing they have in common is my love of story. I have written self—consciously experimental fiction, but prefer fiction that is strong on narrative suspense (by that I mean the wanting—to—know—what—happens—next factor). Writing crime fiction has in fact helped me enrich my other fiction writing in that I use some of the conventions of the genre to good effect (delaying tactics, turning points, mounting suspense, buried secrets, etc.). I often think that many contemporary mainstream/literary novels are under—plotted, and could benefit from the plotting complexity achieved by good crime writers.

Writers should open themselves to all kinds of influences. Certainly a good crime film can teach us a lot about atmosphere and pacing. I can't comment about music, though see that it's used more and more in crime fiction to contextualise and characterise.

Perhaps my father was an influence in the sense that he was a keen reader and there were always books around the house (I was reading adult fiction by the time I was twelve—mainly because books for teenagers didn't seem to exist 30 years ago), but also because he never read to me at bedtime but told me stories he'd make up as he went along, which gave me a sense of how stories, characters and place can be created in the imagination.

I try to achieve a balancing act between the demands of plot and character while I write any type of fiction, but generally a plot incident (e.g., something I've read in a newspaper) around which an absorbing story can be built, rather than a character, is my starting point when I write crime fiction. With my other types of fiction I start with a character facing a certain situation and write to see what happens.

I've had two very good freelance editors to help me over the years. The early drafts of my first Wyatt novel taught me a very good lesson. I began as I do with my 'literary' fiction, with a character in a certain situation, and let the story unfold as a voyage of discovery, and found myself relying on coincidence and unconvincing character motivation to find my story. I was torn apart by the publisher's reader for eighteen months before I finally scrapped everything and sat down and mapped out a storyline. I now plan my crime fiction minutely. I think a certain amount of planning is vital—how else can we create suspense, release information at the right moment, subvert the readers' expectations, etc. (all vital elements of writing crime fiction).

I'm dismayed by the tendency to sell the writer rather than the work. And it's not only publishers but journalists, critics, media heavies and literary festival spindoctors who sell the writer. Books should (and do) stand or fall according to their merits, but there will always be writers who may write like angels but be crippled by shyness, appearance or manner and never get the recognition they deserve.

My next book is the first novel in a new series, a police procedural along the lines of John Harvey's Inspector Resnick novels (an ensemble cast but one central investigator; one compelling central crime but a series of minor crimes; a glimpse of the working and domestic lives of a range of characters). It was absorbing to write. My Wyatt novels gain their suspense from the questions: Will he get away with it? Who betrayed him? Will he get his revenge? And it was instructive to work around the question: Whodunit?

Gary Disher

comics

THE LONG HALLOWEEN, WRITER: JEPH LOEB, ARTIST: TIM SALE, TITAN BOOKS, £24.99

ONE CRITICISM levelled at comics, in general, is that they don't hold up to close scrutiny: unlike film, there isn't enough going on to warrant detailed analysis of titles and issues. *The Long Halloween* is possibly the most ambitious Batman project ever published making *The Dark Knight Returns* look small in comparison. This thirteen chapter epic retells an early year of Batman's career, interweaving it with a lengthy gang war between Gotham's two crime families, the Falcones and the Maronis. Batman's rogues gallery—The Joker, Catwoman, Two Face, Penguin *et al* twine through the story as they involve themselves in the criminal power struggle at the heart of Gotham.

At the dark heart of *The Long Halloween* is a serial killer, Holiday, who is murdering members of the Falcone crime family. As a trademark Holiday leaves an item related to the public holiday on which the murder is committed. The murder committed on American Independence Day, for example, sees a miniature Statue of Liberty left near the victim.

Loeb and Sale have framed the story so that with each chapter a month passes. You feel, as a reader, that strict adherence to this keeps the series grounded and firmly focused on its final objective.

There are so many things that are notable in *The Long Halloween*: Loeb drawing our attention to the Waynes and the Falcone crime family humanises both the gangsters and the Wayne family. Sale's art has a remarkably European feel to it, reminding us of the Munoz and Sampayo of *Mr Wilcox, Mr Conrad* and *Sinner*.

His work describes perfectly an expressionist vision of Gotham and it's dark inhabitants. Holiday's murders in are seen in grey, with small elements picked out in colour, giving us a 'steadicam' view of the killings.

The Long Halloween is one of the most cinematic Batman story ever published: extreme close-ups, panoramic sweeping views and fast, manic action sequences abound. Loeb has written a number of forgettable films but uses the disciplines learnt as a screenwriter here to great effect. Every member of the creative team has worked in concert to come up with a unique and at times disturbing read.

The Long Halloween is also about the relationship between Captain Gordon, Harvey Dent and Batman /Bruce Wayne. It delves into the emotional differences between Wayne and the Batman persona. It charts the decline of Dent and we see the incident which it could be argued made Dent into Two-Face: Maroni throwing the acid into the lawyer's face.

This series is about so many different things it's genuinely difficult for me to do justice and encapsulate it for you. It bears comparison with films like *Godfather* I and II: the gang war is brutal and well-framed: we see the gangsters as petty and venal but well-proportioned in terms of characterisation. Harvey Dent is dedicated to the point of obsession, Batman is just learning how to deal with situations. One of the most telling scenes is at the end of Book One, where Batman and Harvey Dent track down the Falcone family's stash of illegal money and raze it to the ground. This is an act that Batman would never consider these days.

The Holiday mystery is built up, piece by piece, and the tension is maintained with supreme agility. Sale and colourists Greg Wright and Heroic Age bring so much to this: pages are muted and elegant where they need to be and hard-hitting and action-packed where it's necessary.

The Long Halloween is squarely in class of the *Dark Knight Returns* and *Year One*, with its filmic sophistication and ingenious plotline. To good in fact to easily convey in a review. As a Batman story, it is enigmatic, brilliantly executed and wonderfully illustrated. As a piece of fiction in its own right, it is a gripping slice of modern prose.

Joel Meadows

SUPERMAN: THE COMPLETE HISTORY BY LES DANIELS, TITAN, £24.99

Anyone who's read any of Les Daniels' various books on the history of comics will know what to expect here – a comprehensive retelling of the origins and development of the Man of Steel in the comics and other media. What may come as a surprise is the design of the book. Chip Kidd, who produced last years gorgeous Batman Collectibles volume is the designer of the present book and as a result has propelled Daniels' opus into the 'must have' bracket for Superman fans. If any era in Superman history goes unillustrated, it's not Chip Kidd's fault. He's unearthed a set of visuals as stunning as any you'll see.

The text is as competent as you'd expect from an old hander like Daniels, and as he has the co-operation of DC Comics (this is a DC project) much inside information, especially about recent years, is one display. Less time (this *is* a DC project) is given to the fight of Superman creators Siegel and Shuster for recognition, or to the Captain Marvel lawsuit that removed DC's only major competitor (dealt with in half a sidebar). Having said that, what remains is a first-rate celebration of the character, which any fan will treasure.

Peter Mann

film

books on film
michael carlson

LONDON FILM FESTIVAL

JAMES WHALE: A WORLD OF GODS AND
MONSTERS
JAMES CURTIS, FABER, £14.99
NOSFERATU IN LOVE JIM SHEPARD FABER &
FABER, £9.99

DURING THE London Film Festival it's difficult to do much reading at all, but there are compensations. Adrian Wooton is the new director of the festival, and he brings a deep love of crime movies to it. So it's no surprise that *Brown's Requiem* should be one of the centrepieces of the two-week reelathon.

Brown's Requiem is the third feature-film based on an Ellroy book. James Harris' *Cop*, with James Woods in the title role was based on *Blood On The Moon*, and last year's *La Confidential* shot Ellroy into the mega bigtime of properties who are muy caliente.

First time director Jason Freeland's is probably the first of these films to set out to be a faithful adaptation of Ellroy. Fans of the Demon Dog will argue forever about the fidelity of *La Confidential*, whether in spirit or in look, but close as it stays to Ellroy's basic story, *Brown's Requiem* brings a neo-noir sensibility to Ellroy which gives it an interesting spin of its own.

Freeland encountered Ellroy listening to one of his patented manic interviews on the radio in LA, and decided to start at the beginning with his books. When he thought he was ready to adapt Ellroy for the screen, he found *Brown's Requiem* was the only property available, in the post-*La Confidential* rush to option his work.

The two biggest changes Freeland does make are both beneficial. First he changes the female lead from a woman who gets involved with Fritz Brown to a younger girl who doesn't. This is both more realistic, given Brown's personality (truer to the real Brown than even Ellroy was!) and it also provides a better plot motivation, particularly in encouraging Brown's fantasies of being the white knight, and theoretically a more shocking hook (which, sadly, is somewhat dissipated).

Second, he loses the musical sub-text, by which Fritz Brown and Bruckner combine to make him a sensitive tragihero. This was a bit too literary a conceit, and one which Ellroy soon abandoned in his own writing. Only at the end of the film, where Brown gives his friend Hank an imaginary Viking funeral, do we get a hit of that grandiose dream.

Neo-noir puts its emphasis on the dumbo nature of its would-be heroes. Michael Rooker, as Fritz Brown, is a cross somewhere between John Malkovich and Woody Harrelson on the intensity meter (see Crime Time 2.2 for a review of Harrelson in the neo-noir *Palmetto*), and if occasionally he remains too sure, and too strong, his physical presence is always undercut by a knowing voice- over narration. Freeland has done an excellent job casting other roles: there are welcome cameos for Valerie Perrine (excellent in bringing depth to a brief part), Barry Newman, and Brad Dourif.

Also impressive is 23 year old William Sasso, as 'Fat Dog', who sets the story in motion, and who is, to my mind, the Ellroy figure in this book. Freeland admitted this was a tough part to cast: agents told him repeatedly *"my client isn't fat, he's big."* Sasso leaps into the part with such vigour it's a shame he can't carry a bigger load. This highlights the soft spot of this film: in following out the plot, Freeland has to short change some of the supporting cast. In the same way we only get hints of the incestuous cesspool lurking under the story, so things like Brown's relationship with Hank is never really given the depth to carry the force of Brown's final regrets. This, however, is a small criticism of an assured first feature film. Freeland has the feel, and an excellent score by Cynthia Millar helps build the emotional tension. This is an adaptation of Ellroy which will surely please fans of the books.

Another of Adrian Wootton's crime films in the Festival was *Playing God*, with X-Files star David Duchovny as a surgeon who's been struck down for abusing drugs, and who is now a full-time addict. He hooks up with a gangster (Timothy Hutton hamming it up big time) and his girlfriend (Angelina Jolie, a large set of lips with a face and body attached) doing medical repair work on demand. You can guess the rest. The starting point for this British-made thriller, directed by Andy Wilson, was the story of the 'Doc' who appears in so many film noirs, though he's rarely as laconic and healthy as the supposedly junkie Duchovny. In fact, the point you lose interest in this story is precisely the spot where Duchovny kicks his habit and looks and acts exactly the same as before. Well, maybe its when your British gangster uses designer pistol techniques to shoot up a Japanese garden. Or the cycle-gang who assist in the operation on a pool table with a big product placement lamp overhead. This one is a Vespa, not a Triumph, of style over substance.

My own favourite film in the Festival was *High Art*, an assured first feature by Lisa Cholodenko, dealing with a photographer brought back into the working limelight through an affair with an ambitious assistant editor at an art magazine. That the affair is lesbian, and that the photographer and her current girlfriend are languishing in a lazy world of drugs, adds irony to the story, balancing off its cutting look at the pretensions of the New York art scene. Ally Sheedy as the artist and Patricia Clarkson as her German actress girlfriend are both formidably good, while Radha Mitchell as the young editor brings believability to a difficult role.

Another Festival highlight dealing with a homosexual success who turns his back on his profession was *Gods And Monsters*, Bill Condon's portrait of director James Whale in his last days in Hollywood. It's based on *Father Of Franken-stein*, a 1995 novel by Christopher Bram, which is concerned primarily with Whale's sexuality. Ian McKellan plays Whale, and plays him brilliantly, moderating the fruity overtones of the performance with a real sadness. Playing off a sub-plot involving the sexuality of the yard man Whale be-friends, Condon and McKellan build a portrait of a man forgotten and ignored by the industry which once idolised him.

The comparisons with Gloria Swanson in *Sunset Boulevard* are apt. Like William Holden in that movie, Whale was found dead in his swimming pool. It was 1957, and he had not directed a feature film since 1941, a mere decade after *Frank-enstein* made him famous. Yet starting with *Journey's End* in 1930, Whale had a six-year run which included *Waterloo Bridge*, *The Invisible Man*, *Bride Of Frankenstein*, and *Showboat*, during which he was one of Hollywood's best paid and best regard-ed directors.

James Curtis' sensitive biography of Whale makes it clear Hollywood was an unlikely resting place for a boy from the Black Country. Whale was a blast furnace-man's son, raised in a strict Methodist fam-ily in the slums of Dudley. As a boy he studied art, but it was as a prisoner of war in Germany that he discovered the thea-tre. Returning to England in 1918, he be-gan in provincial theatre, eventually turn-ing to directing and scoring a huge hit with *Journey's End*, starring a young Ol-ivier, and showcasing Whale's brilliance at atmospheric staging.

Whale's good fortune was to tour America with *Journey's End* precisely at the point when Hollywood needed stage directors to guide them though the transi-tion to talkies. Whale grasped quickly how camera movement and editing could work with set design to tell a story. Even today, one is struck by the sense of movement in Whale's best films and their cinematic economy.

Whale's decline in Hollywood has of-ten been attributed to discrimination against his open homosexuality. Curtis takes pains to point out, and in the film McKellan also admits Whale's own ease with his sexuality led to general accept-ance in the studios. His difficult reputation was more the result of his tendency to go over budget and schedule, in part by in-sisting on breaks for tea during shooting. When he couldn't repeat the box office success of *Showboat*, he became a liabil-ity. The film *Gods And Monsters* works best when recreating Whale at work on his masterpiece, *Bride Of Frankenstein*, and when staging his return to Hollywood society at a reception thrown by George Cukor for Princess Margaret. It's both fun-ny and touching. We forget the sense of *Frankenstein*'s monster as an outcast, look-ing for a friend. It's not an exclusively ho-mosexual metaphor, and this film is the better for reminding us of that. It is better come to after Curtis' excellent biography, but they do complement each other well.

Horror movies and homosexuality also go together in Jim Shepard's novel about the German director FW Murnau. Born Friedrich Lumpe, Murnau was a 'sensitive' provincial boy sent to school in Berlin, where his schoolmate Hans Ehrenbaum introduced him to both art and society. Murnau's pre-war Berlin, working under Max Reinhard, resembles Whale's Lon-don in the 20s: with Conrad Veidt serving like a young Olivier, and Murnau, like Whale, revelling in the discovery of this exotic demimonde.

Hans' death in the Great War haunted Murnau all his life; he had betrayed Hans with a mutual friend and suspected Hans sought death deliberately. This haunting underpins Shepard's story, and the sense of Murnau using the vampire Nosferatu as a metaphor for his own unhappy sexuali-ty carries far more credence than the theories about Whale and his filmic monsters.

The best scenes are during filming. The emotional apex comes when the brilliant cameraman Karl Freund finally discovers a gyroscopic process which allows his camera to move. This freedom seems to be the only one Murnau ever found in his life.

Murnau's career in Hollywood was unsuccessful; he spent much time in the South Seas, including an doomed attempt to collaborate with Robert Flaherty. It seems the bright light of California washed out the expressionist shadows of Murnau's life. With his latest Filipino houseboy at the wheel, he died in a car crash in 1931.

VERTIGO—THE MAKING OF A HITCHCOCK CLASSIC BY DAN AUILER, TITAN, £19.99, ISBN: 1840230657

IF THERE IS SUCH a thing as a book every Hitchcock fan should have I'd guess the Truffaut book on Hitchcock would be it. Other works have been published, but few have had the impact on how we think about Hitchcock and the way he made films. *Vertigo—The Making of a Hitchcock Classic* is a second such book.

In the years since Hitchcock's death it has become evident how difficult it is to make suspense movies. What director since has produced more than a couple of successful suspense movies in a row? *Vertigo* is acknowledged as one of the defining films (if not *the* defining film) of a career, and now Dan Auiler is here to tell you all, and possibly more, that you want to know about it. Auiler seems to have talked to everyone – from the Hitchcock family and surviving crew members to the film's restoration team – and read everything that could have any bearing on the film. What we end up with is one of the most detailed examinations of the creative process to see print. We see the film emerging butterfly-like from the collaborative process, starting with the purchase of the Boileau and Narcejac novel (*The Living and the Dead*(1956)), through drafts by Maxwell Anderson, Angus McPhail and Alec Coppel, to the final version by Samuel Taylor through to the filming and final edit. At every stage Hitchcock is involved in the process, taking the source material and changing it into something that, no matter how many others are involved, is unmistakably his.

Throughout this the authorial voice rarely intrude, as Auiler covers filming, postproduction, the film's premier and finally the triumphant restoration of what is now recognised as one of the finest films ever made. This is a book to read and reread—even if you're not a Hitchcock fan (there are such people I believe) or don't like *Vertigo* (!) if you like film you should have this book. It's simply one of the best books about film I've ever read.

Peter Mann

a chalk outline of crime film
mike paterson

"As far back as I can remember I've always wanted to be a gangster"— Henry Hill, *Goodfellas*

IN THE BEGINNING was the gun. And the gun was pointed at the camera. And the audience shrieked as the trigger was pulled and smoke blew even though the only sound was that of a cheesy piano.

The year was 1903 and with the release of *The Great Train Robbery* (as well as *Kit Carson and The Pioneers*) cinema had its first real narrative. While music hall blended into the slapstick two-reeler and trains pulled into stations for celluloid entertainment, crime was already beginning to influence the subject and shape of cinema. Indeed, the very first film to be exhibited in Britain was *The Story of the Kelly Gang* in 1906, a 60 minute feature about the iron-clad bushranger Ned Kelly (Unfortunately it was still felt necessary to soil our screens with a Mick Jagger remake).

And *The Great Train Robbery* begat westerns begat John Wayne begat Unforgiven – an anomaly, as the Western now largely seems to be an exhausted genre.. But *The Cabinet of Dr Caligari* begat *M* begat *Maltese Falcon* begat Hitchcock begat *Chinatown* begat *Lost*

Highway. And from these unions the richest strand of cinema was born.

THE CABINET OF DR CALIGARI

As close to downright scary-weird as early cinema gets. Caligari the psychoanalyst with psychopathic tendencies hypnotises his patient into performing his murderous deeds across the rooftops of the city. This is as disturbing a depiction of insanity (which only Lynch in *Lost Highway* has come close to matching) as has appeared on celluloid. There is something uniquely European about the theatricality and deliberate artificiality of its angular rooftop sets and pantomime acting. Its anti-authoritarian theme in an era of intolerance were partly responsible for the dissolution of Germany's most creative personalities. Producer Fromm later worked with Hitchcock and Conrad Veidt's svelte persona appeared in many Hollywood films including *Casablanca*. The art design took experimental theatre into the cinema and popularised the term 'expressionism.' Fritz Lang, associated with the production at an early stage, used similar darkness and twisted themes that would later inform Hollywood with a European slant. To this day, *Caligari* retains the power to disturb, and as a work of creative vision its influence is subtle but widespread.

The crime film, probably more than any other genre, reflects the core of 20th century western society. As social documents, films like *Once Upon a Time in America* and *Godfather II* are peerless in their depiction of the migrant experience in turn of the century US. In Britain *The Long Good Friday* is as good a summation of the tearing apart of city living through pernicious commercial developments and organised terrorism as any academic tract.

Cinema more than any other artistic medium has the ability to provoke an emotional reaction. The combination of image and sound tap directly to our cortex with an immediacy lacking in other art forms. Music can evoke emotion, art stimulates imagery and literature insinuates passion but cinema can combine stimuli to much stronger effect. As a director who grasped the potential for film to shortcut directly to the core of human emotional response Hitchcock is acknowledged as the master of the art. Within his films we can see the archetype of storytelling on celluloid. The ability of the camera to insinuate, to suggest and to shock provided the suspense and thrill that is the essence of cinema. In *Rear Window* the simple elements of James Stewart's (and through the objective telephoto lens, our) witnessing of events across his apartment suggest that a murder has been committed. But we do not see this take place. Hitchcock nudges us to fill in the gaps. Film narrative is all about filling in the gaps. The cliché of art mirroring society is true. And society is mired in crime. America has provided the model for the images of crime in film. The tough-guy role models from the Chicago prohibition gangs were fed back to audiences by Hollywood and the adopting of style became a spiral of influence. From "dirty rats" to "reaching out" the cadence of slang entered the language from film dialogue to street slang. American literature worked in tandem with Hollywood to propagate the image.

From James M Cain, Chandler, Hammett and the pulp magazines to Richard Price and James Ellroy a celluloid vocabulary has been written.

Europe after originally pioneering became an imitator. As the devastating consequences of world war forced an artistic migration to the Land of the Free few originators remained. The influence of Europe on American film is unquestionable. The lineage from Lang, Hitchcock and Melville to Polanski and Neil Jordan is as rich and important as any in Hollywood. Indeed the very first examples of the genre in any form were in English literature (Wilkie Collins and Conan Doyle). Here, Britain's genre path took a divergence from that of America's. This was the path of the gentleman detective, the Hitchcock thriller, Graham Greene, The Blue Lamp and wartime spies. It is America though that historically has come to dominate. In 1939 Hollywood produced The Roaring Twenties, a seminal gangster film with Cagney and Bogart. In the same year Britain produced The Arsenal Stadium Mystery. Cute, but no contest. Get Carter came later.

As cinema became the dominant popular art form and entertainment it was only natural that it would plunder the front pages of newspapers to feed itself. Growing almost in parallel, Hollywood and organised crime began to set the template for the familiar imagery of the genre.

Prohibition in the States had quickly led to an underworld of criminal cabals and a news media hungry for copy were making anti-heroes of their leaders. The age of the jazz speakeasy, the pinstripe fashion and cheap munitions gave us the gangster.

This was the age that spawned Cagney and Raft, Edward G Robinson and a glut of fast-talking wiseacres. Film as social realism was taking over. Films such

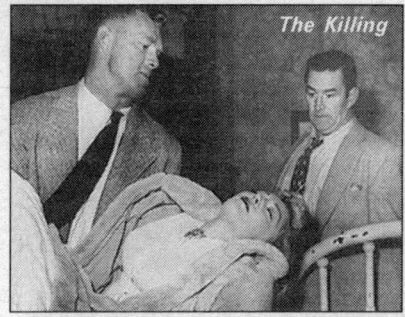
The Killing

as The Roaring Twenties, Scarface and Little Caesar crammed the screen with all the Tommy-gunning, Fedora-wearing, Moll-loving gangsters the public craved. These characters provided a dangerous glamour in an age of depression and cynicism. Musicals provided light escapism, screwball comedies lifted the spirits—but gangster films were cool. These wiseguys were peers for a downtrodden generation. Despite the Hays Code demands on filmmakers to depict crime and criminals with moral redemption it was obvious that crime paid. There was glamour in the street punk who crawled his way out of the gutter of American cities to become the successful hood. This was The American Dream with machine guns.

THE COTTON CLUB

Coppola's ode to the gangster era and the gangster film. This is a glossy, stylistic distillation of all the elements from the thirties Hollywood mob film but given a technical sheen. Using many of the methods of genre narrative (spinning newspapers, panning superimposition over intercut scenes) it works as a summary of an age and a style in Hollywood and in history. The Cotton Club in Harlem in the thirties was the haunt for the successful mob-boss and the Hollywood star keen to get some street charisma by association. Lucky Luciano would rub shoulders with Chaplin. Duke Ellington would provide the soundtrack for the pioneering, drug-fuelled mania demanded by the decadent guests. This is where jazz became associated with the underworld.

Despite it's failings of story and pacing it is an unjustly criticised work. The production design is sumptuous, the cinematography glowing and the sound editing a marvel. There are some set-pieces that are breathtaking; The Hines Brothers perform a staccato tap-dance while mobsters machine gun their enemies in intercut sequences which echo *The Godfather*. Fred Gwynne and Bob Hoskins are a delightful double-act, James Remarr is a thuggish Dutch Schultz and Nick Cage, Tom Waits, Joe Dallesandro, Larry Fishburne and Giancarlo Esposito add a richness to the supporting cast. Ignore the smugness of Richard Gere and revel in the cinematic elegy of Coppola in love with his subject.

Meanwhile there was something interesting going on before the main feature. While the big budget Hollywood film was bringing in the punter the support movie was becoming an arena for experiment. B Movies had little risk. They were a production line affair. However they provided an opportunity for young writers and directors to introduce new elements within the strict confines of the formula and the tightness of the production. Most B Movies were worthless but provided an experience in which some noble work could be done. From this school graduated names that came to dominate the genre: Jacques Tourneur, Sam Fuller, Robert Aldrich, Nicholas Ray, Don Siegel and character actors such as Elisha Cook Jr, Sterling Hayden, Edmond O'Brien, Marie Windsor and Sydney Greenstreet.

The fast and tight formula of the B Movie was reflected in the rise of the pulp novel. The crime genre was becoming influenced by a shifting society. As prohibition disappeared and the rackets declined, the iniquities in society were being countered by a new set of characters. Where the G-Men of the gangster era battled the mob, in forties America, an underworld of crime threw up the private detective and the heist gang. The loner was translating into the genre from the Western. Fiction was providing us with Marlowe and Spade and newspapers were providing more murder and corruption than ever before. This was the era of the true-crime dime magazine and the DC comic. People wanted dirt. Things were getting sleazier.

THE KILLING

From out of the pages of Look magazine came a young photographer with a stare like a hawk and a vision of humanity framed by the camera lens. Stanley Kubrick was twenty-seven when he made the film which would get him noticed by the film community. From unpromising sources he produced something with a freshness and verve which is still plundered to this day for ideas. His telling of a racetrack robbery is done within the superficial formula of the B Movie; a *Dragnet* narration introduces the characters, familiar actors from the world of supporting quirks populate it and a heist goes wrong. With these elements however Kubrick twisted the expected. The narrative becomes a sequence of character- perspective flashbacks; the camera participates in the interaction rather than observing. Kubrick's chess skill sets the tone for the time reordered plot structure. His finesse in the depiction of the mechanistic actions of his characters is already evident. The script is unremarkable but there's a bluntness and believability in the dialogue and the characters have an unglamorous seediness. Elisha Cook Jr whines to good effect, Timothy Carey is a sharpshooting, sharp-suited psychotic and Sterling Hayden is the hard-boiled ringleader with a grimly dignified work ethic. The inevitable failure of the heist due to human weakness is a theme that came to dominate Kubrick's cinematic philosophy.

There is much visually striking detail; the clown masks worn during the heist, the FBI advancing in synchronous steps on the defeated Sterling Hayden and the roving eye of the camera as it follows the speech from character to character in the claustrophobic hotel room. As an example of the heist-gone-wrong movie it is peerless. Its influence is unavoidable in *Reservoir Dogs*, which plundered many films but used most from this.

THE CRIMES OF PEDRO ALMODOVAR

When the Spanish director Pedro Almodovar decided to film a novel by the very English crime writer Ruth Rendell, it might have been predicted that the results would be very strange indeed. In the event, *Live Flesh* turned out to be even more bizarre than anyone might have expected, and Rendell was apparently bemused by the results. One would hope that she would also have been pleased, as her vision of psychosexual strangeness (while not as *outré* as Almodovar's) has been perfectly transmuted into a heated Latin setting. And Rendell, famous for her unblinking portrayal of violence, would certainly have approved of Almodovar's hair-trigger way with the gunplay.

Almodovar was born in the province of Cuidad Real. A strict religious upbringing had the effect (as so often) of causing Almodovar to completely reject the church, while at the same time becoming a compulsive cinema-goer. At the age of 16 he moved to Madrid with a strong desire to make films. But as Franco had closed the Official Film School, it took him some time to create his first feature. *Pepi, Luci, Bom* was a full-blown example of the director's outrageous style, totally mirroring his powerful rejection of bourgeois values and enthusiastically embracing the kind of aberrant sexual behaviour his critics would be so shocked by. This first film explored many of his favourite subjects: sexually frustrated housewives, male and female genitals, flamboyant costumes, and a kitsch vision of Spanish housing estates. And along with the eyebrow-raising sexuality, he introduced his female alter ego Carmen Maura, whose operatic performances were to become a mainstay of his cinema. *Labyrinth Of Passion*, while equally outrageous in its treatment of carnality, seemed a little like marking time before the hilarious and powerful *What Have I Done To Deserve This?* with Maura in an erotic and scabrous black comedy. In 1985 his most disturbing film, *Matador*, appeared. Starting with the protagonist involved in auto-erotic activities while watching a grisly horror movie on television, Almodovar examined the crushing legacy of Catholic guilt with Assumpta Serna as an angel of death, killing her lovers at the point of consummation with a hat pin driven into the nape of the neck.

By now audiences thought they knew what to expect from Almodovar. Those with delicate sensibilities had long since turned away, while many more film lovers had come to enjoy this totally unique Latin vision. Like his great predecessor Luis Buñuel, Almodovar enjoyed his cor-

rosive reputation, but was in danger of repeating familiar tactics. However, with 1989's *Tie Me Up, Tie Me Down* he achieved one of his greatest commercial successes, while managing to get liberal sensibilities as hot under the collar as he had the more easily shockable. But the director had the courage not to be politically correct and followed the less successful *High Heels* with the more tender and warmly characterised The *Flower Of My Secret*.

With *Live Flesh*, however, he has added a new level of incisive characterisation to his armoury, while keeping the more camp elements on the back burner. The conflict between a young man Victor (Liberto Rabal) and the policeman he accidentally crippled (Jose Sancho) is played out against the usual background of unbridled sex, with an unobtrusive social consciousness strongly at work. Almodovar has clearly realised that it's time to move into new areas, and his Rendell adaptation gives every appearance that a new era of beckons for his movies: one that will continue to delight his admirers and shock his detractors.

Barry Forshaw

THE X FILES

With *The X Files* we have a format of FBI procedural drama that uses the best of a selection of related influences yet appears to be of shining freshness: we have such short memories. *The Night Stalker, The Avengers, Silence of the Lambs, Twin Peaks*, anyone? (for the literary inspiration read the *Illuminatus* trilogy. Go on.) This is a world of genre crossovers. The pop culture generation are creating their own strands of genre from a kaleidoscope of influences and filters. Too much rigidity and homage becomes fromage.

What gives it the freshness is in the intelligence of characterisation and dialogue and a chemistry of subtle nuance between two actors that shines in an age of dumb buddy dramas. That *The X Files* has chosen to blend the procedural with the supernatural is what defines it as the zeitgeist drama of our time. It's sexy detectives investigating sexy crimes.

After five seasons where the suggestion and speculation of unknown extra terrestrial forces at work within the sphere of earth- bound conspiracy has gradually become more and more explicit with each episode we finally have the movie to explain all. Or rather we don't. That would be too simple. It was inevitable that with the growing success of the series and the control that originator Chris Carter has over his franchise, a big budget, special-effect laden film would appear. But with this control comes the ability to continue the conspiracy theorising rather than provide neat answers. To his credit Carter has refused to make concessions to a wider audience demanding simple explanations requiring little thought. Thanks Chris. Keep the faith.

From the Nigel Kneale inspired opening sequence in prehistoric Antarctica the sign of visceral shocks to come are placed. Later we see Mulder and Scully, so suave and impressive in widescreen, on anti-terrorist duty in Dallas. After a devastating explosion in a federal building, links are gradually made to conspiracies of cover-up. Bodies recovered from the wreckage are discovered to have died elsewhere. Mystery ensues, suspicion is aroused, Mulder is accused, Scully reassigned. Mulder pouts. Scully frowns.

Martin Landau makes an impressive cameo as a conspiracy nut with insider knowledge who helps Mulder on his trail for the truth. With a hearing convened to decide the fate of the agents and information on the source of a virus discovered in the bodies always just out of grasp the chase continues. The shadowy conspiracy group convenes and Mr Smoking Man

and Mr Well-Manicured man start spinning their web. So far, so TV. For the aficionado, there is much to enjoy. The production values and larger budget open out the scope of the world of Mulder and Scully. Special effects add some spectacular scenes out of reach of the TV budget. Where the series seems to be bathed in shadows and permanent dark the film has a brightness and gloss and with the use of anamorphic lenses and steadicams a whole new dimension of cool has been added. Like the series however the tendency to recycle plots from other sources results in a sense of deja vu. Here there are elements of *Quatermass*, *The Hot Zone*, *The Andromeda Strain, The Thing* and the great plot stealer of them all; *Alien*. But *The X Files* does it with it's own sense of style and intelligence. Add to the mix a blend of events familiar from recent news stories and a largely smart and compelling drama is created. Until the end. But that would be spoiling things. Suffice to say that villagers burning down the village is becoming technically very refined these days.

Duchovny's laconic humour is present but there is an overbearing seriousness to the film that could have been lightened by some familiar touches. Maybe for the follow up. Darren Morgan, the outstanding writer of the more comedic episodes, could add Leslie Nielsen as a co-star. As the Foo Fighters beautiful song runs over the closing credits you realise that over all the alien abduction and global conspiracy, at the heart of this story is the suppressed love of two people for each other. In their performances Gillian Anderson and David Duchovny give a sense of intelligence and dignified work ethic completely lacking in any other two-handed action film. Their professionalism denies the declaration of love that is boiling under the surface. This is a love story for the terminally cynical.

Mike Patterson

music

music to kill by...
frank thielmann

THE TAKING OF PELHAM 1, 2, 3, DAVID SHIRE,
RETROGRADE FSM-80123-2, $16.95
THE WILD BUNCH JERRY FIELDING, WARNER
HOME VIDEO, $19.95

IN ITS EVER-CONTINUING quest to report on all things dark and wonderful, *Crime Time* brings you from now on a column that deals with film music, specifically music created for thrillers, detective movies, pulp fiction and the like. Everything from Batman to Bond, really—even the *Wallace & Gromit* music, if it's ever released on CD (fascinating 1940s pastiche ... no, really!).

Prepare to be dazzled—there's a lot more interesting stuff out there than you thought there was, covering all kinds of musical styles and techniques. What you will *not* find reviewed here is the latest Tarantino pop song compilation or anything recorded by an orchestra with the word 'Starlight' in its name. We are talking about film music in its strictest sense—original scores, composed exclusively to enrich and support the movie they go with, and how they are presented on CD. And just to show you how serious I am about this, I'd like to kick off this column with two recent releases that you won't find at your local HMV; both titles are only available directly through the label that released them.

Come back with me, then, if you will, to a time when movies about terrorists didn't feature Bruce Willis in a shirt and two hundred ear-shattering explosions that just about everybody miraculously survives. Instead, let us remember a film that, though cliched, is so deeply grounded in reality that the events it depicts could almost really happen. Such a movie is *The Taking of Pelham 1-2-3*, which deals with a gang of terrorists who've hijacked a subway train, demanding one million dollars from the city of New York. Hardly what we've come to consider an action movie, *Pelham* instead concentrates on the dry logistics of an urban hostage crisis, pitting the wits of wrinkly-faced Transport Authority officer Walter Matthau (in one of his all-too-rare serious roles) against the cold-blooded criminals led by Robert Shaw and deriving much suspense from it.

Today, a film like that would feature a full orchestral score (and most likely a vapid Celine Dion song), shouting 'DANGER! SUSPENSE! DRAMA!' in a desperate and unsuccessful attempt to compete with the sound effects. Back in 1974, though, composer David Shire could afford to concentrate on creating a musical backdrop for New York City that is never intrusive and yet manages to keep the tension rising. Shire, who has provided effective and memorable music for dramas such as *Norma Rae* and *All the President's Men*, thrillers like *Farewell, My Lovely* and *The Conversation* as well as the disaster movie *The Hindenburg*, talks in the CD's liner notes about wondering *"what New York sounds like;"* what he came up with is a rhythmic, yet chaotic and dissonant blend of contemporary jazz and swing music, enhanced with percussion. Musicologists could probably wax eloquently about his clever use of the twelve-tone method of composition (as pioneered by Arnold Schönberg). Don't let that scare you off. Luckily, I myself cannot even read notes, which is why I must confine myself to pointing out that the music for *Pelham* confidently and successfully combines the acoustic atmosphere of the big city with the demands and the dramatic tension of the plot. This is the kind of music to read a good hard-boiled novel to (if you're into this sort of thing); down-to-earth, no-nonsense Seventies stuff, on par with classics like *Shaft* and *Taxi Driver* which surely are on everybody's CD shelf by now. Or at least they should be.

Jerry Fielding, who is probably best known for his music for Eastwood's *Dirty Harry* films, used a similarly serious and realistic approach for Sam Peckinpah's shootout-of-the-century, *The Wild Bunch*. Finally recognised as the classic it is, *Bunch* is probably one of the most (over-)analysed films of all time, but so far only little attention has been paid to its music. Instead of the usual syncopatic Elmer Bernstein fanfares that you would somehow expect from a western, Fielding created a minimalistic but sinister musical image of Mexico caught in the grip of the revolution, hinting at the violence to come. Turn-of-the-century Mexican folk music is contrasted with military rhythms and Fielding's own particular blend of action music, thus slyly and subversively converting the jollyness of the source material into an elegy for William Holden's doomed gang of outlaws.

This release of the *Wild Bunch* music was produced to accompany the US laserdisc box set of the movie. Separated from that, it is only available—as a legitimate release—through the good people at Film Score Monthly who've also rescued the *Pelham* music from oblivion. Unlike earlier releases, this version of *The Wild Bunch* was mastered directly from the original tracks in Warner Brothers' archives and is as complete as possible, as well as up to modern audio standards.

For audio samples and ordering information about these two CDs (and others), point your web browser to www.filmscoremonthly.com. Alternatively, you can email *FilmScore Monthly* editor Lukas Kendall at :

lukas@filmscoremonthly.com.

THE CRIME SCENE (ULTRA LOUNGE VOLUME 7, CAPITOL RECORDS)

From *Ultra Lounge*, the hipsters who brought us *Cocktail Capers*, *Organs in Space* and *Bachelor Pad Royale* comes *The Crime Scene*. In colour!

Subtitled Spies Thighs and Private Eyes this is a repackaged, remastered CD collection of the coolest sounds in the genre. 18 tracks of finger-popping insouciance that name-checks all that is great in the modern soundtrack; from Joe Meek, Elmer Bernstein and John Barry to Henry Mancini, Lalo Schifrin and Nelson Riddle. As Hitchcock himself says on track 18— *"Mood music in a jugular vein."*

You may think this is more nostalgia for the age of irony or another lurid slice of lounge music in a Pink Panther package, but this is beyond kitsch. This is the real thing. I defy anybody not to break into a goofy grin at the sound of the fanfare of horns that announces *Dragnet* in the opening track. Or feel the hair on the back of the neck stand up when *The Man With The Golden Arm* kicks in. This is the original Big Beat. Who needs a sequencer when you've got Gene Krupa.

Certainly there are some humorous moments for lovers of the lounge-core scene; Nelson Riddle's *Untouchables* theme and Leroy Holmes take on James Bond (from *"The Incredible World of James Bond"*) to name two. Crank that reverb up to 11, Leroy. There are also some delicious touches; Count Basie puts the foot on the accelerator for a barnstormingly swinging version of *From Russia With Love* that will have David Arnold chewing carpet. And as a beautifully judged parody of the spy theme, the trumpet on Spike Jones' *Harlem Nocturne* is an essay in sleaze. Banjo Noir.

For the admirers of manly style we have the theme from The Silencers. Dean Martin IS Matt Helm; *"She measures 38. Where it's great. To measure 38."* Chandler behind a mike. Things are rounded off by the gorgeous Tchaikovsky parody that is *Music to be Murdered By*. Can you honestly imagine the theme from *The Bill* resonating as much as that?

This is music to construct your own films to. Brando smirks at Deano. Deano checks out Connery's threads. Hitchcock directs, Nelson Riddle arranges and Lalo Schifrin scores. Oscars all round.

The remastering is excellent Trumpets kick, reeds rasp and hi-hats insinuate. Turn the volume up and the bottom end of the horns will blow your door off. Separation and orchestration that kicks ass. Even the sleeve notes are done with care, knowledge and humour. A stylish package right down to the cocktail recipes. And not so much as one shaken, not stirred gag.

Mike Paterson

GET CARTER. AN ORIGINAL SOUNDTRACK RECORDING. ROY BUDD CD (AND VINYL) WITH POSTER AND SLIPCASE CINEPHILE CIN 001 £13.50

A LOT OF PEOPLE have tried to make a convincing British gangster movie. If you have been weaned on pop videos you might think *Lock Stock And Two Smoking Barrels* is the real thing but few would disagree that *Get Carter* is infinitely superior, and growing in stature and significance as the years go by. As I have the book and the video it's supposedly embarrassing admitting that I actually bought this CD with real money -obsessive or what?—but the prospect of having the film poster plus some of the dialogue and the music was too good to resist. I have spotted several other copies of this product sticking out of shopping bags in central London, some belonging to young women, so perhaps the appeal of *Get Carter* is not confined to overgrown adolescents. Trainspotters will indeed enjoy the extensive sleeve notes and perhaps even the train sounds on Jack's journey home over the opening titles. Roy Budd's jazz-flavoured theme tune is the highlight; very effective, very memorable. At last it can be told that the haunting opening motif is played on a harpsichord mixed in with the sound of a hand stroking open piano strings, although you may find the information that Roy Budd once recorded an album of Gilbert O'Sullivan tunes haunting in a different way—it's certainly been giving me nightmares.

Director Mike Hodges has contributed an informative and amusing essay on the genesis of the film, namechecking Crime Time 9 where he wrote about the script-writing process.

The telephone sex scene with Britt Ekland is included here, (giving me a chance to mention that she propositioned me in Maunkberry's night club circa 1978. Well, she was falling-down drunk and I was about the only heterosexual man in the entire club.)

The main theme and snippets of dialogue are likely to turn up on a lot of dance products soon, now they are available in easy-to-sample form. And many pop journalists will no doubt think that is creative. Whether they would be so happy to have their work photocopied and distributed without payment is debatable.

The original film poster is not over-large and some of the dialogue has been edited but it's worth it if you need a quick fix of the title music on long car journeys or on your walkman headphones. Plus you get telephone sex with Britt Ekland. More importantly, this sends you back to the film, the stunning performance by Michael Caine and ultimately to the book and the terse magic of the great Ted Lewis—on top form when he wrote *Jack's Return Home*. If you haven't read the book, the back story of Jack Carter's childhood and his troubled relationship with his family give added depth and poignancy to the revenge tragedy portrayed in the film.

Mark Ramsden

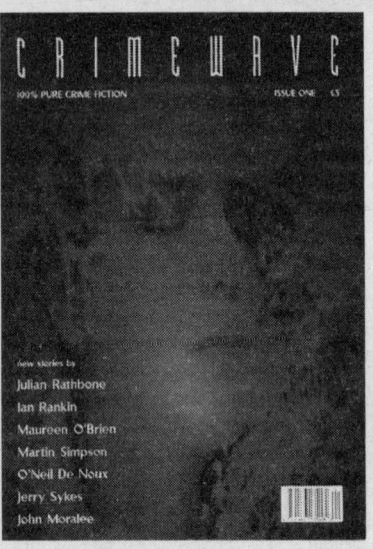

...and finally
john kennedy melling

IN MY OWN WORDS, COPPER....

GEORGE BERNARD SHAW said the alphabet was so poor that Napoleon and Shakespeare looked alike from a distance. GK Chesterton in *The Club Of Queer Trades* had one member inventing a new alphabet. At least three crime writers have invented their own language.

Robert Leslie Bellem (1902-1968) was a racy Writer in the 1930's Spicy Detective. He not only invented terms for the sound of a bullet from the 'Roscoe' (a handgun—not quite the same as the Saint's sidekick Hoppy Uniatz with his 'Betsy') but he specialised in descriptions of glamour girls. He emphasised the pectoral mammary glands, then quite shocking but mild today compared with television plays. His account of one murder victim. *"'The upper slopes of her breasts were squeezed upward and partly overflowed the tight bodice, like whipped cream",* prompted SJ Perelman in The Most Of SJ Perelman (1959) to refer to her as the 'charlotte russe'. Bellem's roscoes explode to 'Ka-Chaow', 'Chow-chow', 'Chow'—men are 'gazabos' or 'ginks' in his slang.

For more prolific invention few can touch for authenticity Damon Runyon (1884-1946) with his immortal gallery of guys and dolls on Broadway from the innocent to the criminous. Runyon was a writer from his teens, a first-class war correspondent, and an acute observer of murder and crime trials, including the Hall-Mills Case in 1926, the Snyder-Gray Trial in 1927, and two years later the alleged killers of The Brain, Arnold Rothstein, the great gambler, portrayed in Runyon's short story The Brain Goes Home (and as Nathan Detroit?) and by Scott Fitzgerald as Meyer Wolfsheim, in The Great Gatsby. Runyon and Fitzgerald were probably the two greatest influences on American writing. Runyon always wrote in the historic present *("I am standing outside Mindy's restaurant...")*—indeed in his foreword to More Than Somewhat Bentley says the solitary past tense stands up to hit you—and it does.

Many of Runyon's stories transferred to the screen, including Million Dollar Ransom (1934) *Tight Shoes*, *Little Miss Marker* (1934), *and The Big Street* (1942, based on *Little Pinks*). *Lady For A Day* (1933, based on *Madame La Gimp*), The *Lemon DROP KID* (1951), and of courses greatest of all, *Guys And Dolls* (1955), based mainly on the short story *The Idyll Of Miss Sarah Brown*, echoing *The Belle Of New York*. He wrote a play with Howard Lindsay, *A Slight Case Of Murder*, not premiered in Britain till June, 1991, but a Warner film in 1938 with Edward G. Robinson, and remade with Broderick Crawford in 1953 as *Stop, You're Killing Me*.

RUNYON'S LANGUAGE

His nouns, verbs, adjectives and adverbs

are fascinating in their originality and strict appropriateness. A girl friend is a 'sweet pea' reminding us of Popeye's adopted child. A girl is a 'bim', decades before the use of 'bimbo', possibly from 'bambino'. A man is 'smooth in the tooth in the matter of age'; a woman is 'half-past thirty-eight to give her a few hours'. Money is 'cucumbers', 'potatoes', 'moolah', 'beesom' or 'moo' A gun is a 'Betsy' (see supra). Nonsense is 'ackamarakus'. Girls rank from a 'pretty' to a beautiful' or a 'gorgeous' to a 'marvellous'. The head is the familiar 'noggin' or the 'pimple'. A negro is a 'zaggaboo', the origin of which is very obscure. A wallet is a 'leather', handcuffs are 'darbolas', the goal is the 'canneroo' and next year is 'come next grass'.

Runyon's Broadway characters are based on real people. Dave the Dude is Frank Costello, the Prime Minister of the Mafia, Waldo Winchester, Walter Winchell; Miss Missouri Martin is Texas Guinan of course; Sky Masterson was Bat Masterson. Dapper Dan was Ratsy Toorbillon, Dapper Dan Collins; Lt. Brannigan was John Broderick, and Nathan Detroit, portrayed so splendidly on Broadway and West End by Sam Levene was also based on Schnozzle Durante's onetime partner Lou Clayton. Harry the Horse, Benjamin Caplan, lived till 1973. Big Black Marrio—Al Capone; Regret was Otto 'Abbadabba' Berman, murdered with Dutch Schultz in 1935 in Newark. Mindy's is Lindy's and each time I visit New York I just have to dine there, but only a few days ago a New Yorker sitting beside me on the plane from Nice told me Lindy's of Broadway is no more.

SAN ANTONIO

For sheer volume of invented language we must award first prize to 'San Antonio'— Frédéric Dard. Over two hundred novels about his sleuth San Antonio, eight pseudonyms (noms de plume is out of date now) between 1948 and 1955, and two prestigious claims to fame for invention of words!

Les Pensées De San Antonio a 204-page book of quotations from his books, classified, with a -bibliography, published 1996 by Le Cherche Midi Editeur. *A Dictionnaire*, of 612 pages describing the words, persons, slang, etc., from all the books. I possess the hardback two inches thick, but the paperback reminds readers of the weekly San Antonio Crossword in a leading French magazine.

He claims to use only 300 words, the rest he invents. Some are his own slang. A 'Fillasse' is a petite fille, a 'kodakon' is a tourist, 'monocules' are monocle wearers, a 'Tournedos Rossini' is subtly a homosexual, the 'abbé-baissé' is the BBC (!), 'chamberlain' an umbrella, the guillotine is 'Abbaye de Monte-au-Regret' or 'La Veuve'. Real people appear in his books under other names; Cecil B de Cent Mille, J'aime le-Steward, J'abonde, A grappa Christina, Chatqu'espere or (William) J'expire, Scotch, or Ichetecoque, Si-mais-Non, Franck Sinapisme—but Mrs Thatcher, Chirac, Mitterand and Achille Zavatta, the great circus clown, appear as themselves. There are three pages of names and nicknames for Inspecteur Rinaud, twenty-one for San Antonio and six for Inspecteur Berurier. Of course, there are dozens of pages about his characters' amorous activities, with which we will not delay, but as with Bellem he is preoccupied with various areas of female anatomy. One neat, apt quote in *Penseés* is that he likes to see a woman's derriere making 88888 as she walks—I wonder if he knew Marilyn Monroe achieved her famous wiggle by shaving a quarter inch off her right heels? Of the pectorals he has literally dozens of terms, ranging from the fairly obvious 'dunlopillos' to the character who called them the Brother-Karamazov, until he found there were three brothers, so now he nicknames them Brothers Goncourt, with many others peculiarly French.

And I thought fiction was just a matter of writing!!

back issues

Crime Time 1 Our debut issue contains interviews with John Harvey, Martina Cole, Derek Raymond, Andrew Klavan (*True Crime*). Plus, features on *Cracker*, Colin Wilson, Griff, Dannie M Martin, and our notorious reviews section.

Crime Time 2 Sorry, sold out.

Crime Time 3 We interview Robert Rodriguez (*Desperado*) and Michael Mann (*Heat*), investigate the transvestite hitman fiction of Ed Wood Jr, talk the talk with Elizabeth George, Elliott Leyton, and Lawrence Block, give the low-down on German crime fiction, and feature an article by Booker prize nominee Julian Rathbone.

Crime Time 4 'The Violence Issue' Reservoir Dog, ex-con and writer Edward Bunker tells us how it is, Ben Elton takes the piss out of it, Joe Eszterhas exploits it, Morgan Freeman abhors it. Plus *Mission: Impossible*, *Heaven's Prisoners* (Phil Joanou), *Curdled*, Kinky Friedman, *The Bill* and *The Verdict*!.

Crime Time 5 Female Trouble! Interviews with Patricia Cornwell, Michael Dibdin, James Sallis and William Gibson. *Feisty Femmes And Two-Fisted Totty* gives the lowdown on women PIs, Ed Gorman talks about Gold Medal books of the Fifties, Hong Kong filmmakers Wong Kar-Wai & Christopher Doyle discuss *Fallen Angels*, and Michael Mann (*Heat*) is examined.

Crime Time 6 The Mean Streets issue contains interviews with writers James Ellroy, Gwendoline Butler, Sara Paretsky and Joseph Hansen, and film directors George Sluizer and Andrew Davis. Articles include Post-War Paperback Art, Batman, Crime Time: The Movie, and Steve Holland's excellent Pulp Fictions.

Crime Time 7 Val McDermid, Hong Kong Cinema, Phillip Margolin, Molly Brown, Ian Rankin, Michael Connelly, Daniel Woodrell and a cast of 1000s in this special 96 page issue!

Crime Time 8 Fantastic! Homicide, Faye and Jonathan Kellerman, Mark Timlin, Anthony Frewin, Gerald Kersh, Gwendoline Butler, Chandler on Celluloid, James Sallis on Chester Himes, The Payback Press and the biggest review section yet!

Crime Time 9 We *Got Carter*, with *Get Carter!* director Mike Hodges writing about making the film and Paul Duncan profiling the man who wrote *Jack's Return Home*. This plus scads of good stuff and the inimitable review section...

Crime Time 10 *Sin City*, Ed Gorman interviewed, Lawrence Block in the Library, Stella Duffy, Lauren Henderson, Sean Hughes, Denise Danks, Jerome Charyn and a cast of squillions...

Crime Time 11 Shut It!!! *The Sweeney* cover feature with those cheeky chappies Regan and Carter, Colin Dexter, Sparkle Hayter, David Williams, Gary Phillips, Janwillem Van De Wetering and the Great Grandam of kid's crime Enid Blyton.

Crime Time 12 The Last Time! (In floppy format anyway!) Joe R Lansdale, Simon Brett, Jay Russell, Steve Lopez, James Patterson, *Black Mask* magazine and the late Derek Raymond on Ted Lewis.

Crime Time 2.1 We re-invent ourselves in shorter, thicker trade paperback format, with interviews with features and fiction including James Sallis, Mark Timlin, Gwendoline Butler, Colin Dexter, Alan Moore, Jerry Sykes, Edward Bunker and more! 288 pages of sheer crime pleasure

Crime Time 2.2 Ed McBain, Mark Timlin, Steve Aylett, Fred Willard, Gary Phillips, Jason Starr, Russell James, Neil Jordan, Stuart Dawson, Paul Duncan and a host of others make this the most enjoyable 288 pages since the last issue of *Crime Time*.

Each issue up till number 12 is £3.00 post paid in the UK (please add £3.00 p&p per order overseas and Southern Ireland). Issues 2.1 and 2.2 are £5.00 each. Make cheques payable to 'Crime Time' and send your orders to: Back Issues (Dept CT23) Crime Time, 18 Coleswood Rd, Harpenden, Herts AL5 1EQ.